THE *Joys of Hebrew*

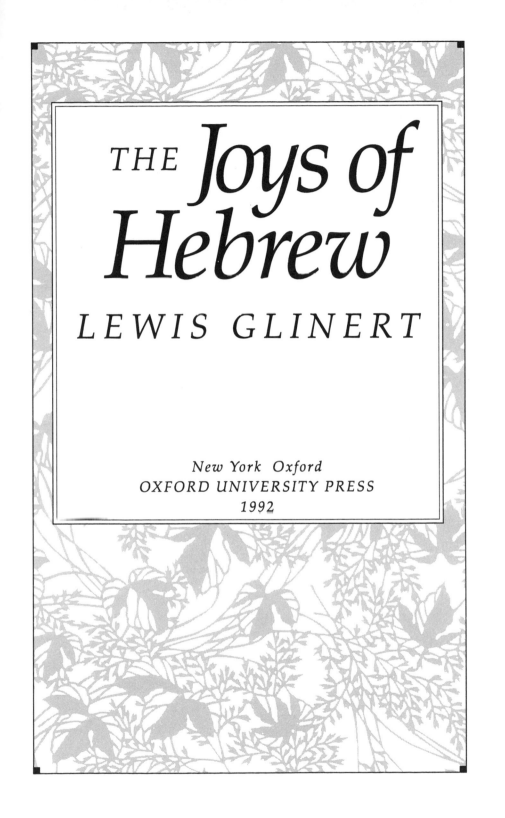

THE *Joys of Hebrew*

LEWIS GLINERT

New York Oxford
OXFORD UNIVERSITY PRESS
1992

Oxford University Press

Oxford   New York   Toronto
Delhi   Bombay   Calcutta   Madras   Karachi
Kuala Lumpur   Singapore   Hong Kong   Tokyo
Nairobi   Dar es Salaam   Cape Town
Melbourne   Auckland   Madrid

and associated companies in
Berlin   Ibadan

Copyright © 1992 by Lewis Glinert

Published by Oxford University Press, Inc.
200 Madison Avenue, New York, New York 10016

Oxford is a registered trademark of Oxford University Press

Library of Congress Cataloging-in-Publication Data
Glinert, Lewis.
The joys of Hebrew / Lewis Glinert.
p.   cm.
ISBN   0-19-507424-6
1. Proverbs, Hebrew—Dictionaries.   2. Proverbs, Jewish—Dictionaries.
3. Bible, O.T.—Quotations—Dictionaries.   4. Rabbinical literature—
Quotations, maxims, etc.—Dictionaries.
5. Jews—Folklore—Dictionaries.   6. Judaism—Quotations, maxims, etc.—
Dictionaries.   7. Hebrew language—Terms and phrases.   I. Title
PN6414.G58   1992
398.9'924—dc20   92-28624

1 3 5 7 9 8 6 4 2

Printed in the United States of America
on acid-free paper

To Shalva, Yeshurun, and Tsivya

Contents

Acknowledgments

Thanks are due to the following authors, or their representatives, and publishers for permission to quote from the sources listed: Elie Wiesel for *Souls on Fire*, copyright © 1972 by Elie Wiesel; Herman Wouk for *This Is My God*, copyright © 1949 by The Abe Wouk Foundation, Inc., copyright renewed 1987 by Herman Wouk; The Balkin Agency for *Israel and the World* by Martin Buber, copyright © 1948, 1975 by Schocken Books; the Rabbinical Council of America for *Orthodox Judaism in a World of Revolutionary Transformations* by Eliezer Berkovits and *Sheliach Tzibbur: Historical and Phenomenological Observations* by Gerald Blidstein, both from *Tradition*, copyright © 1965, 1971 by the Rabbinical Council of America; Rabbi Norman Lamm for permission to quote from his writings, copyright © by Norman Lamm; Rabbi Jack Riemer for *So That Your Values Live On* by Jack Riemer and Nathaniel Stampfer, published by Jewish Lights, Woodstock, VT, 1991; quotations from Adin Steinsaltz, Yeshayahu Leibowitz, Aharon Lichtenstein, Aviezer Ravitzky, and Robert M. Seltzer, reprinted with permission of Charles Scribner's Sons, an imprint of Macmillan Publishing Company, from *Contemporary Jewish Religious Thought*, Arthur A. Cohen and Paul Mendes-Flohr, editors, copyright © 1987 by Charles Scribner's Sons; Random House, Inc., for quotations from Joseph B. Soloveitchik, Jacob Neusner, and Deborah Lipstadt in *Jewish Reflections on Death*, edited by Jack Riemer, copyright © 1974 by Schocken Books, for *Jewish Mystical Testimonies* by Louis Jacobs, copyright © 1976 by Schocken Books, for *The Kerchief* by S.Y. Agnon, copyright © 1970 by Schocken Books, and for *On Judaism* by Martin Buber, copyright © 1948 by Schocken Books; Curt Leviant for translations of Sholom Aleichem; Naomi Shemer for *Yerushalayim shel Zahav*, translation copyright © by Naomi Shemer; Moshe Yess for *David Cohen's Bar Mitzvah* and *That's My Boy*, copyright © by Moshe Yess; Shraga Arad and the Jerusalem Post for *Randomalia* by Miriam Arad, copyright © 1988 by Shraga Arad; a quotation from Emanuel Rackman in *This I Believe: Documents of American Jewish Life*, edited by Jacob Rader Marcus, reprinted by permission of the publisher, Jason Aronson, Inc., Northvale, NJ, copyright © 1990; Thames &

Hudson, Ltd., for *Major Trends in Jewish Mysticism* by Gershom Scholem, copyright © 1955 by Thames & Hudson; *The Jerusalem Report* for a quotation from Ya'acov Kirschen, copyright © 1991 by Ya'acov Kirschen; Crown Publishers, Inc., for translation of Sholem Aleichem's *The Old Country* by Julius and Frances Butwin, copyright © 1946 by Crown Publishers, Inc.; excerpts from *A Passion for Truth* by Abraham Joshua Heschel, copyright © by Sylvia Heschel as Executrix of the Estate of Abraham Joshua Heschel, reprinted by permission of Farrar, Straus & Giroux, Inc.; excerpts from *World of Our Fathers*, copyright © 1976 by Irving Howe, reprinted by permission of Harcourt Brace Jovanovich, Inc.; excerpts from *How to Run a Traditional Jewish Household*, copyright © 1983 by Blu Greenberg, reprinted by permission of Simon & Schuster; excerpts from *What Is Judaism?*, copyright © 1987 by Emil L. Fackenheim, reprinted by permission of Simon & Schuster.

Introduction

All manner of people wish they knew a few Hebrew words and phrases—or a few more:

> Those who feel a sentimental attachment to Jewish life and who wish they could just put a name and meaning to some of those customs—and millions more with Jewish friends and colleagues or simply with a taste for Woody Allen or Barbra Streisand.

> The Jewish-educated graduate who knows full well that Hebrew is a treasure-house of wisdom.

> People planning a trip to Israel, who wish they knew just a little bit more "Israeli"-style Hebrew than just "shalom" and "falafel."

> Speakers planning an after-dinner speech to a Jewish audience, who would love to slip in a spicy Hebrew witticism.

> Bible-conscious folk who sometimes wonder how the language of the Psalms must have sounded in the original.

The Joys of Hebrew is a celebration of Hebrew It brings together the best-known and most lovable Hebrew words and sayings, as used today in the Diaspora, in a manageable English transcription—with little tidbits of Bible, Talmud, folklore, and literature to illustrate them, and a measure of humor from the Old World and from the crazy, zany side of life in Modern Israel.

Within living memory, Hebrew has been reborn as the spoken language of Israel; and around the world, when Jews of different backgrounds come together, Israeli Hebrew is increasingly what they use as a lingua franca—where once they might have used Yiddish or Spanyol.

But this is not to say that Israeli Hebrew is the only Hebrew. The grand old Ashkenazi Hebrew heritage is still alive and thriving in New York, Toronto, London, and throughout the Diaspora—with its distinctive pronunciations and charming semantics. *The Joys of Hebrew* gives full acknowledgment to this tradition; and to the fact that in Ultraorthodox circles outside Israel the Ashkenazi tradition reigns supreme.

Some may fancy that words like *mazl tov* and *meshuge* are not Hebrew at all but Yiddish. No—they're both the one and the other. They're some of the hundreds of common Hebrew words that were kept alive for a millenium in a fruitful symbiosis with Yiddish, pronounced in a Yiddish way but all this while written in a distinctive Hebrew way, and now relaunched on a new life as a kind of Yiddishized Israeli Hebrew. To all of them, *be-sha'a tova*

Of course, giving an Ashkenazi pronunciation has been an almighty headache. There still survive in fact as many Hebrew pronunciations as there were dialects of Yiddish—ranging, for example, from *Reysh ha-Shono* (Lithuanian) through *Roysh ha-Shunu* (Central Polish) to *Rowsh ha-Shono* (German). But out of the mishmash of mass migrations has emerged something like a typical Anglo-Ashkenazi pronunciation, with an underlying American sound pattern all its own. This seems to be what one generally hears in conversation, and this is the form that I have sought to represent in this book. (For *writing* the word or phrase, however, the predominant convention is to use the Israeli pronunciation.)

Six hundred or so words and phrases have surely not exhausted the treasury of Hebrew as used in Diaspora daily life today. There were probably a few more common phrases and sayings that I could have added—and many more that I would like to see more widely used. But, as Rabbi Tarfon put it a long, long time ago, *lo alecha hamlacha ligmor* ("Yours is not the duty to finish the work").

Guide to Transliteration

"a"	as in *Bach*	"ey"	as in *hey!*
"ay"	as in *Cairo*	"i"	as in *pit*
"ch"	as in *Bach*	"o"	as in *Gorbachev*
"e"	as in *Jerusalem**	"u"	as in *bush*
"e"	as in *pet*		

* Please note that subsized "e"s (representing schwas) and acute accents (indicating stressed syllables) are used only in the boldfaced entry terms as pronunciation aids.

THE *Joys of Hebrew*

Prologue

The story of Hebrew is much like the story of the Jews: Misty origins, ancient splendor, sudden eclipse followed by centuries of alien domination, staunched somehow by an infinite ability to adapt and survive—and culminating, in our century, in a dramatic paradox of ruin and rebirth.

The beginnings of Hebrew are bound up with the Jewish Bible. In fact, for most people ancient Hebrew *is* the Hebrew of the Bible, an august and infinitely subtle language, meticulously cultivated by the biblical schools of prophets over hundreds of years. One can study it, after a fashion. Indeed, the number of biblical grammar books and dictionaries must surely run into thousands. Yet the complexities of the biblical tenses or word order have never been fully fathomed, nor the precise shades of meaning in all those words for "righteous" or "loving-kindness" or "sin."

However, the Bible is not the whole story of Hebrew, not even of ancient Hebrew. There are the hosts of inscriptions and messages unearthed by excited archaeologists. Schoolchildren's calendars, engineers' plaques, army mayday calls, and the leftovers of Israelite bureaucrats . . . all in a kind of biblical Hebrew. They, and the biblical scrolls discovered after two millennia in the Judean Desert (the Dead Sea Scrolls), are witness to a remarkable tradition: The Bible as copied and recopied by 2,000 years of Jewish scribes is the same Bible. Even the Jewish traditions of pronunciation—the so-called pointing—are now rated by scholars as a superb freeze-frame of ancient pronunciation.

What of the Hebrew of the Israelite-in-the-street? History, of course, rarely records the language of people-in-the-street. Intriguingly, however, a kind of after-echo of that Hebrew has indeed come down to us, and actually forms the basis of the Hebrew of our own day: The vast writings of early postbiblical times—the Talmud, the Midrash, the Dead Sea Scrolls—were in many respects a new, semipopular Hebrew, drawn from the dialects and colloquial styles of an earlier time. This Hebrew, generally called Mishnaic Hebrew, was as rich in vocabulary as the Bible is sparse. It was as simple in style as the Bible is subtle. The whole of Jewish life is there, an encyclopedic vocabulary of everyday housekeeping, medicine, farming, warfare, business, law. In one letter by Shimon Bar-Kochva, the commander of a Jewish revolt against Rome, researchers have even discovered a grammatical "mistake" hitherto only known in Israeli Hebrew, and condemned as a modern horror by every grammar teacher in the land.

At the same time, however, in this postbiblical age, Hebrew was under threat. Masses of Jews had been exiled to Babylon, where they now spoke Aramaic. Some remained in the Holy Land, and others eventually returned; but many of them spoke a mix of Hebrew and other languages. Aramaic, the official language of the occupiers, was a serious competitor; Greek, too, began to weave its spell. For some 600 years, during the Second Temple period, Hebrew battled for survival as a spoken and written tongue. Many Jews had to read the Bible in translation or in a vulgarized Hebrew.

And then came the War against Rome, the destruction of Jerusalem in the year 70, and another devastating revolt in 132—famine, deportation, and the sword. Spoken Hebrew died. No one knows precisely when, and no one wrote its obituary. But the Talmud records how leading rabbis had to ask their servant girls the meaning of certain basic Hebrew words whose meaning they no longer knew. Hebrew might be the Holy Tongue, and the key to the Torah and the Prophets, but they could not keep spoken Hebrew alive.

However, those rabbis' efforts succeeded in keeping the sounds of Hebrew in Jewish homes for 2,000 years. They had the foresight to standardize the wording of Jewish prayer and Jewish law in a popular Hebrew, and thereby sent a message to Jews in all places and all times: Study Hebrew, teach your children Hebrew, and use Hebrew in your synagogues and your houses of study.

The message got through. Right up to modern times, whenever Jews wrote a letter or a document—be it in Arabic, Spanish, German, or Persian—it was in the Hebrew alphabet. The hours of daily study that young Jewish men devoted to the Bible, the Talmud, the Kabbalah, and their commentaries involved the original language. The poetry written in Jewish Spain, Byzantium, Italy, and France was invariably in Hebrew. A Hebrew linguistic science flourished. In the late medieval Rhineland, the ancient mystical practices of chanting Hebrew letter combinations were set down, and scholars pondered the cosmic meaning of the holy tongue as a language above language, a code and blueprint of creation.

Amid all this, however, there was also, for a time, a deep sense of failure: The worldly and sophisticated Jews of the Islamic Empire did all their writing on science and medicine and much of their writing on Judaism in Arabic. How, they asked, could poor old Hebrew possibly express the new thoughts of the day? But fortunately for the future of Hebrew, there were other great Jewish communities in southern France, in Italy, and in northern Europe who had faith in the holy language. They had little knowledge of Arabic (or of Latin, for that matter) and hundreds of great works of science, by Jew and non-Jew, were translated into a new scientific Hebrew. Thus was the basis for today's thoroughly modern Hebrew laid down in medieval Europe. The Hebrew language ranks alongside Arabic and Latin as one of the three great media of the medieval intellect.

But again we must return to the Jewish man and woman in the street. Most were probably Hebrew-literate, in that they could read and partly understand their daily prayers. But beyond that?

Beyond that, Hebrew continued to bubble and ferment in every Jew's speech. Throughout the Diaspora, down until the end of traditional Jewish society in the nineteenth century, every Gentile language spoken by Jews was in some way a Jewish language, by virtue of the hundreds, and sometimes the thousands, of Hebrew and Aramaic words and expressions by which Jews expressed their Judaism and their very Jewishness. To hear the snippets of Psalms, the Talmudic witticisms, the names of the laws and the customs and the *objets*, or just plain Hebraic miscellanea, in the aging verbal memories of one-time inhabitants of Salonika or Oran or Minsk is still a delight—things like Judeo-Español *gannab*, "thief," *enka'asarse*, "get angry," *yimmah semo vezixro*, "may his name and memory be wiped out," and Yiddish *balabos*, "householder," *yam*, "sea," *gedile*, "joy." To listen to a Yiddish conversation, to this day, is to be amazed at how much Hebrew has been kept alive in the language. It was a kind of open-ended symbiosis, in fact; the more learned or the more creative you were, the more Hebraisms were likely to decorate your Yiddish. If you were a man, the Bible and the Talmud seemed veritably to be under your breath. Women and children, too, exuded the popular Torah anthologies and translations that they learned week in and week out.

The sound of Hebrew was itself a token of just how alive and lively the language was. Every corner of the Jewish world had its own Hebrew accent, constrained naturally by the sounds of the local Yiddish or Arabic or whatever, but more distinctive than just that. The word for "peace" known today the world over as *shalom* was typically *salom* when Spanish Jews recited the Torah, *sholowm* for Germans, *shuloym* for Poles, *sholeym* for Yemenites, and so on. And the way it was pronounced when you were ceremoniously reciting the Torah generally bore little resemblance to the multitude of ways in which it was pronounced when you were reading prayers or chanting Talmud or just slipping it into your conversation. Each community guarded its Hebrew traditions jealously—like all the other local customs that made Jewish life so colorful and chaotic.

With the nineteenth century, this all began to change. Jews were slowly gaining admittance to European society. They were gaining the right to live where they chose, work at what they chose, pray as they chose. But at a price: They had to abandon their self-contained lifestyle— for example, the ancient practice of recording communal affairs in Hebrew. They were pressured to abandon the old full-time all-Hebrew religious schools and devote many hours to secular studies designed to make them economically more useful to the state. Many Jews exulted: German and Russian were the languages of the future. And French, too, for the emerging Jewish bourgeoisie of North Africa and the Middle East. Hebrew, it was felt, could safely be left to the synagogue, to the narrow confines of "religion." One could admire it as a classical language, to be sure, but the classics mattered less and less than progress and modernity. As for Yiddish and Judeo-Spanish, the less said about them, the better. Were they not illegitimate, mongrel languages, a bit of this and a bit of that?

And so began, across the Diaspora, the steady, inexorable collapse of Hebrew literacy, and of Jewish languages in general. Progress and modernity were not entirely to blame. The mass migrations to America, the havoc wrought by World War I, and finally the Bolsheviks and Hitler: Yiddish all but vanished (so too Judeo-Español). Knowledge of Hebrew in the Diaspora was reduced to little more than the Bar Mitzvah ritual.

But at the eleventh hour—and by a double twist of irony remarkable even by Jewish standards—Hebrew and Yiddish have been saved, indeed reincarnated. A spark plucked from the flame, by the forces of Zionism and traditional religion.

Russian Zionism, in its desperate attempt to save the Jews from persecution or assimilation, had the almost inconceivable idea of restoring Hebrew as a spoken language in the Holy Land—and succeeded. When the British marched into Palestine in 1917, they found a younger generation of 20,000 to 30,000 Jews already speaking Hebrew as their main language. How did it happen? A few hundred idealists, led by Eliezer Ben-Yehuda, determined to set up a revolutionary school system in which Yiddish would be obliterated in favor of Hebrew; a general population of Jews speaking a babble of tongues, in desperate need of a lingua franca to bridge the gulf; a few intellectuals who had already been experimenting for decades with modernizing Hebrew for science and the humanities; and most important of all, a generation of Jews—both Ashkenazi and Sephardi—who had been given the old-style, full-time Hebrew schooling and thus had the linguistic capabilities to make the whole thing work. As the historian Cecil Roth put it, they had always been *able* to speak Hebrew; now, they were *willing*.

Thus, at the last moment possible, Hebrew was reborn. In its new role, it is called *Ivrit*. It is now the main language of a whole country, and of maybe half a million Israelis living abroad. In many ways, modern Hebrew and modern Israel are one and the same logic-defying phenomenon of history.

To hear a toddler produce the same verb forms as Isaiah is a thrill, but no more so than to hear the Hebrew for things like tomato, dictionary, rhinoceros, lighthouse, orchestra, software, all new coinages built on biblical words. It wasn't long before colloquialisms, slang, and shortcuts with the old grammar were the order of the day (the Israeli equivalent of "I ain't" and "I don't know nothing"). And there are those ubiquitous Americanisms . . .

For the Jewish Diaspora, unfortunately, the now *Ivrit* is to all intents and purposes a foreign language. Any hopes the Israeli founding fathers had for Modern Hebrew to become a new universal Jewish language, a substitute for Yiddish, have been disappointed. The fact is that when two American Jews communicate, it's in English.*

And yet, a taste of the old Hebrew lives on in the Diaspora—thanks to Yiddish, to *Ivrit*, and to the resurgence of traditional Judaism and Jewish learning. The Yiddish of the Ellis Island generation has left a resonant chord in the English of its children and grandchildren, and within it many, many Hebrew words—words like *pesach* and *mazel tov*, *chutzpah* and *meshuge*. The Modern Hebrew of Israel has made its mark, too, through identification with Israel: *chag sameach* and *shabbat*

---

*See Alan Mintz, ed., *Hebrew in America* (Detroit: Wayne State University Press, in press).

shalom, for example. And—who could have predicted it forty years ago?—there are the rapidly burgeoning Orthodox and Ultraorthodox communities in New York, Los Angeles, London, and many other centers. They are bringing back a new wave of mother-tongue Yiddish, and above all a new Jewish learning and an English enriched with the juice of Hebrew. Young people are again devoting eight hours a day to the ancient sources and again proud to be heard "talking Jewish." The story of Hebrew goes on.

The Entries

Acharón, pl. **Acharoním** (Ashkenazi: **Áchren**, pl. **Achróhnim**)   Latter-day religious authorities

"Before you check it in the *Acharonim*, look up the *Rishonim*."

See *Rishon*.

Jews did not traditionally talk of "medieval" or "modern." They talked of *Rishonim* versus *Acharonim*.

Rishonim (literally "First Ones") denotes the Torah scholars of medieval times; *Acharonim* (literally "Latter Ones") are the scholars of the Renaissance and later times. Bridging the two, in the early sixteenth century, was Rabbi Yosef Caro. His great code of practice, the *Shulchan Aruch*, has become "final" and more or less binding on all generations since.

To be cited as an *Acharon* is no mean thing. The Gaon of Vilna and Rav Kook were both *Acharonim*. But the flowchart of Jewish history is generally seen as flowing downhill—and that gives the *Rishonim* a distinct advantage.

— ❧ —

Acharón acharón chavív (Ashkenazi: **Áchren áchren chóviv**)   Last but not least

"I'm sending invites to Joseph, John, Danny, Lenny, and *acharon acharon chaviv* to Norman."

I've translated *acharon acharon chaviv* as "last but not least," and that's essentially how you use it, but actually it's more than that: It's "the very last is lovable"—or "last is best."

The classic *acharon acharon chaviv* was, I suppose, the creation of mankind, on the last day of creation. Another was Jacob's youngest son Benjamin. Many parents have probably felt like him about their youngest offspring, and perhaps that's what gives the whole expression its force.

— ❧ —

Adár (Ashkenazi: **Áder/Óder**)   The month of Adar

The last month of the Jewish year is also the most lively—with the feast of *Purim*.

When *Adar* comes in, it's time to make merry.

The Talmud, Megila

– ✣ –

Adón Olám (Ashkenazi: **Adóhn Ohlóm**)   The hymn *Adon Olam*

"Before we conclude with *Adon Olam*, I have a few announcements to make."

Alhough it seems to have been written as a bedtime hymn, *Adon Olam* has come to be the standard song to end the Sabbath or festival service. The words are simply superb. And given a fitting tune (and I can think of several very unfitting tunes), *Adon Olam* can stir the soul. Nothing comes as a greater shock to Americans in an Israeli synagogue than to discover that Israelis (and Sephardim) don't sing it at all.

Master of the World [Adon Olam], *who reigned*
Before any creature was created—
Only when all had been made at His wish
Was His name proclaimed King.

And after all has ended
He will reign alone and fearsome,
He was, He is, He will be
In splendor . . .

Translation of the opening stanzas of Adon Olam

– ✣ –

Afikomán (Ashkenazi: **Afikóhmen**)   Last piece of *matzo* at the Passover *Seder*

"Uncle Marty always hides the *afikoman* in the same place every year."

The last thing eaten on the Passover *Seder* night is a piece of *matzo*, called by the curious name *afikoman* (probably Greek, but don't ask me why). After having consumed vast quantities of *matzo*, plus a filling meal, you eat the *afikoman matzo* and endeavor to enjoy every morsel of it. It is, after all, the last thing you'll eat tonight (or ever, some people are probably thinking). Some Sephardim ask their children to hold the *afikomun* on their shoulder throughout the proceedings. Most Ashkenazim hide it for their kids to find. And they always do.

After the meal is over one eats the *afikoman* in memory of the Passover sacrifice, which was eaten at the end of the meal after eating one's fill. . . . and one eats it reclining and after the *afikoman* one eats nothing more. . . .

Kitsur Shulchan Aruch

Aggadá (Ashkenazi: **Agóde**)　Talmudic stories or philosophical material

"We studied an interesting *aggada* about the *shofar*."

The Talmud is a massive canvas of *halacha* (law) and *aggada* (philosophical and folkloric material). The *aggada* sometimes appears to be easier; *yeshiva* students tend to skip it. In fact, it's often far more esoteric and harder to understand than the *halacha*, but the images contained in the *aggada*, and the way it tries to explain the laws and customs, are the daily stuff of every Jewish school and kindergarten.

Halacha and *Aggada* are two sides of Judaism, not just two literary genres, constantly intertwining and mutually challenging. *Halacha* gives the *Aggada* its social and public expression; *Aggada* gives the *Halacha* its spontaneity and extralegal spirit.

Michael Fishbane

Ahavát Yisraél (Ashkenazi: **Ahavas Yisróel**)　Love of one's fellow Jew

"Those guys who volunteered for the Entebbe Raid showed such *ahavat yisrael*."

Running like a thread through the Torah and tying the whole package together is the precept of *ahavat yisrael*, the essence of which is the verse *ve-ahavta le-reacha kamocha*: "You shall love your fellow as yourself." Where the Jewish people are disunited, the unity of the Torah and of Creation itself comes under threat.

I am grateful to God that He filled my heart with *ahavat yisrael*. I was granted this love not on account of any wisdom or righteousness I might possess but on account of His infinite mercy and love.

Rav Kook

(The) **Akedá** (Ashkenazi: **Akéyde**)   The binding of Isaac

The *Akeda*, literally "binding," as described in the Book of Genesis is the climax of Abraham's journey of faith. On Mount Moriah he makes ready to go through with God's command to sacrifice Isaac, his and Sarah's only son, but learns at the last moment that the whole thing was a test. God does not seek human sacrifice.

The memory of the *Akeda* is woven into Jewish life, into the prayers, and most famously into the ceremony of blowing the *shofar* (ram's horn) on the New Year. And in modern secular Israeli writing, a kind of *Akeda* trauma, repressed, surfaces again and again.

The synagogue management decided to fire the *shamash*. But they were afraid to tell him. So they asked the rabbi to tell him. But the rabbi refused.

"Why, rabbi?" they asked. "You're the *rav* and he's just a *shamash*."

The rabbi replied, "Don't you recite daily the chapter about the *Akeda*? How does God command Abraham to sacrifice his son? He tells him Himself. But how does He command him to stop? Through an angel! But then why didn't God send an angel at the outset? Because the angel would have said, "If You want to kill a Jew, O Lord, do it Yourself . . .""

— ✺ —

Al Chet (Ashkenazi: **Al Cheyt**)   The Al Chet confession

A leitmotif running through the prayers on *Yom Kippur* (the Day of Atonement) is the *Al Chet*—a mass confession of collective sins, recited again and again, evening, morning, and afternoon. Jewish thought regards spoken confession as a vital prelude to the process of *teshuva* (repentance). A custom associated with *Al Chet* is to beat the heart while saying the words *al chet*.

For the sin [al chet] *we have sinned to You by compulsion and free will.*
And for the sin we have sinned to You by closing our heart.
For the sin we have sinned to You unwittingly.
And for the sin we have sinned to You by utterance of the lips . . .

Translation of the opening of *Al Chet*

— ✺ —

Al ha-Nisím (Ashkenazi: **Al ha-Nísim**)   The prayer *Al ha-Nisim*

". . . and remember to add *Al ha-Nisim* for *Purim*."

On the festivals of *Chanukah* and *Purim*, the *Al ha-Nisim* prayer is inserted into the daily *Amida* prayer in thanksgiving for the miraculous deliverance from Greek-Syrian and Persian persecution.

For the miracles [*al ha-nisim*], the redemption, the mighty acts, the triumphs and the wars that You performed for our fathers in those days at this time. In the days of Mordechai and Esther in the great city of Shushan, when the evil Haman rose up against them, and sought to liquidate all Jews, young and old, women and children, on a single day . . .

Translation of the beginning of *Al ha-Nisim* for *Purim*

. . . nowhere in Jewish sources is there any of the reverence for the heroism of the fighter that is so prevalent in many non-Jewish cultures, even the most enlightened. Nor on *Chanukah* would we recite the added prayer *Al ha-Nisim* for the Maccabees if they had not fought the Lord's war and saved the holy law. Their heroism in battle is not mentioned at all; it is taken for granted.

Yeshayahu Leibowitz

Al régel achát (Ashkenazi: **Al régel áchas**)　Standing on one leg

"Look, you can't expect me to answer a question like that *al regel achat*!"

To answer a question or deal with a query very briefly and cursorily has been described as answering *al regel achat*, "standing on one leg." It all goes back to one of the most amusing stories in the Talmud, in which a Gentile wagered that he could get the sage Hillel to lose his proverbial patience, and proceeded to ask Hillel to teach him the whole Torah while standing on one leg.

He lost.

Al tiftách peh la-satán (Ashkenazi: . . . **la-sóton**)　Don't tempt Providence (literally "Don't open your mouth to Satan")

"But what if I fail?"
"Nonsense, *al tiftach peh la-satan*."

For more on *Satan* (if you'll pardon me for mentioning him), see under S.

Whatever the ultimate "real" meaning of this ancient expression (superstition? or a fear of self-fulfilling prophecies?), it's always had an effect. When mentioning something bad that might happen, Jews have always been quick to add a prophylactic *chas ve-shalom* or a *rachmana litslan*.

Aláv/aléha ha-shalóm (Ashkenazi: **Ólev/olého ha-shólem**)   May he or she rest in peace (literally "peace upon him or her")

"The other television used to belong to Mrs. Cohen, *aleha ha-shalom*."

See also *Zichrono livracha*, "May his memory be a blessing."

This phrase is commonly added when mentioning the name of a deceased friend or relative.

— ✣ —

Álef-Bet (Ashkenazi: **Álef-Beys**)   The Hebrew alphabet

"All my brothers and sisters knew the *Alef-Bet* by the age of four."

All Jewish communities today use roughly the same shape of letters: one set for the printed or scribal word and another (often called *script* or *cursive*) for handwriting. Some people, perhaps most, never look beyond the purely functional use of the letters. A few may see the sheer beauty of them—scribes, graphic artists, inveterate doodlers. And a select few are aware of some hidden metaphysical meaning in the very shape of each letter.

It is fascinating to compare the shapes of our English alphabet, and its order, with the *Alef-Bet*—they are very distant relatives.

On the hearth a fire is burning,
In the room it's hot,
And the Rebbe's *teaching little children*
The Alef-Beys.

Remember, children,
Remember, precious ones,
What you're learning here.
Say again, and once again,
kumets alef "u."

From the traditional Yiddish song "Oifn Pripetchik"

Why does the *Torah* begin with the letter *bet*? To teach you that we still have not reached *alef* in understanding it.

Rabbi Israel Baal Shem Tov

— ✣ —

Aléynu (Ashkenazi: **Oléynu**)   The prayer Aleynu

"Make room for yourself to kneel during *Aleynu*."

Even prayers have good or bad luck. Take *Aleynu*. It was probably specially composed as a climax to the *Musaf* prayer on the High Holy

Days. And to this day worshippers on these days feel a *frisson* of awe as they kneel and fall on their faces during the *Aleynu* prayer. However, it was subsequently chosen to round off the three weekday services every day of the year—and try as I may, I can't get that *frisson*.

It is our duty [aleynu] *to praise the Master of All,*
To proclaim the greatness of Him who shaped the Beginning . . .
And we bend the knee and throw ourselves down and avow it
Before the Supreme King of Kings, the Holy One blessed be He . . .

Translation of part of the *Aleynu* prayer

Aliyáh Immigration to Israel

"We're planning to make *Aliyah* next month."

See also *Oleh,* "Immigrant" and (*lehavdil*) *Yerida,* "Emigration from Israel."

There was a time shortly after 1948 when Ben-Gurion, Israel's first premier, expected all Western Jews to "make *aliyah*" (as the Americans say) or to "go on *aliyah*" (as the British say) in a short space of time. Indeed, mass *aliyah* has been a major goal of Zionism, and there have been many mass waves, starting with the so-called First *Aliyah* in the 1880s. The latest is the mass "Gorbachev" *aliyah* from Russia.

   Aliyah is more than a word, it's a dream slogan—it means "ascent." And it wasn't some Zionist politician that dreamed it up but the Author of the Bible, who talks of the Israelites ascending from Egypt to Israel, since (as the ancient Midrash puts it) the Land of Israel is higher than all other lands.

Aliyáh (Ashkenazi: **Alíye**)   Calling to the reading of the Torah

"Weren't you proud when Daddy had an *aliyah*?"

Not by chance does *aliyah* mean both "immigration to Israel" and "calling to the Torah reading"—the basic meaning of *aliyah* is "going up."

Once long ago, to be given an *aliyah* meant to be called up to the platform to recite a part of the Torah reading. No longer. Most people can't read it off the cuff, so it's given to a professional reader, the *baal koré*. But members of the congregation are still given the honor of being called up by name to stand next to the *baal koré* (and the honor of making a donation to the synagogue).

Alyá ve-kóts ba (Ashkenazi: **Ályo ve-kóhts bo**)   "There's just one little problem"

This piquant Talmudic expression means literally "a sheep's tail with a thorn in it." Sheep shearers working on the sheep's tail found one little problem: a small protrusion ending in a kind of spike.

   Alya ve-kots ba is good for any kind of "you've heard the good news, now here's the bad news" situation. Or render it "a fly in the ointment."

– ❧ –

Am ha-Árets (Ashkenazi: **Am ho-Órets**, pl. **Amrátsim**)   Ignoramus

"Some of these colleges almost seem to breed *amratsim*."

It's a strange word, *am ha-arets*. It literally means "people of the land," but it has always meant "peasants" in the most derogatory sense of the word. And, like so many Hebrew words, Yiddish adopted it and gave it a peculiarly Ashkenazi plural, *amratsim*.

It was in the *beys medresh* [study hall]. Three *yeshiva bocherim* [rabbinic students] were stuck over a line of Talmud. In walked one of the locals, no *am ho-orets* but not exactly a *lamden* [scholar] either—and they called him over to explain it to them. Now no one wants to appear an *am ho-orets*, but what could he do? So he shouted:

   "Ask a total stranger, would you?! I happen to be a *lamden*, but I might have been an *am ho-orets* and then look how you'd have embarrassed me. So I *won't* explain it!"

– ❧ –

Amén! (Ashkenazi: **Oméyn!**)   "Amen!"

"He's a marvellous kid. He should grow up to be a credit to you."
   "*Amen!*"

Another word from the same root is *emuna*, "faith"; the basic idea of the root may be "strength."

Apart from its use in prayer, *Amen!* is often said piously in response to an informal prayer voiced on one's behalf.

If I knew that I had said one *Amen* properly in my entire life, I would never worry again.

                                                                    Rabbi Moshe of Kobryn

– ❧ –

Amidá (Ashkenazi: **Amíde**)   Silent standing prayer

"During the *Amida* you could hear a pin drop."

Every day Jewish men, and many women, have traditionally recited the *Amida*, a prayer said standing, under one's breath, and with intense concentration. It is essentially a cry for help—for wisdom, health, peace, prosperity, return to Zion. It is also called *Shmoneh-esre* ("eighteen"), having originally consisted of eighteen blessings. (Eighteen is the numerical value of the word *chay*, "life.")

A pious man was saying the *Amida* by the roadside, when up rode a Roman officer and called out a greeting. No reply. The officer allowed the man to finish his *Amida*, but then challenged him: "Idiot! Doesn't your Torah tell you 'Look after your life'? For not greeting me I could have sliced off your head . . ."

Replied the Jew: "If you were having an audience with an emperor and turned to answer someone's greeting, what would happen to you? Meanwhile, I just happened to be having an audience with the emperor of emperors."

The officer smiled and rode off.

The Talmud, Berachot

— ❧ —

Aním Zemirót (Ashkenazi: **Ánim Zmíres**)   The hymn *Anim Zemirot*

"Goldstein Junior, would you like to sing *Anim Zemirot*?"

Most synagogue regulars know and love *Anim Zemirot* as a tuneful hymn sung by one of the young lads, with the congregation joining in responsively—bringing the *Shabbat* morning service toward a cheerful close.

What few realize is that this hymn, known also as *Shir ha-Kavod*, "the Hymn of Glory," was deliberately omitted in many circles because its praise of God was felt to be excessive (the Talmud cautions against excessive paeans of praise). And so other circles responded by having a child, an innocent, sing it. A case of "out of the mouths of babes and sucklings."

I shall sing sweet hymns [anim zemirot] *and weave songs,*
For my heart thirsteth for Thee.
My soul desireth the shade of Thy hands,
To know all the mystery of Thy secrets . . .

Translation of the opening of *Anim Zemirot*

— ❧ —

Apikóres, pl. apikórsim   Nonbeliever

"The writer Bialik had a good *yeshiva* education, but he soon became quite an *apikores.*"

"Nonbeliever" is perforce a vague translation. How *can* you translate *apikores*? The *apikores*—both as classically defined by Maimonides and in popular usage—is essentially someone who denies the authority of the Rabbis.

There are lots of *apikores* jokes. Maybe it's a healthy thing, although Jews have certainly suffered enough persecution at their hands. In any event, there's a sly regard for the *apikores*: He has at least studied the things he rejects, by comparison with the *am ha-arets*, the ignoramus who can barely distinguish one *mitzvah* from another.

The *apikores* denies, among other things, the very possibility of prophecy in general and the veracity of Moses' prophecy in particular. . . . The term *apikores* is taken to refer also to someone who "denigrates the Sages."

Gershon Weiler

Know how to answer the *apikores.*

The Talmud, Avot

— ❧ —

(The) Aravá   The Arava valley

The *Arava* is the arid valley stretching southward, along the Israeli-Jordanian border, from the Dead Sea to the Red Sea at Eilat. It has just a handful of villages and just one town, Eilat. In the 1950s, the *Arava* became something of a Wild West frontier for Israelis chafing to break out of their total siege by undertaking cross-border dares to reach the famed deserted city of Petra.

Arava, Arava *without end.*
The herdsman's eye prowls,
Not a juniper, not a thorn-bush, not a tree.
Wind comes to the desert . . .

From a 1950s Hebrew ballad

— ❧ —

Aravót (Ashkenazi: Aróves)   Willow twigs

"Come on, beat those *aravot* till there isn't a single leaf left!"

The penchant of willows for water is well known. And on *Sukkot*, the harvest festival when the world is judged for rain, tradition requires that one take *aravot* (willow twigs) together with three other plants (the *arba minim*, the "Four Species") and wave them in the synagogue prayers. Finally, we come to *Hoshana Raba*, the last day of *Sukkot*, and the *aravot* are beaten, as if to beat away one's sins. This day is the final, final deadline in the annual process of repentance.

Why the *aravot*? The leaf is similar in shape to the lips, and atones for the utterance of the lips.

The Midrash

— 🦋 —

Árba kánfes   Four-cornered garment

"Before you put your *arba kanfes* on, Benjy, check that you have eight strings on each corner."

Arba kanfes, literally "four corners," is a popular Ashkenazi name for the *tallit katan* (see entry).

— 🦋 —

Arbá kosót (Ashkenazi: Árba kóhses)   The four glasses of wine drunk on Passover

". . . and get three crates of Concord wine for the *arba kosot*."

The *arba kosot* are a major feature of the *Seder* night ceremonies of Passover. Everyone is meant to drink four glasses of wine (or the best part thereof) in celebration of freedom, each glass representing a stage in the Divine liberation. But this is no occasion for wine connoisseurs—you're meant to down it and enjoy it, not savor it.

— 🦋 —

Arbá miním (Ashkenazi: Árba mínim)   The four plant species used on *Sukkot*.

"Did you buy your set of *arba minim* in Israel or in Brooklyn?"

Since Bible times, Jews have celebrated the harvest festival of *Sukkot* by acquiring *arba minim*, literally "four species," and waving them ceremonially during their prayers. The *arba minim* are the *lulav* (palm branch), *etrog* (citron), *hadasim* (myrtle twigs), and *aravot* (willow twigs), each one full of symbolism.

Every year, Israeli markets are piled high with them—and with Orthodox Jews seeking the perfect *arba minim*. And every *Sukkot* morning, the cops in Brooklyn and L.A. have to be reminded that these guys walking around with long narrow boxes are carrying palm branches and nothing more deadly.

— ❧ —

Arón kódesh (Ashkenazi: **Óren kóhdesh**) Holy ark

"Mr. Katz, could you open the *Aron kodesh* please?"

In some ways the synagogue is modeled on the ancient Temple. In the Temple Holy of Holies stood the *Aron kodesh*, a golden chest containing the ten commandments. Today, in its place, on the Jerusalem-facing wall of every synagogue is a modern-day *Aron kodesh*, containing the Torah scrolls, the holiest spot in the synagogue.

— ❧ —

Asará be-Tevét (Ashkenazi: **Asóro be-Téyveys**) Fast of the tenth day of Tevet

"They're learning about the Warsaw ghetto uprising in school, because next week is *Asara be-Tevet*."

Asara be-Tevet is the first of three annual fast days commemorating the downfall of biblical Judea and the destruction of the Temple. *Asara be-Tevet*, which falls in the early winter, marks the beginning of the end— the arrival of armies from Babylon to commence the final siege. In some circles, *Asara be-Tevet* also serves to memorialize the Nazi Holocaust. An edition of the *Selichot* (prayers for forgiveness) published in Britain includes a memorial prayer for the Six Million, but it is doubtful if such a modern theme is much heard in traditional synagogues.

— ❧ —

Aséret yeméy teshuvá (Ashkenazi: **Aséres yeméy teshúve**) Ten Days of Penitence

"Daniel, don't forget to add the extra bits to the prayers for the *Aseret yemey teshuva*."

The ten days from *Rosh Hashanah* to *Yom Kippur* are known as the *Aseret yemey teshuva*, the "Ten Days of Penitence"—with extra-early morning prayers for forgiveness and extra lines about "the book of life" to add to the regular prayers.

Ashkenazí, pl. Ashkenazim (Ashkenazi: **Ashkenázi, pl. Ashkenázim**)
a. Jew of Northern European background; b. Pertaining to Jews of
Northern European background

"Most *Ashkenazim* have a deep affinity for *Ashkenazi* food."

The word *Ashkenazi* betokens all the expulsions (and population expan-
sions) of European Jewry. Originally the Hebrew name for German
Jews, it followed them eastward to Poland and Russia, west to Britain
and France, and across the seas to the New World. Even in Israel, a siz-
able population regards itself as *Ashkenazi* in certain ways—food,
looks, religious customs.

  Ashkenazim don't feel that to be an *Ashkenazi* in and of itself is a cul-
tural cachet—you can leave that to the *Sephardim*. But by a twist of history, the grand old *Sephardi* community in Israel have found that their
Ashkenazi brethren have the power, the numbers, and the sense of
superiority.

— ❧ —

Asúr (Ashkenazi: **Óser**)   Forbidden

"Keeping quiet when you have important evidence is plain *asur!*"

Some people imagine that in traditional Judaism there's very little that
isn't *asur*, but they should go and read the local traffic regulations
some time. There are quite a few things that are *mutar* (permitted) too.

What's *asur* is *asur*. And as for what's *mutar* [permitted]—don't be in a rush to
do it either.

                                                            Rabbi Yisroel of Rozhyn

— ❧ —

Av (Ashkenazi: **Av/Ov**)   The month of Av

The fifth month of the Jewish year, *Av* falls in July-August. It starts on
a sour note, with the "Nine Days" of semi-mourning leading up to the
dark fast day of *Tisha be-Av*, but it soon brightens up and everyone can
then enjoy their vacation.

When *Av* comes round, one cuts down on merriment.

                                                            The Talmud, Ta'anit

— ❧ —

Avatíach Watermelon

"There's an *avatiach* stand at the junction coming up. Let's pull over."

Oh for *avatiach* now that summer's here! In a miserable age where you can buy anything from anywhere at any time, the appearance of the *avatiach* men in the Machane Yehuda market in Jerusalem, in the Carmel *Shuk* in Tel Aviv, and on every street corner in the country is a bracing reminder that there are still some things that don't come easy.

The Israeli *avatiach* may not be bigger than watermelons in other climes (I've never taken their vital statistics), but it's sold with a panache and bravura that lend it Rabelaisian proportions. The cries of the shirtless men on their barrows echo up and down the land: *A-va-ti-ach!* In a language where nearly all words have two syllables, the word *avatiach* seems to be a pure miracle—for yes, it is there in the Bible, and people even then were pining for it.

Unfortunately, they were pining for the Egyptian *avatiach*, and asking themselves why they had ever left Egypt for the Promised Land.

Sign seen on an *avatiach* barrow near Beersheba:
  Kol avatiach doktor [Every *avatiach* is a Ph.D.]

— ❧❧ —

Avél, pl. **avelím** (Ashkenazi: **Óvel**, pl. **avéylim**) Someone who is in mourning
Avelút (Ashkenazi: **Avéylus**) Mourning

"He can't use the tickets to the show because he's an *avel*."

See *Nichum avel*, "Consoling the mourner."

Avelim—those who have recently lost a next of kin—traditionally find expression for their *avelut* by observing seven days' confinement at home ("sitting *shiva*"), forgoing new clothes and musical entertainment, and reciting the *kaddish* prayer.

But the words *avel* and *avelut* are also used to refer to national acts of mourning, the fasts commemorating the destruction of the Temple and so on. In a way, the bereaved *avel* feels that "we are all *avelim*."

May the Almighty comfort you among the *avelim* for Zion and Jerusalem.
> The traditional words of comfort
> said to a mourner after the burial

An avel has no mouth to speak.
> The Talmud, Bava Batra

— ❧❧ —

Averá, pl. averót (Ashkenazi: **Avéyre, pl. avéyres**)   A sin

"When they don't see their parents from one year to the next, they just don't realize what an *avera* it is."

"Don't you dare do that again, you little monkey! It's a terrible *avera!*"

An *avera* is an infringement of the Torah, the opposite of a *mitzvah*.

The reward for a *mitzvah* is one more *mitzvah*, and the penalty for an *avera* is a further *avera*.

The Talmud, Avot

Within an *avera* itself are holy sparks. When one does *teshuva* [repentance], one raises the sparks.

Rabbi Israel Baal Shem Tov

— ✺ —

Avínu Malkénu (Ashkenazi: **Ovínu Malkéynu**)   The Avinu Malkenu prayer

Avinu Malkenu is a high point in the *Rosh Hashanah* and *Yom Kippur* prayers. It reads like a plea from the heart, for all the things that a Jew might wish for in the coming year—and ends on a famous haunting melody that lifts and bonds.

. . . Our father, our king [avinu malkenu], act for the sake of those who went
through fire and water to sanctify Your name.
Our father, our king, avenge the spilt blood of Your servants.
Our father, our king, do it for Your sake, if not for ours.
Our father, our king, do it for Your sake, and save us . . .

From *Avinu Malkenu*

— ✺ —

Avrahám Avínu (Ashkenazi: **Avróhom Ovínu**)   Our father Abraham

"The whole Jewish concept of hospitality comes from *Avraham Avinu*."

Avraham Avinu, "Abraham our father," is the age-old name for Abraham, father of the Jewish people and in every sense the first Jew. Abraham, his son Isaac, and his son Jacob are collectively known as the *Avot*, "the fathers."

When King Nimrod sallied forth to the field,
He looked aloft and scanned the stars,
He saw a holy light in the Jewish people,
For Avraham Avinu had just been born.
Avraham Avinu,

Dearest father,
Blessed father,
Light of Israel.

Translation of a Spanyol (Ladino) ballad

– ৹ৼ৹ –

Áyin ha-rá (Ashkenazi: **Áyin hóre**)   The evil eye
Bli áyin ha-rá   "Let there be no evil eye"

"Hey, your husband's looking really well, *bli ayin ha-ra*."

Some have seen it as a paranatural evil eye, and some merely as an embodiment of envy, but in any event Jewish custom has always sought to allay the *ayin ha-ra*, for example by not counting heads or by not calling a father and son in straight succession to the Torah reading. The phrase *bli ayin ha-ra* is frequently heard among Israelis when children are the topic of conversation. Yiddish took over *ayin ha-ra* and pronounced it *eynore*.

The sage Rav went up to the graveyard, performed certain actions, and declared: "Ninety-nine percent were by *ayin ha-ra* and one percent by a natural death."

The Talmud, Bava Metzia

A young woman had given birth. The neighbors began visiting. Her mother, fearing an *ayin ha-ra*, crept over to the crib and switched the baby with a little dog. An old woman shortly came to visit. Peering shortsightedly into the crib, she exclaimed, "*Bli ayin ha-ra*, he looks just like his father!"

Ayin ha-ra and *yetser ha-ra* [the evil impulse] and hatred of others dispatch a person from the world.

The Talmud, Avot

– ৹ৼ৹ –

Báal ga'avá (Ashkenazi: **Báal gáave**)   Arrogant person

"He didn't 'forget' to mention you in the credits, he's just a plain *baal gaave*."

It's no accident that the everyday talk of traditional Jews has always been peppered with Hebrew words having to do with moral psychology, like *baal ga'ava*. The study of human behavior and how to improve it is a central plank in Jewish study.

When I see a *baal gaave*, I feel a physical urge to vomit.

Rabbi Yisroel Salant

– ৹ৼ৹ –

Báal ha-báyit (Ashkenazi: **Báal ha-báyis, Balabós** pl. **Balebátim**)
Homeowner, head of household; boss

"A lot of *balebatim* in this neighborhood are against the new mall."

N.B.: In *baal ha-bayit* and the words that follow, *baal* means literally "owner, possessor."

The word *baal ha-bayit* has a secure ring about it, the ring of being able to build a house and raise a family without threat of poverty or expulsion. Yiddish created a delightful feminine form of the word: *baleboste*, meaning "Jewish housewife" (shades of piety, pickles, and chicken soup). And some say that the Jewish immigrants to New York shortened *balabos* to plain *bos*, thus giving the world the word *boss*.

— ❧❧ —

Báal koré (Ashkenazi: **Báal kóhre**)   Reader of the Torah in the synagogue

"The *baal kore* skipped a word, so the rabbi corrected him."

See *Kriat ha-Torah*, "The reading of the Torah."

The *baal kore* is the unsung virtuoso of Jewish life. Every Sabbath, on the synagogue rostrum, he has to open a Torah scroll, consisting of words with no vowel signs, commas, or periods, and read it fluently, clearly, and musically, with a highly complex traditional chant that has to be learned in advance and is virtually impossible to predict from the words themselves—and all this in front of an audience of perhaps hundreds, some of whom will not hesitate to interrupt him if he makes the slightest mistake on a letter.

— ❧❧ —

Báal tekiá (Ashkenazi: **Báal tekíe**)   *Shofar* blower

"You'll excuse me if I practice the *shofar* every evening, but I'm going to be the *baal tekie* in the synagogue this year."

See *Tekia*, "Blast of the *shofar*."

The *baal tekie* has to produce 100 blasts of the *shofar* (ram's horn) on both days of *Rosh Hashanah*. In his white robe, he stands on the synagogue platform, trying before each blast to choose exactly the right aperture for his lips. *Baal tekie* is not a job for brass players. I knew a professional trumpeter who couldn't get a sound out of the *shofar*. The *baal tekie* will be mindful not only that hundreds of people are wondering if he'll produce the expected sounds but also that the blowing of the *shofar* is a mighty responsibility before God, the great occasion.

Báal teshuvá, pl. Baaléy teshuvá (Ashkenazi: **Báal teshúve, pl. Báaley teshúve**)   Newly religious Jew; penitent

"What can I tell you about Fran? Well, she's married to a *baal teshuva* and she lives in Jerusalem and she has four kids . . ."

See *Teshuva*.

The 1970s and 1980s saw a big wave of *baaley teshuva*, typically students from well-to-do homes in the United States and Israel who felt that they had grown up with an empty lifestyle and wanted to find their Jewish roots. This meant going to men's or women's *yeshiva* (seminary) to study the classic Jewish sources and the observances. The wave is still building.

Where *baaley teshuva* stand, even the most saintly cannot stand.

The Talmud, Berachot

Bal tashchít (Ashkenazi: **Bal táshchis**)   "Waste not, want not"

"Will you stop scribbling in that book? It's *bal tashchit*!"

I doubt if any of the world's languages can produce so powerful an ecological rallying cry as *bal tashchit!* Deriving from the biblical ban on destroying fruit trees in pursuit of military scorched earth, *bal tashchit* means literally "do not destroy," and at the same time evokes images of the generation of Noah corrupting (*hishchit*) its way upon the earth and condemning an entire world.

   In Jewish law, smashing things in anger comes under *bal tashchit!* So, too, any destruction that serves no useful purpose, even absent-mindedly plucking leaves from a bush.

Balagán   Mess

"Don't even look into his room. It's a total *balagan*."

"First you say Friday, then Wednesday! You've made a real *balagan* . . ."

The noun *balagan* is an import, from Russian. But like all well-adjusted imports, it has already produced a verb *hitbalgen* "make a mess," an adjective *mebulgan*, "messy," and another noun *balaganist*, "mess-maker." (What about the biblical word for "mess"? Well, there seem to have been no messes in the Bible, except for Jacob's "mess of pottage.")

However, a Slavicist I know informs me that the Russian comes from the Persian, where it meant "balcony" (in fact, so does the English: *balcony, balagan*). And it is of course on the balcony that the Israelis put all their mess, all of which shows that Israeli language imports are exceedingly well planned.

– ✿ –

Ba-Midbár (Ashkenazi: Ba-Mídbor)   The Book of Numbers

Ba-Midbar is the fourth book of the Torah. Like the other books, its present-day name is based on the first phrase, and means "in the wilderness." *Ba-Midbar* charts the moral experiences of the Israelites during thirty-nine years of desert wandering from Mt. Sinai to the borders of the Promised Land—taking in Korach's rebellion, the striking of the rock, Bilam's talking ass, and much else.

Cecil B. de Mille managed to cram it into three minutes. Jews nowadays read it on *Shabbat* in synagogue from late spring through the summer.

The Torah was given in *esh* [fire], in *mayim* [water], and in *midbar* [wilderness].
The Midrash on *Ba-Midbar*

Thanks to these experiences of the fiery furnace into which Abraham was thrown, the waters of the Red Sea, and the *midbar* which the Israelites crossed in answer to the word of God, the Torah was given to them for all time.
Rabbi Meir Shapiro of Lublin

– ✿ –

Bar Mitzváh (Ashkenazi: Bar Mítzve)   Ceremony of a Jewish boy's coming of age; boy who has reached that age

"So you've decided to hold his *Bar Mitzvah* at the Western Wall?"

"We'll have the *Bar Mitzvah* stand just there, with his hand round his mother's shoulder. Hold it . . . perfect!"

"We need someone to read from the Torah—are you *Bar Mitzvah* yet?"

See *Mitzvah*, "Religious responsibility" and *Bat Mitzvah*, "Girl's coming of age."

In some parts they fear 13 so badly that they number houses 12, 14, 15. For Jewish boys, however, 13 is a magic age, the age of becoming *Bar Mitzvah*: the age at which they will read from the Torah in the synagogue, give their parents heaps of *nachat* (fulfillment) and receive heaps of presents in return, be the center of a huge party, start putting on *tefilin*, fasting the whole day on *Yom Kippur*, and doing all sorts of other duties incumbent on Jewish men. For now, technically, they are "men."

Unfortunately, most Jewish boys in the United States also look forward to 13 as a magic age at which their parents will allow them to quit Jewish schooling and say goodbye to the synagogue.

I nearly forgot. *Bar Mitzvah*—essential meaning: subject to religious responsibilities.

Uncle Abe flew in from Cincinnati,
Aunt Becky drove up from Miami Beach.
The Rabbi was watching with a tear in his eye
As David Cohen read his Bar Mitzvah speech.

"I want to thank the Rabbi, my mother and my father.
Today I am a man by Jewish law.
I accept all of my obligations.
I acknowledge that there is only one God."

From Moshe Yess, "David Cohen's Bar Mitzvah"

Bar Mitzvahs would be much better if they had a little bit less of the "bar" and a little bit more of the "mitzvah."

Anon.

Barúch dayán ha-emét! (Ashkenazi: **Bórech dáyan ho-émes!**)
"Blessed be the True Judge!" (said on news of a bereavement)

"Listen, Izzie's sister passed away last night."
  "What, really? *Baruch dayan ha-emet!*"

The traditional response on being informed of the death of a friend or acquaintance is *baruch dayan ha-emet!* embodying the Talmudic philosophy that one must bless God for the bad as well as for the good. One may also hear Israelis saying *baruch dayan ha-emet!* when (if only it were just "if") they hear on the radio about some tragic loss of life or terrorist atrocity. English is poorer for not having something similar.

Barúch habá! (Ashkenazi: **Bóruch habó!**)   "Welcome!"

"Hi, Vivian, I wasn't expecting you—*baruch haba!*"

The first time a Jew (well, a Jewish boy, in fact) hears the words *baruch haba* is when he's borne into the room for his *brit mila* (circumcision).

It's also a general way of saying welcome, on any occasion, and the words often adorn the hallway in a Jewish home. It literally means "blessed is the person that comes in." To two or more people, you say *bruchim haba'im!* (Ashkenazi: *bruchim habo'im!*).

— ❧ —

Barúch ha-Shém! (Ashkenazi: **Bóruch ha-Shém!**) "Thank God!"

"Shimon's cough's a bit better this morning, *baruch ha-Shem!*"

Orthodox Jews say *baruch ha-Shem* a lot. It's often more than just an expression of relief, uttered with a verbal exclamation mark. It can be an expression of faith, uttered quietly, almost solemnly. I know people who answer every "How are you?" with a simple *baruch ha-Shem*, whether they're very well or they're not. But there again, how often does anyone answer "How are you?" with "Not very well, thank you"?

— ❧ —

Barúch she-petaráni (Ashkenazi: **Bóruch she-potráni**) "Good riddance!"

"Has she gone? *Boruch she-potrani!*"

Literally "blessed be He who has released me." *Baruch she-petarani* is taken—with a wink and a sparkle—from the blessing traditionally uttered by a father in the synagogue as soon as his son has recited his Bar Mitzvah reading. Up until that moment, the son's sins and merits were deemed to rest on the shoulders of his father. From that moment on, they are deemed his own (fathers' lib). Hence, its general use as "good riddance."

— ❧ —

Batél be-shishím (Ashkenazi: **Bótl be-shíshim**) Of no significance

"Don't worry if you made a few mistakes—it's all *batel be-shishim.*"

Batel be-shishim is Hebrew at its cutest. At heart a legal term for when a small amount of a forbidden food falls into a kosher food (if it comes to no more than a sixtieth, it's usually deemed null and void), *batel be-shishim* was—as you might imagine—an everyday concern for the Jewish housewife. And it came to be a metaphor for anything undesirable that pales into unimportance.

— ❧ —

Batlán, pl. batlaním (Ashkenazi: **bátlen, pl. batlónim**)   Layabout

"If you ask me, the whole board should resign—they're a bunch of *batlanim*."

Where would Hebrew be without Yiddish? For a thousand years, Yiddish gave houseroom to hundreds, even thousands of Hebrew words, an expression of the bond felt by Jewish men, women, and children to their religion and its writings. Often, whole new sets of Hebrew words were hatched *within* Yiddish. And words got new meanings, with a folksy or slangy touch.

One was *batlan*. In ancient times it meant "man of leisure (always on call to attend the synagogue)." Nowadays: "layabout."

— ✀ —

Bat Mitzváh (Ashkenazi: **Bas Mítzve**)   Ceremony of a Jewish girl's coming of age; girl who has reached that age

"They've decided to have Charlotte's *Bat Mitzvah* on the cruise ship?"

"If you're *Bat Mitzvah*, Melissa, you have to fast like everyone."

Bat Mitzvah means subject to (literally "daughter to") commandments.

Everyone, from Chasidim in Williamsburg to (*lehavdil*) Reconstructionists out in Utah, holds a *Bar Mitzvah*. Not so with a *Bat Mitzvah*. That a girl comes of age at twelve is a hallowed idea, of course, and twelve is the age at which girls start keeping the Torah for real. But the idea of celebrating it like a *Bar Mitzvah* is a modern one, a tampering with the past in some people's eyes, even a sellout to feminism.

And so the Ultraorthodox ignore it, the Modern Orthodox go for a special girl's ceremony quite different from the *Bar Mitzvah* (and called *Bat Chayil* or *Bat Mitzvah*), and the non-Orthodox go for the full works.

— ✀ —

Báu máyim ad néfesh (Ashkenazi: **Bóu máyim ad nófesh**)   Things are critical; it's make or break

When King David began the sixty-ninth psalm with the cry *bau mayim ad nafesh*, he was saying literally, "The waters are up to my neck," and he went on, "I drown in the muddy deep . . ." He presumably meant it metaphorically—as we do today.

— ✀ —

Bechirá (Ashkenazi: **Bechíre**)   Free will

"Some of these Nazi war criminals even claim they were forced to do it, as if they were animals with no *bechira*."

To what extent does a person have *bechira*? This issue was high on the agenda of Jewish thought in the Middle Ages, and again, in modern times, with the rise of the creed of determinism and behaviorism and popular notions of the chemical mind. That every human being has a fundamental *bechira* between good and evil is never in doubt.

– ❦ –

Bechiyá le-dorót (Ashkenazi: **Bechíye le-dóres**)   A cause for eternal regret

"If they allow that reactor to be built there, it'll be a *bechiya le-dorot*."

Bechiya le-dorot literally means "a moaning for generations." The wailing was the moaning of the Israelites, in the wastes of the wilderness, after rumors were spread that the Promised Land was a land of giants and freaks. The rumors were swiftly discredited. But the moaners went on and on. And that date became *Tisha be-Av*, the date on which the Temple was destroyed.

Meanwhile, *bechiya le-dorot* came to denote anything that's likely to be regretted by generations to come (such as our environmental policies?).

– ❦ –

Bedikát chamétz (Ashkenazi: **Bedíkes chómetz**)   Checking for leaven

"While we were doing *bedikat chametz*, we found a whole Entenmann's doughnut behind the couch."

See also *Chametz*, "Leaven" and *Bi'ur Chametz*, "Destroying leaven."

Bedikat chametz usually takes place on the evening before the *Pesach* (Passover) festival. It's the final check to ensure that there'll be no *chametz* (leaven, such as bread and cake) left in one's house during the festival, traditionally done with a candle, a feather, and kids getting under foot and making a pain in the neck of themselves. Actually, the checking for *chametz* will have been going on for several days already—in offices, schools, farms, El Al planes, Israeli army bases, in short anywhere where food may have been.

Personally, I find doing *bedikat chametz* in my car the hardest.

One must check every place, every nook, every cranny, as far as is feasible, and the pockets in one's clothes and in the children's clothes require *bedika* too and should be shaken out the following day during the *bi'ur.*

Kitsur Shulchan Aruch

Be-ezrát ha-Shém (Ashkenazi: **Be-ézras ha-Shém**)   With God's help

"We'll buy some land in Israel and grow our own food, *be-ezrat ha-Shem.*"

Used mainly by the Orthodox, this phrase is also abbreviated in writing as the letters *bet-heh* and placed at the top of any letter or other piece of writing. Bar-Ilan, the religious university near Tel Aviv, incorporates *bet-heh* into its letterhead.

Bereshít (Ashkenazi: **Beréyshis**)   The Book of Genesis

Bereshit is the first book of the Torah, named after its first word, meaning "in the beginning." It describes the Creation and humankind's moral history from Adam to the emergence of the Jewish people.

Why was the world created with the letter *bet?* Just as the *bet* is closed on all sides except forward, so too we are not at liberty to interpret what is above and beneath, before and after, except from the day of Creation forward.

The Midrash on Genesis

Said Rabbi Yitschak: "The Torah should surely have begun with the first commandment to the Jewish people. Why then does it begin with *Bereshit?* Because if the world's nations should say to the Israel: 'You are robbers, because you have seized the lands of the Canaanites,' they can retort: 'All the Earth belongs to the Almighty. He created it and gave it to those whom He deemed worthy; and when He willed, He took it from them and gave it to us.' "

The first comment on the Torah
by the revered medieval commentator, Rashi

Besamím (Ashkenazi: **Bsómim**)   Spices (for the *Havdala* ceremony)

"Shari, bring me the wine and the *besamim* box. Bobbie, bring me the candle."

Besamim "spices" are the traditional antidote to the passing of the Sabbath and the return of the workaday week on Saturday evening. As part of the *Havdala* ceremony marking the end of the Sabbath, *besamim* are passed round and whiffed—commonly cloves but they can be anything. The mystical idea is that the *neshama yetera* (the "extra soul") granted during *Shabbat* has been withdrawn and some kind of symbolic compensation is in order.

— ❧ —

Be-séder   OK

"From your hotel to the beach: fifteen shekels, OK?"
   "*Be-seder.*"

"You can't start changing the arrangements now, John. It's not *be-seder.*"

Literally "in order." Israelis' every other word is *be-seder*. Try to use it too. If you can't remember it, think of the Passover *Seder* night, so called because it follows a particular order of ceremonies.
   When you're in Israel, however, you'll find that Israelis also seem to say *OK* all the time. So say *OK* too, but with a nice Israeli accent.

— ❧ —

Be-sha'á tová!   "Good luck!"

"Has Sue gone into labor? Well, *be-sha'a tova . . .*"

Ashkenazi Jews traditionally used a Yiddish version of this phrase: *in a guter sho!*

Be-sha'a tova is the standard Israeli (and Sephardi) good luck greeting. As its literal meaning "in a good hour" suggests, *be-sha'a tova* contains echoes of a traditional astrological mindset—the same echoes as the universally loved *mazel tov!* "congratulations!" which literally means "good constellation!" But don't mix them up: *Mazel tov!* is said upon a joyous event, for example after Sue has come out of labor with a bouncing baby.

— ❧ —

Be-shem omró (Ashkenazi: **Be-shem ómroh**)   Giving credit for an idea

"Jeff, I don't mind if you use my idea on your client, but say it *be-shem omro.*"

If you're going to use someone else's idea, it might be a good idea to say it *be-shem omro*, literally "in the name of the person who said it." *Be-shem omro* makes the world a nicer place. If not every joke in this book is given *be-shem omro*, it's because Jews have been telling the same morbid jokes for hundreds of years.

Said Rabbi Chanina: "Anyone who says an idea *be-shem omro* brings redemption to the world, for it is written: 'And Esther said to the King, in the name of Mordechai. . . .'"

The Talmud, Megila

Be-siyáta di-shmáya (Ashkenazi: **Be-siyása di-shmáya**)   With the help of Heaven

"Stop worrying! *Be-siyata di-shmaya* you'll be able to sell the house."

Be-siyata di-shmaya (strictly speaking, it's Aramaic rather than Hebrew) is a common expression among Sephardim. Among Ashkenazim, it's the Ultraorthodox who like to use it, but mainly in abbreviated form at the beginning of letters and other writing.

Bet Din (Ashkenazi: **Beys Din, Bézdin)**   Religious court

"If you both go to *Bezdin*, Jim, it'll probably save you a fortune in lawyers' fees."

There was a time when two Jews with a dispute automatically took it to a *Bet Din*, a rabbinical court, which could rule on anything from a quarrel over a fence to murder most foul, and fine or imprison the culprits. But nowadays that's a thing of the past; Western governments have long ago done away with Jewish legal autonomy, except in the sphere of religious ritual.

Nowadays, to most Jews, a *Bet Din* is something to do with getting a Jewish divorce. The only time it exercises its traditional broad powers is when two religious Jews agree among themselves to use it for a civil dispute (which may work out to be a bit cheaper and much quicker).

Be-teyavón   "Enjoy your meal!"

"Wow, this looks delicious—*be-teyavon*, everyone!"

Literally "bon appétit!" This is an automatic way of beginning a meal in Israel. *Be-teyavon* creates a sense of togetherness—as well as serving the useful function of an "on your mark, get set, go!" Israelis may not say *bevakasha* as often as English speakers say please, but their *be-teyavon* makes up for it.

— ❧ —

Bet ha-Mikdásh (Ashkenazi: **Beys ha-Míkdesh**)   The Jerusalem Temple

"Can you imagine how many people will want to live in Jerusalem when the Third *Bet ha-Mikdash* is built?"

The Orthodox Jewish world lives in a state of perpetual expectation that the Third *Bet ha-Mikdash* will be built by the *Mashiach* (Messiah) in its own lifetime, and mentions this in virtually all its prayers. The First and Second *Bet ha-Mikdash* were constructed in Jerusalem around the years 1000 and 500 B.C.E., respectively. Both were destroyed, and the *churban* (destruction) and subsequent dispersion are still lamented amid much self-searching; until the Ingathering and the Rebuilding (in whichever order), much of Jewish observance remains suspended.

Today, certain circles in Israel are actively preparing for the *Bet ha-Mikdash* and the resumption of sacrificial ceremonies on *Har ha-Bayit* (The Temple Mount).

Whoever never saw Jerusalem in its splendor never saw a beautiful city; and whoever never saw the *Bet ha-Mikdash* while it yet stood never saw a magnificent building.

The Talmud, Suka

Erets Yisrael is the navel of the world, and Jerusalem is its center, and the *Bet ha-Mikdash* is at the center of Jerusalem, and the Holy of Holies is at its center, and the Holy Ark is at the center of the Holy of Holies, and in front of it is the Foundation Stone on which the world was founded.

The Midrash

— ❧ —

Bet midrásh (Ashkenazi: **Beys médresh**)   Study hall

"The Talmud class will meet on Tuesday in the *bet midrash*."

The traditional epicenter of Jewish life is not the synagogue but the *bet midrash*, a building, or hall, or even just a cozy little room, lined with learned tomes and devoted to *shiurim* (seminars), *chavruses* (twosome study), and every other kind of intellectual activity.

In many American communities, miserable to relate, the *bet midrash* has degenerated into little more than the library or the place where the rabbi writes his sermons. But in all kinds of unexpected places, the *bet midrash* is still alive—an entree into the Jewish fifth dimension.

That implacable opponent of early Reform Judaism, Rabbi Moshe Sofer, proposed ostracizing the whole movement. But Rabbi Yisrael Salanter strongly disagreed:

"First, let's use force of reason," he said. "If that fails and they go on building modern temples with pulpits and organs, I say we agree to it. But what we do then is this: We put ten learned men in every one of their new temples and sit and study Talmud. By them, it's a 'temple'—by us, it's a *bet midrash!*"

— ❦ —

Bevakashá   Please; go ahead; you're welcome

"If you're determined to do it, then *bevakasha.*"

Contrary to some reports, everyone in Israel says *bevakasha*, but not necessarily in the same places that an English speaker might expect to hear *please*. You can easily purchase five bus tickets, thirteen cans of Coke, and ten kilos of sunflower seeds without once saying *bevakasha*, but just let someone say *toda* (thank you) to you, and you'll feel an overwhelming need to respond *bevakasha*. If you think it all sounds oddly reminiscent of German *bitteschön*, you may be right; if you want to blame it on Russian *pazhalsta*, you're probably right too.

— ❦ —

(The) Biká   The Jordan Valley

The *Bika*—or *Bikat ha-Yarden*, to use the full name—is the narrow valley through which the tiny Jordan River (marking the border between the Israelis and the Jordanians) winds its way down from the Sea of Galilee to the Dead Sea. Hundreds of feet below sea level, rainless, and searingly hot, the *Bika* nevertheless supports a growing number of Israeli villages, with their miles of vineyards and tomato fields—and the town of Jericho.

— ❦ —

Bikúr cholím (Ashkenazi: **Bíkur chólim**)   Visiting the sick

"The kids will be along later—they're doing *bikur cholim.*"

Bikur cholim is one of the classic elements of *gemilut chasadim* (good works). Halacha (Jewish Law) pays great attention to how to visit the sick, when to visit, and what to say. There is even a hospital in Jerusalem today called *Bikur Cholim*.

Said Rav Huna: "Visiting the sick takes away a sixtieth of their sickness."

The Midrash on Leviticus

The main point of *Bikur Cholim* is to find out what the patient needs and to pray for their recovery.

Kitsur Shulchan Aruch

— ❧❧ —

Bimá (Ashkenazi: **Bíme**)   Platform for the Torah reading

"Don't let the children run around up on the *bima* during the reading!"

In the center of every synagogue is a *bima*. Ancient custom has the prayer leader or cantor standing at ground level—praying "from the depths"—while the *bima* is used primarily for reciting the Torah, blowing the *shofar*, making announcements, and so on. But a newer practice is for the cantor to stand on the *bima* at all times.

The name *Ha-Bima* was also selected for the world-famous Hebrew theater founded in Moscow and spirited to Tel Aviv under Stalin. *Bima* in fact means "stage," which isn't a bad description of the synagogue *bima* when certain cantors are on it.

— ❧❧ —

Birkát ha-Mazón (Ashkenazi: **Bírkas ha-Mózen**)   Grace after meals

"Let's first say *Birkat ha-Mazon* and then have coffee and ice cream in the den."

The popular Ashkenazi Yiddish word for *Birkat ha-Mazon*, "bentshing," is not Hebrew and goes back to a Jewish Latin dialect of sorts.

Birkat ha-Mazon is traditionally said after any meal taken with bread. Although its name means "blessing for food," it is actually far more: a lengthy series of blessings and prayers about *Erets Yisrael* (the Holy Land), the ruined Temple, the Messiah—in fact, the whole Jewish spiritual shopping list.

And hardly surprising—having a meal is itself meant to be a spiritual experience. Anyone who has listened to *Birkat ha-Mazon* being sung at a summer camp will never forget it.

— ❧❧ —

Birkát Kohaním (Ashkenazi: **Bírkas Kohánim**)   Priestly blessing

"There were about ten priests to say *Birkat Kohanim* in the synagogue today."

Great mystique surrounds the biblical tradition of *Birkat Kohanim*, blessing the people. The *kohanim* (priests) take up position in front of the Holy Ark, the worshippers lower their gaze, men sometimes wrapping their face in their *tallit* and nestling their children beneath it; and then the *kohanim* form their fingers into the customary shape, and in a slow and haunting chant they pronounce the three short blessings as prescribed in the Book of Numbers. In the Diaspora, the priests generally *duchen* (to use the popular Ashkenazi-Hebrew term for saying *Birkat Kohanim*) on festivals; in Israel, they *duchen* every day.

How ancient these words are was underlined by the recent find in Israel of the only known biblical verses dating back to preexilic times: a tiny charm bearing the *Birkat Kohanim*.

May the Lord bless you and protect you.
May the Lord make His countenance shine upon you and be gracious to you.
May the Lord show you favor and grant you peace.

Translation of the *Birkat Kohanim*

Bitachón (Ashkenazi: **Bitóchen**)   Trust (in God)

"Sure there are big risks, but you have to have *bitachon*."

Bitachon was the first special quality instilled in the fathers of the Jewish people: Abraham's *bitachon* that God would grant him an heir, Isaac's *bitachon* that he would not truly be a human sacrifice, Moses' *bitachon* that millions could cross the wilderness.

Bitúl zman (Ashkenazi: **Bítl zman**)   Time wasting

"Don't watch TV so much. It's such a *bitul zman*."

In traditional Jewish eyes, time was created for the performance of *mitzvot* (religious deeds). And so *bitul zman* is not just wasting time, it amounts to the heinous offense of killing time.

They say that the Chafetz Chayim, a revered prewar sage, used to keep an account at the end of every day of how he had spent every minute—the ultimate response to *bitul zman*.

Biúr chamétz (Ashkenazi: **Bíur chómetz**)   Ceremonial disposal of *chametz*

"Dump all the cornflakes and bread and things on the ground, and we'll do *biur chametz*."

See *Chametz*, "Leaven" and *Pesach*, "Passover."

On the morning before *Pesach* (Passover), the last of the *chametz* (leavened food) has to be disposed of; there must be no *chametz* in Jewish possession for the next eight days. What gets sold to a Gentile has been sold. The remainder is disposed of via *biur chametz*. The favorite method is to burn it. All over Jerusalem, *biur chametz* takes place in the street, much to the delight of crowds of small boys and all frustrated arsonists.

— ❧ —

Bli néder (Ashkenazi: **Bli néyder**)   "I'll do my best"

"OK, I'll drive you to the airport on Monday, *bli neder*."

Literally "without vowing," this is added to any casual promise to avoid it being taken as an absolute undertaking.

Judaism was traditionally very much opposed to people making vows at the drop of a hat but without being able to do much about it. So the *Halacha* (Jewish Law) recommended adding the phrase *bli neder* whenever one made a resolution to oneself or a casual promise to someone else. (A solemn promise is, of course, a promise and must be kept.)

Orthodox Jews still habitually add *bli neder* to casual promises.

— ❧ —

Brachá, pl. **brachót** (Ashkenazi: **Bróche**, pl. **bróches**)   Blessing

"His granddaughter already knows how to say the *bracha* for eating fruit."

"You know, that new hard disk is a real *bracha*."

Saying *brachot* in recognition of Divine *brachot* is one of the most ingrained of traditional Jewish habits. The *bracha* over wine, the *brachot* for eating bread, cereals, vegetables, fruits, the *bracha* on seeing the first fruit blossom of spring . . . and the hardest one to say, the *bracha* on hearing tragic tidings (see *Baruch dayan ha-emet*).

"Rabbi, give me a *bracha* to have a child," said the attractive young woman.

The rabbi half closed his eyes, spread his hands over her head, and gave her a *bracha*, but he made every effort to avoid the slightest touch.

The woman was upset. "Can't you actually lay your hands on my head?" she asked. "The closer the *bracha*, the stronger it will be . . ."

The rabbi shook his head. "Show me how you kindled the *Shabbat* candles yesterday," he said. "When you said the *bracha*, did you touch the flames?"

"Of course not," she said. "I'd burn my fingers!"

"Me too," said the rabbi.

Blessed art Thou, O Lord our God, King of the Universe, who made the great sea.

The traditional Hebrew blessing on seeing the ocean

– ✺ –

Brit milá (Ashkenazi: **Bris mile** or simply **Bris**)   Jewish circumcision

"I'll be in late today, Chris, I have to go to a *bris*."

Compare the expression *B'nai B'rith*, literally "children of the covenant."

The *brit mila* ceremony is usually held on the eighth day of a baby boy's life—in the presence of family and friends. Literally "circumcision covenant," it is the most ancient and arguably the most powerful of Jewish rites.

A young man left the Old Country for America. When, years later, he returned to see his mother, she could hardly recognize him.

"Where's your beard, Dovid?"

"Ach, nobody wears a beard in America."

"But you do keep *Shabbes* still, don't you?"

"Look, Momma, in America the whole country works on *Shabbes!*" The old lady grasped his hand. "Then tell me, what do you eat?"

"Ach, Momma, I know what you're getting at—but it's just so complicated to keep *kosher* in a modern country . . . life is too hectic."

For a few seconds, his mother reflected on this. Then she took a deep breath: "Tell me the truth, my son—do you still have your *bris*?"

– ✺ –

Brógez (Ashkenazi: **Bróyges**)   Cross (with someone); bad blood

"Just smile, Norm, and try to forget that you're *brogez* with her."

"Don't even think of inviting them both. There's a *brogez* that's been going on for years."

I'm no psychologist, but I'll vouch that to be *brogez* is not a mood or an emotion but something verging on a personality trait. It must be, or else how can I (and most other people I know) have aunts and cousins that have been *brogez* with one another for years? So ethnic and indigenously Old Worldly is the sound of *brogez/broyges* that few realize that it's originally Hebrew. Nor, I'll wager, do Israelis, who do their best to keep up the glorious tradition of the *brogez*.

For the fact that *brogez* occurs nowhere in the Bible there can be only one explanation: the ancient rabbis, who delicately edited explicit obscenities out of Scripture, clearly felt that a *brogez* was one too. Jewish history has proved them right.

As Mr. Rabin once observed, there's no predicting Middle East affairs. No one foresaw Sadat's trip to Jerusalem, the Iran-Iraq war, the split in the PLO and the *brogez* between Arafat and Assad. . . . Not only did no one foresee any of it, they foresaw a whole lot of other things that never happened.

Miriam Arad

— ৽৻৽ —

Buréke, pl. **burékes**   Savory pastry

"Two *burekes* with spinach, please, and four with cheese."

The *bureke* may be Turkish, but that, as they say, is history. If you are attacked in a Tel Aviv street by hunger, and you can't face another *pitta* and *falafel*, try the *bureke*, a pastry that's savory and quite a surprise to the Ashkenazi palate. But make sure you ask for some *mapiyot* (napkins) too.

— ৽৻৽ —

Bushá (Ashkenazi: **Búshe**)   Disgrace

"What, he ran away with a graduate student? And in the middle of a semester? What a *busha*!"

Busha means shame or disgrace. It's funny how different cultures have different views of shame. When something happens to prompt an English speaker to declare "What a shame!" it's hardly the sort of thing to bring anyone into disrepute. But when a Jew cries, "What a *busha*!" . . .

— ৽৻৽ —

Chad Gadyá (Ashkenazi: **Chad Gádye**)   Name of the last song in the Passover *Haggadah*

"Little Esti fell asleep in the middle of *Chad Gadya*."

Chad Gadya is literally "one little goat," the opening words of a song universally sung to round off the Passover *Seder* night. The song is a ballad about a little goat who is eaten by a cat who is eaten by a dog who is eaten by, and so on, until the Almighty Himself comes and saves the day. Entirely appropriate to the Passover story and loved by children, who are invariably asleep all over the place by the time you get to *Chad Gadya*.

The words *chad gadya* and indeed the entire song are in Aramaic, a Jewish popular language in ancient and medieval times. But to all intents and purposes Aramaic has always been included with Hebrew as part of *Leshon ha-Kodesh*, "the Holy Tongue."

Chad Gadya, Chad Gadya,
Which Father bought for two pennies,
Chad Gadya.

And along came a cat
And ate the little goat,
Which father bought for two pennies,
Chad Gadya . . .

Translation of the opening of *Chad Gadya*

The next step, the lawyer said, would be for the rich man to sue Birnbaum, Birnbaum me, I my brother, my brother the monk. Like the Passover song *Chad Gadya* . . .

Sholom Aleichem

Chag, pl. chagím   Festival

"The buses in Jerusalem stop running much earlier today, because it's a *chag* this evening."

"We're renting a place in Netanya for the month of the *chagim*."

Chagim in the plural often denotes the holy day season from Rosh Hashanah through Sukkot.

Chag refers to any of the festivals, the big ones and the little ones, the ancient ones and the modern ones. *Chag* is *the* biblical word for festival, yet it has a decidedly modern ring to it, because from postbiblical times Jews tended to use the word *yomtov* (or its Yiddish form, *yontef*) instead, until the Zionist rebirth of spoken Hebrew put *chag* back on the map and unceremoniously dumped *yontef*.

Chag saméach!   "Happy festival!"

Chag sameach! is the Israeli greeting on a festival. It has also been picked up and adopted by modern circles, if only to be different from Ashkenazi traditionalists and old-timers, who prefer *good yontef* or its Yiddish equivalent. Sephardim traditionally say *moadim le-simcha!* ("festivals for joy!").

— ✿ —

Chaláv yisraél (Ashkenazi: **Chólev yisróel**)   Jewish-supervised milk

"They won't eat this milk chocolate because it doesn't contain *chalav yisrael.*"

There is a long-standing practice, strictly adhered to in Ultraorthodox circles though less so elsewhere, of only drinking *chalav yisrael* milk, that is, milk which has been milked under Jewish supervision. The practice stems from a fear of non-*kosher* milk being added, as does indeed happen in some countries.

— ✿ —

Chalitsá (Ashkenazi: **Chalítse**)   Ceremony releasing a man from levirate marriage

"Harvey had to do *chalitsa* last week for Rachel."

One doesn't hear a lot about *chalitsa* but it still takes place. A married man dies childless. If there is a brother, he would in former times have been expected to marry his widowed sister-in-law (levirate marriage). Nowadays, instead, the widow is asked by the Jewish court to perform an ancient symbolic act: she draws a sandal off her brother-in-law's foot. This is called *chalitsa.* Now she is free to marry anyone.

— ✿ —

Chaltúra, pl. chaltúrot   A job on the side, moonlighting

"Dear Mom and Dad,
    We're doing all right in Ramat Gan. With my main job, Diane's teaching, and two *chalturot,* we're just about breaking even . . ."

For years, economists have wondered how, on an Israeli salary, Israelis are able to feed a family and a Fiat. The secret is in a Hebrew word that is not to be found in any Hebrew-English dictionary: *chaltura.*

— ✿ —

Chalútz, pl. chalutzím   Zionist pioneer

"With his khaki shorts, grimy sandals, tousled hair, and splendid moustache, he looked every inch a *chalutz*."

Some would argue that the *chalutz* has passed into Zionist history. There are no more malarial swamps, marauding bedouin, or hostile authorities. But some, seeing two adults and five children in a tiny caravan on a barren windswept mountain with no central heating, car, or clothes dryer, would say, "These are today's *chalutzim*."

Chalutzism is not sacrifice but fulfillment. It is the marriage of innermost, subjective strivings and objective values.

The *chalutz* is an "Individualist." His act satisfies his very own, basic drives for a new life.

The *chalutz* is the socialist (commune man) *par excellence*. He wants the commune, because without it he could not be an individual; for only within the commune can the "new life" flower, *among* humans and not merely *within* them.

A manifesto of 1923

Chamétz (Ashkenazi: **Chómetz**)   Leavened food

"You can't use whiskey on *Pesach*—it's pure *chametz*!"

The word chametz has the same letters as matzo, except that the letter heh has been closed into a letter chet. For matzo signifies humility whereas chametz signifies a closed, arrogant mind.

Chametz is what Jews traditionally don't eat on Passover: any leavened food, which means anything deriving from grain, unless it's been specifically prevented from rising (such as *matzo*). So bread and cookies are out, as are hosts of manufactured foods. But up pop a whole range of specially kosher-for-Passover foods guaranteed *chametz*-free, and even nicer—or at least the packaging is.

Matzo shall be eaten for these seven days, and no *chametz* shall be seen in your possession; no leaven may be seen within your borders.

Exodus 13

Chanukáh (Ashkenazi: **Chánuke**)   The festival of Chanukah

"I've got a few *Chanukah* candles left over from last year, but not enough for eight days."

Chanukah means "inauguration," referring to the Temple. The same root gives you *chinuch*, "education."

Millions of people on the American East Coast probably know what *Chanukah* is, but for the benefit of the other 99 percent of the world's population, *Chanukah* is a festival in December commemorating the successful Jewish spiritual-military revolt, over 2,000 years ago, against a Greek-Syrian attempt to stifle Judaism and ram Greek paganism down their throats. And in memory of the Temple *menorah* (candelabra) defiled by the pagans but miraculously relit, Jews light a special *Chanukah* candelabra on eight successive evenings by a window or front door—for all the world to see. The song for the occasion is *Maoz Tsur,* and parents give their children money or presents.

The days of Chanuka, *the inauguration of our Temple,*
Fill our hearts with glee and joy.
Night and day we spin our tops,
And also eat lots of doughnuts . . .

From an Israeli children's *Chanukah* song

– ✿ –

Chanukiyá, pl. **chanukiyót**   Chanukah candelabra

"Did you see the giant *chanukiyu* in the terminal building at Newark International?"

Chanukiya is a modern Israeli word (borrowed actually from the Sephardim). European Jews traditionally called it a *Chanukah menorah.*

A *chanukiya* is a candelabra used for lighting the *Chanukah* lights: on the first evening of *Chanukah,* one light; on the second, two; and so on, until you light eight lights on the eighth and last evening. The lights are usually wax candles, but some keep up the delightful tradition of using olive oil with a cotton wick. There is, in fact, practically no limit on the design of a *chanukiya.* Here and there you're also bound to see large electric *chanukiyot,* set up in public places (particularly by *Chasidim* of the Lubavitch organization) to proclaim the miracle of *Chanukah* as a festival of religious liberty to the world at large. They've even managed to set one up in the Kremlin, but not yet (as I write) in the Beijing Hall of the People.

– ✿ –

Charatá (Ashkenazi: **Charóte**)   Remorse

"Rivka called me to say she has real *charata* over what she said at the *Sheva Brachot* last night—it just kind of came out."

Charata is identified by moralists as the first stage in the process of *teshuva* (repentance). Next comes the apology. Kids, of course, often act as if saying "sorry" can absolve them from having to have *charata* at all.

At the end of every quarrel comes *charata*.

Solomon ibn Gabirol

— ❧ —

Charedí, pl. **Charedím** (Ashkenazi: **Charéydi**, pl. **Charéydim**)   Ultra-orthodox Jew

"I think some *Charedim* have moved out of Brooklyn to Jersey now."

Literally "God-fearing." This is a cover term (used particularly among themselves) for the Ultraorthodox, that is, those who keep up a stringent religious lifestyle and keep the modern world—and modern education—at arm's length, even though they often have to make a livelihood out of it. Many, though by no means all, *Charedim* are *Chasidim*.

— ❧ —

Charóset (Ashkenazi: **Charóhses**)   A sweet spread eaten at the Passover *Seder*

"Can I have a bit more *charoset* and a bit less *maror* on my *matzo*, please?"

I have never met a person who didn't love *charoset*, a mix of apples, walnuts, cinnamon, and wine (Ashkenazi recipe) eaten with *matso* and *maror* on the *Seder* night. I know that it's meant to embody the mortar that the Israelites in Egypt spread between the hated bricks, but it tastes downright delicious. Might it subliminally also embody the way Jews have learned to sweeten their suffering?

— ❧ —

Chas ve-shalóm! (Ashkenazi: **Chas ve-shólem!**)   "Heaven forbid, perish the thought!"

"If there's ever a fire, *chas ve-shalom*, keep all the doors closed."

"Are they thinking of getting a divorce?"
  "*Chas ve-shalom!*"

Hebrew, even in its skeletal Diaspora form, is well stocked with prophylactics, words that seek to head off misfortunes, disasters, and catastrophes. There's *chas ve-shalom* (literally "mercy and peace"), *chas ve-chalila*—both in common use—and the more erudite *rachmana litslan*. And also *lo alenu.*

– ℐℰℛ –

Chashásh   A fear, a danger

"Of course, if you take a Friday flight there's always a *chashash* that you'll be stranded somewhere on *Shabbat.*"

It's hard to be a Jew, the saying goes, and one of the harder parts is the *chashash*, the danger that you may overstep the rules. Many of the well-known laws were actually introduced by the rabbis of old as precautions to obviate any *chashash*. Thus you remove all bread and *chametz* before Passover, even if you've sold it, because of a *chashash* that you may eat it inadvertently. Of course, *chashash* can get out of control. The Talmud was thinking of this when it said not to worry too much about mice bringing back indoors the bread you've just cleaned out. On the other hand, think how much happier Oedipus would have been if only he'd had a bit more *chashash*.

– ℐℰℛ –

Chasíd, pl. Chasidím (Ashkenazi: **Chósid, pl. Chasídim**)   Chasid

"We sell a lot of this style of wig to wives of *Chasidim*—in fact, that woman over there is married to a Lubavitcher *Chosid.*"

See *Chasidut.*

Literally "pious one." All kinds of people may be pious, of course, but the word *Chasid* generally refers nowadays to Ultraorthodox groups perpetuating the heritage of the Chasidic movement. Arising in eighteenth- and nineteenth-century eastern Europe, Chasidism (in Hebrew, *Chasidut*) sought to emphasize the value of piety and spontaneity rather than dry intellectualism—with charismatic rabbis holding court to adoring followers. Today's *Chasidim* live mainly in New York and Israel, maintaining a pre-Holocaust eastern European ambience and bucking the birth rate.

The word *Chasid* generally refers to men. Hebrew does have a word *chasida*, but it means "a stork."

My father, an enlightened spirit, believed in man.
My grandfather, a fervent Hasid, believed in God.

The one taught me to speak, the other to sing.
Both loved stories.
But when I tell mine, I hear their voices.
Whispering from beyond the silenced storm,
They are what links the survivor to their memory.

Elie Wiesel, *Souls on Fire*

Chasíd shotéh (Ashkenazi: **Chósid shóhte**)   Pious fool; blind follower

"Some of these political TV ads are so bad that only a *chasid shoteh* would believe them."

Chasid originally meant anyone who was pious, not just *Chasidim*; and the phrase *chasid shoteh* (literally "mad pious") is a fitting description for anyone who takes piety, or faith, to absurd lengths.

What is a *chasid shoteh*? Someone who sees a child floundering in the river and says, "When I've taken off my tefilin I'll rescue him."

The Jerusalem Talmud, Sota

A *chasid shoteh* is someone to whom Heaven decided to grant stupidity, except that he went beyond the strict letter of the law and decided to be even more stupid.

Rabbi Menachem Mendl of Kotsk

Chasidéy umót ha-olám (Ashkenazi: **Chasídey úmes ho-óhlom**)
The pious of the world

"Raoul Wallenberg will go down in history as one of the outstanding *chasidey umot ha-olam*."

To a people condemned to such isolation, the thought that out there somewhere are hosts of *chasidey umot ha-olam* is a precious consolation. Jewish folklore treasures the memory of Jethro, Moses' father-in-law, of the many pious Romans in the Talmud, and others down the centuries. Maimonides ranked all Gentiles abiding by the seven basic Noahide Laws (see *sheva mitzvot livney noach*) as *chasidey umot ha-olam*.

The term has recently been applied in Israel and the United States to all those countless Christians who rescued Jews from the Nazis.

Chasidút (Ashkenazi: **Chasídes**)   Chasidism

"Jerry goes with some of the guys from the office to a *shiur* [seminar] in *chasidut* every lunchtime."

For *Chasidim*, the very essence of Torah is *Chasidut*, the philosophy of God and the human soul derived from Kabbalah, which seeks to read every Jewish observance and every biblical verse from a particular spiritual angle.

The study of Kabbalah *lifts the Jew to Heaven.*
The study of Chasidut *brings down Heaven to the Jew.*

Rabbi Shneur Zalman of Ladi

– 🙣 –

Chatán (Ashkenazi: **Chósn**)   Bridegroom

"Would the *chatan* please come this way to lift the veil?"

See also *Chatuna,* "Wedding" and *Mechutanim,* "In-laws."

Being a *chatan* involves certain minor challenges, like fasting before the wedding ceremony, lifting the veil of the *kala* (bride) to make sure she is who she is, stamping a glass underfoot, and, in Orthodox circles, surviving *sheva brachot* (a week of banquets).

A *chatan* is like a monarch.

The Midrash

– 🙣 –

Chatán Bereshít (Ashkenazi: **Chósn Bréyshis**)   Bridegroom of Genesis

"Why are they making Mr. Greenspan *Chatan Bereshit*—what has *he* done for the synagogue?"

Every year the honor of being called up to the reading of the opening lines of the Torah on the festival of *Simchat Torah* is given to an important member of the community. He is proclaimed *Chatan Bereshit* , the "bridegroom of Genesis." The relationship between the Jewish people and the Torah is traditionally described as that of two lovers. In the synagogue I attended as a child in London's East End, the *Chatan Bereshit* and his fellow *Chatan Torah* would be led in with all the pomp and circumstance of a real wedding.

    The whole thing is consummated the following *Shabbat* with a big party.

– 🙣 –

Chatán Toráh (Ashkenazi: **Chósn Tóhre**)   Bridegroom of the Torah

"I hope you can come along to the synagogue this *Simchat Torah*—my father's going to be the *Chatan Torah*."

As with the *Chatan Bereshit* (see entry), to be proclaimed *Chatan Torah* is a great honor. He is called up to the reading of the closing lines of the Torah. He, too, throws a party.

— ❦ —

Chatuná (Ashkenazi: **Chásne**)   Wedding

"I checked with the band but they're already booked for two *chasnes* on that date."

Although for a *chatuna* you really only need one *chatan* (bridegroom), one *kala* (bride), and two *edim* (witnesses), in practice you'll want to have one *rav* (rabbi), one *chazan* (cantor), one *shomer* (kashrut supervisor), one caterer, one florist, one keyboard player, and about five hundred guests.

   And of course one *chupa* (wedding canopy).

— ❦ —

Chavrúta (Ashkenazi: **Chavrúse**)   Twosome for religious study; a partner in such a twosome

"Every afternoon, Ira and I had a *chavruta* in *Tenach* [Bible], but he's started college now."

"Cheryl, I'm looking for a *chavruta* to study with during the week. Know anyone?"

The *chavruta* is the secret of the old Jewish study skill, but a secret that Jews would willingly share with the world's Secretaries of Education, if only they would ask.

   Two people, at roughly the same level, get together to study a text (they may have prepared it, they may have not), taking turns to read and explain it as they see it, discussing, debating, even questioning it—for half an hour, an hour . . . The net result is that they know it inside out, generally far better than if they'd studied it singly. Of course, they may permit themselves a few digressions, but sleep they won't; nor will they doodle.

   The *chavruta* still thrives in *yeshivot* and wherever traditional study survives. The *chavruta* is probably also why Israeli school students like to study in pairs.

A *chavruta* is like a stone: A stone in itself has no value. But when you start rubbing one stone on another, sparks fly.

Rabbi Mordechai of Lechovitz

– ✾ –

Chay [rhymes with "sky"]   Alive; name for a kind of pendant.

"We're buying her a beautiful *chay* to wear around her neck."

It is ancient Jewish practice to wear charms with Hebrew lettering or Scriptural verses. Today the custom is widespread to wear a pendant with the word *chay*, meaning "alive," around the neck—and as the numerical value of its letters is eighteen, gifts on *Bar Mitzvahs* and other such occasions frequently feature the value eighteen.

The people of Israel is chay!
Our Father is still chay!

Translation of the most enduring of the Jewish Refusenik songs of
the Brezhnev years

– ✾ –

Chazák u-barúch!   Words of congratulation to someone honored in the synagogue

See *Yishar koach!*

Chazak u-baruch! (literally "strong and blessed!") are the traditional Sephardi words of congratulation to anyone who has been granted an honor in the synagogue, such as being called to the reading of the Torah. A typical reply is *gam tihye!* ("so may you be!") or *chazak ve-emats!* ("be strong and courageous!"). To Ashkenazi ears it all sounds exotic and vaguely macho, but perhaps that's how Sephardim feel about an Ashkenazi *yishar koach!*

– ✾ –

Chazaká (Ashkenazi: **Chazóke**)   Automatic presumption

"What, she said *Mazel tov* when you told her I had a baby? Then there's a *chazaka* that she's Jewish."

Chazaka is actually a legal term. (Hebrew's full of them, because Jewish life was always full of Talmud study.)

When there are strong grounds for making a certain assumption, one talks about there being a *chazaka*. If you walk into a board room and someone is sitting in the chairperson's seat and everyone is listening intently, there's a *chazaka* that it's the chairperson. There's a *chazaka* that an incumbent president will be reelected. Abba Eban once said there was a *chazaka* that if a nonaligned country at the United Nations proposed that the world was square, they would get a two-thirds majority for it.

— ℘ —

Chazál   The Rabbis of the Talmud

"Much of the Passover *Haggadah* dates back to *Chazal*."

Based on the initial letters of *Chachameynu Zichronam Livracha* ("Our Sages of Blessed Memory"), this is the word usually used in Orthodox circles for the Rabbis of the Talmud.

— ℘ —

Chazán, pl. **chazaním** (Ashkenazi: **Cházn**, pl. **chazónim**)   Cantor

"He's an old-style *chazn*—you know, the sort that made them cry rather than talk."

Time was when every Jewish mother dreamed of her daughter marrying a successful *chazn*—to fill the synagogue with that breathtaking blend of operatics and folk known as *chazanut* (or *chazones*) was one of the most wondrous things any Jewish vocal artist could aspire to. But everybody knows what happened to Al Jolson's *chazn*'s career, and everybody knows what has happened to popular tastes in music. Now we have guitar-strumming *chazanim* with the latest selection of Israeli hits.

Reb Melekh, the *Chazn*, a handsome long-bearded, thick-necked man, had been standing on his feet since early that morning. He stood before the Creator with outstretched arms, praying devotedly, crying and pleading for mercy for the people who had chosen him to beg forgiveness for their great sins and ask that they be inscribed for a year of health and peace.

Sholom Aleichem

Motke the baker couldn't sing the prayers, he couldn't even get his tongue around some of the words, but he insisted that he was the *chazn* of the synagogue.
    One day, at the end of the service, an unassuming stranger came up to him and patted him on the back.
    "It's a difficult job we have to do—not so, *chazn*?"
    Motke beamed. "Are you a professional *chazn* too, then?"
    "Oh me? No, perish the thought . . . I'm a clerk."

— ℘ —

Chazanút (Ashkenazi: **Chazónes**)   Cantorial singing

"I always go to the synagogue in the next town—you get better *chazanut.*"

See *Chazan,* "Cantor."

Chazanut was one of those things you either loved or hated. The experienced *chazan* could take the most insignificant-looking word in the Hebrew prayers and transform it into a rhapsody of mode and warble—and emotion. Once upon a time, in the age of vaudeville and music hall, congregations were quite capable of joining in and singing, and crying, with all their hearts. And if they identified with their prayers, there was no such thing as an insignificant word. *Chazanut* records sold in the hundreds of thousands. Will it ever come back?

– ❦ –

Chazír, pl. **chazirím** (Ashkenazi: **Cházer,** pl. **chazéyrim**)   Pig

"He eats non-*kosher* meat in college, but he won't eat *chazir.*"

"Not even a thank-you for the gift! He's a real *chazer.*"

Chazir is probably the final barrier that the assimilating Jew will hesitate to cross. True, pig is just one of many non-*kosher* animals. (And using pigskin leather is perfectly OK.) But *chazir* is a potent symbol: Jews have for so long been persecuted for not eating pig while everyone around them does.

– ❦ –

Chéder, pl. **chadarím** (Ashkenazi: **Chéyder,** pl. **chadórim**)   Traditional small-time Jewish school

"Their school's so run-down, it's almost like a *cheyder.*"

It's almost impossible to be objective about a *cheyder.* Literally "a room," that's what it basically was in the collective memory of American Jews: a privately run small-time religious school, after regular school hours, where chafing children got a smattering of Hebrew reading and Jewish knowledge.

But there is more to *cheyder* than that. In the Old Country, when Jews devoted the full school day to Jewish education, *chadorim* regularly turned out a class of educated Jew who would have found a book like this quite pointless. In Britain, *cheyder* is still a perfectly respectable word for Jewish afternoon school.

Restless after a day in public school, where discipline has to be taken seriously, and bored by the rasping drone of the melamed, the pupils resent the *cheyder* as a theft of time that might better be used in playing stickball; soon they come to see it as a theatre of war in which their aim is to torment the *melamed* as ingeniously as possible.

Irving Howe

— ❧ —

Chérem   Excommunication

"If he really is guilty of fraud, he should be put into *cherem*."

Once, when Jews used to run their own internal affairs in eastern Europe or in the Middle East, it was in no way abnormal for rabbis, with the consent of their community, to put someone in *cherem* for some heinous offense. It involved uttering various curses and a ban of varying degrees.

Nowadays, in Israeli Ultraorthodox circles, the *cherem* weapon is still used.

. . . may Divine wrath end his life, may he choke like Ahitophel in his schemes, may his leprosy be like Gehazi's, may he fall and never arise, and may his grave not be among his people's graves and may his wife be given to others. May _____ be placed under this *cherem*, and may this be his lot, but may I and all Israel be granted peace and blessing . . .

From a traditional Hebrew *cherem* formula

— ❧ —

Cheshbón ha-néfesh (Ashkenazi: Chéshben ha-néfesh)   Soul-searching, self-accounting

"If you're going to sort yourself out, Gary, you'll need to do a thorough *cheshbon ha-nefesh*."

Cheshbon ha-nefesh is literally "accounting of the self." This is the classic Jewish method of self-improvement and character building, and the traditional preliminary to the *teshuva* season between *Rosh Hashanah* and *Yom Kippur*.

All manner of books were, and still are, written as aids to *cheshbon ha-nefesh*. What sales are like, I don't know, but I'm sure they aren't bestsellers.

So much needs doing on that day, quite apart from the *kapara* custom and the special midnight prayers for forgiveness. . . . There is the eating and drinking—to indulge yourself on that day is deemed a *mitzvah* because of the long fast that is to come. You have to do all this by midday; the afternoon is devoted to a *cheshbon ha-nefesh,* a reckoning that is meant to embrace the entire year that has gone by. And it's no easy matter. Look how many days there are in every year and how many imprints of sin one leaves behind as one struggles through each day.

Yehuda Steinberg

– ❧ –

Chévra Kadísha (Ashkenazi: Chévre Kadíshe)   Burial society

"The *Chevra Kadisha* will be coming at eight to prepare the body."

It's difficult to name a nobler body of men and women than the *Chevra Kadisha* (literally, "holy society"). In every major Jewish community, since ancient times, volunteers have prepared the dead for burial. It is, naturally, harrowing work. Volunteers are carefully screened; people who have had no experience of death are hard put to deal with death at close quarters. And, as befits so sensitive a function, they will seek to keep their identity a secret.

Jerusalem's *Chevra Kadisha* is deserving of its name, "the holy society." Those beautiful Jews showed me more of what it means to be a Jew, of what Torah stands for, than all the books I ever read. They tended the corpse gently and reverently, yet did not pretend it was other than a corpse.

Jacob Neusner

– ❧ –

Chèvre   (sing.) Crowd; (pl.) Guys

"I'm so glad that your kids have found themselves a nice *chevre.*"

"Do you know those *chevre* over there?"

Chevre is one of those casual, folksy Yiddishized Hebrew words that the Israelis—though they might profess loathing for Yiddish—have never been able to give up. It goes against all the rules of Hebrew grammar. But it marches on.

– ❧ –

Chévreman   One of the guys

"Being a counselor will be good for you, it'll make you a real *chevreman.*"

Chevreman sounds even more Yiddish than *chevre* (previous entry). But it's as Hebrew as pizza is American. And to call you a *Chevreman* is one of the greatest tributes an Israeli can pay you. (Whether you can call a woman a *chevreman* I can't be sure, but I'd be reluctant to try.)

Chidúsh, pl. chidushím (Ashkenazi: **Chídesh, pl. chidúshim**)   Innovative idea, new information

"You must see the feature I've written. There are some real *chidushim* there."

"Herbie called. They're meeting at 5 P.M."
   "Well? So what's the *chidush*?"

Chidush is drawn from "*Gemara* language," that is, the language of Talmudic analysis and argumentation. In looking at any rabbi's statements, one is trained to assume that their every word was weighed and calculated—nothing was redundant, everything was new information, a *chidush*.
   Another meaning of *chidush*: In the so-called yeshiva world, young men vie with one another to write their own *chidushim* (articles, books) on the texts they've been studying.
   And another, more prosaic: any kind of new information.

Chilúl ha-Shém (Ashkenazi: **Chílul ha-Shém**)   Bringing God's name into disgrace

"If just one single Jew had been involved in that sting, can you imagine the *chilul ha-Shem* it would have created?"

See also *Kiddush ha-Shem*, "Sanctification of God's name" and *Ha-Shem*, "God."

Nothing ever aroused more anxiety in a Jew than the possibility of *chilul ha-Shem*, of Judaism being brought into disrepute as a result of some individual's foolish actions. If the individual is a rabbi or leader, how much worse—noblesse oblige. Worst of all: A *chilul ha-Shem* reaches the outside world and fuels anti-Semitism.
   And so any success by a Jew in politics or big business creates mixed Jewish feelings: pride, and fear of some future *chilul ha-Shem*.

Anyone who causes *chilul ha-Shem*, though he may repent and though the Day of Atonement come and he remain repentant and though he undergo sufferings, cannot gain complete forgiveness until death.

Maimonides, Laws of Repentance

Chilúl shabbát (Ashkenazi: **chílel shábes**).   See **Mechalél shabbát.**

– ✿ –

Chinúch (Ashkenazi: **Chínuch**)   Jewish education

"If you move to Chicago, you'll have no problem with the *chinuch.*"

Chinuch is a high-prestige, high-profile word in the Jewish world today. A pity, then, that the *mechanchim* (educators) are not always paid accordingly.
  Chinuch traditionally started at age 3 or 4 with the *Alef-Bet*, continuing at least up to *Bar Mitzvah* (age 13) with *Chumash* (Five Books of Moses) and practical observances. Girls often made do with less *chinuch*; nowadays it's equal (though perhaps *equal* is a sensitive word).

– ✿ –

Chizúk (Ashkenazi: **Chízuk**)   Encouragement

"Pay him a compliment occasionally when he's at the piano—you have to give the kid a *chizuk.*"

Chizuk is one of a family of Hebrew words that have to do with strength. To wish someone strength is an age-old practice, going back as least as far as Moses who bid his successor Joshua "be strong and courageous"—though not everyone has a task quite so hard as conquering a country and settling a people.

– ✿ –

Chóchem   Wise guy (literally "wise man"; only has an Ashkenazi pronunciation, even in Israeli Hebrew)

"So you thought you could fix it then, did you, *chochem*?"

See also *Chochma,* "Wisdom."

This is one of those beautiful cases where a Hebrew word used within Yiddish has acquired an irony. See *talmid chacham* for the word used in its more literal sense.

– ✿ –

Chochmá (Ashkenazi: **Chóchme,** pl. **chochmes**)   Brains; wisdom; a brilliant idea

"What, he solved it? You know, that guy has real *chochma.*"

"Merv comes to me with all these *chochmes*, but they aren't practical."

See also *Talmid chacham,* "Man of Jewish learning."

Chochma is what Solomon asked for and got. It's the highest rung of wisdom. When the Passover *Haggadah* depicts the four archetypal "sons" and their attitude to their heritage, the *chacham* (wise one) is contrasted with the *rasha* (wicked one).

If one's chochma *exceeds one's good deeds, what is this like?*
Like a tree whose branches are many but whose roots are few.

The Talmud, Avot

. . . for the more *chochma,* the more upset . . .

The Bible, Kohelet (Ecclesiastes)

Rabbi Dov-Ber of Mezeritch used to say:
"For any object to undergo a change, it must first go through a stage of being a nothing. This nothingness is none other than the primal state—the state that came before Creation, a state of chaos that no man can imagine. Take a sprouting seed: before it can sprout in the soil, it must rot away to nothing and lose its very seed-hood. Now the name for this rung is *chochma,* for *chochma* is the stage in thought where nothing is as yet tangible."

Chol ha-Moéd (Ashkenazi: **Chol ha-Móed**)   Intermediate days of a festival

"Let's go to the zoo this *Chol ha-Moed!*"

The festivals of *Pesach* and *Sukkot* begin with one day (outside Israel, two) of the "festival proper" and then come five (or four) days of semifestival, called *Chol ha-Moed,* and finally another one day (or two) of festival proper to round things off. *Chol ha-Moed* is a time to relax.

After all the efforts that go into preparing for *Pesach* and *Sukkot*—cleaning the house of crumbs or of anything whose resemblance to crumbs is entirely coincidental, cooking for the *Seder* night, building the *sukkah*—it's hard not to feel that *Chol ha-Moed* is the Almighty's way of saying, "These days are on Me." Orthodox Jews don't work unless they must, and instead they paint the town, or just hang out. In Israel, schools, colleges, government, and many businesses stay closed, but museums and zoos close at their peril—hundreds of thousands of hyperactive kids and their mothers are roaming the country looking for things to do.

Chumásh, pl. chumashím (Ashkenazi: **Chúmesh, pl. chumóshim**)
Printed version of the Five Books of Moses

"The synagogue is presenting him with a Hebrew-English *Chumash* for his *Bar Mitzvah*."

See *Bereshit, Shemot, Vayikra, Ba-Midbar, Devarim*.

The *Chumash* is a printed book containing the Five Books of Moses that make up the Torah. (The word *chumash* is from *chamesh*, "five.")

Whereas a "Torah scroll," a *Sefer Torah* (see entry) written by a scribe on parchment, is treated with extreme sanctity and rarely leaves the synagogue, a *Chumash* can be found on almost every educated Jew's bookshelf. And when you walk into the synagogue lobby on a *Shabbat* morning, you pick up a *Chumash* from which to follow the recitation of the Torah.

From an early age, traditional Jewish education revolves around studying *Chumash* day in and day out. And inseparable from the *Chumash* is the running commentary by the medieval sage Rashi, written at the foot of the page in a spidery type of script without any vowel marks—bane and joy of generations of schoolchildren. One doesn't just study *Chumash*, one studies *Chumash-Rashi*.

— ❧ —

Chumrá, pl. chumrót (Ashkenazi: **Chúmre, pl. chúmres**)   Stringent rulings

"Do they expect all girls to wear thick tights or is it just their personal *chumra*?"

See *Machmir*, "Stringent."

There are particular Jewish communities or regions of the Jewish world that have their own time-hallowed *chumrot*, stringent customs or interpretations of the law. For example, Ashkenazim will not eat rice and peas on Passover, Chasidim will not marry off their children without a binding engagement, and so on. As times change, *chumrot* may change. On the whole, though, it is easier to add a *chumra* than to take it away.

— ❧ —

Chúmus   Hummus (a dip made from chick-peas and sesame paste)

"Can I have a bit more *chumus* to dip my *pitta* in?"

It's funny how a standard Middle Eastern dish—and the name for it—can, for Diaspora Jews, become so associated with Israel. The same goes for several other food words that I have included here—*techina, falafel, pitta, borekes.*

— ✿ —

Chupá (Ashkenazi: **Chúpe**)   Wedding canopy; wedding ceremony

". . . and here's a beautiful shot of the two of them standing under the *chupa.*"

"Come on, the *chupa*'s at 3 o'clock and you're not even ready!"

The *chupa* has become synonymous with the Jewish wedding. It usually takes the form of an embroidered cloth held up on four poles, under which the couple stand for the wedding ceremony—a symbol of the marital home.

. . . and they position the *chupa* under the open skies, for a good sign that their offspring should be as numerous as the stars of the sky.

> Rabbi Moshe Isserlis, sixteenth century, Poland

May this little child named _____ become great; just as he has entered into the *brit* [covenant], so may he enter into the Torah, the *chupa*, and a life of good deeds.

> From the prayers at a *Brit Mila* (circumcision)

— ✿ —

Churbán (Ashkenazi: **Chúrben**)   Destruction of the Temple

"Some of the walls inside the Old City show burn marks dating back to the *Churban.*"

Literally "destruction." Although many Yiddish speakers have used the Hebrew word *churben* to refer to the Nazi Holocaust, in Hebrew itself *Churban* denotes above all the destruction of the Holy Temple in Jerusalem, first by the Babylonians (586 B.C.E.) and then by the Romans (70 C.E.). The Jewish people have never ceased to mourn the *Churban*—in a series of regular fast days culminating in the bleak day of *Tisha be-Av*, and in all manner of customs, such as breaking a glass underfoot at weddings.

In the postwar era, to the extent that Jews have regrouped in large numbers, they have reshaped contemporary events into new archetypal patterns: *churban* has given way to *Shoah* (Holocaust) . . .

> David Roskies

— ✿ —

Chuts La-árets (Ashkenazi: **Chuts Lo-órets**)   Outside Israel (literally "outside the Land")

"She did her master's in Israel and her Ph.D. in *Chuts La-arets.*"

Chuts La-arets as a term for the Diaspora conveys the centrality of the Land of Israel, which Jews have traditionally called by the affectionate name *Erets*, literally "land."

Rabbi Shimon ben Yochai had a disciple who left for *Chuts La-arets* and came back a wealthy man. His other disciples were envious and also sought to leave for *Chuts La-arets.* Hearing this, Rabbi Shimon led them all to a valley facing Meron and prayed, "Valley, valley, fill with gold coins!" and the valley began to fill.
   Then Rabbi Shimon said to them, "If gold you seek, here is gold. But know this: He who takes now is taking his share of the Next World—for it is there that the reward for Torah study will come."

The Midrash on Proverbs

— ❦ —

Chutzpáh (Ashkenazi: **Chútzpe**)   Breathtaking cheek

"They bring cold soup and get angry with you for complaining? What a *chutzpah!*"

I translated it as breathtaking cheek, but can you really translate *chutzpah*? Even the Yiddish for *chutzpah* is *chutzpe*.
   The only way to visualize it is to have a taste of it—or, if you're not so lucky, then to digest the following example.

One definition of *chutzpah*: The man who shoots his parents and then begs for *tsedaka* [charity] because he's an orphan.

In the run up to the *Mashiach* [Messia], *chutzpah* will mount, prices will rocket . . .

The Talmud, Sotah

— ❦ —

Daf Yomí (Ashkenazi: **Daf Yóhmi**)   Daily set page (of Talmud)

"What's that about the rabbi introducing a *Daf Yomi* class every evening?"

In the global *shtetl*, it's cheering to see Jews of all sorts and in all kinds of places studying the very same page—or *daf*—of the Talmud on any particular day. This concept of the *Daf Yomi*, the daily page, was launched in 1923, the goal being that everyone should complete the entire Talmud once in seven years.

At the very least, *Daf Yomi* gives an opportunity for total strangers sitting side by side in cramped airplanes or chafing in line at the bank to discover that they have some baffling legal or philosophical problem in common.

Dáled amót shel halachá (Ashkenazi: **Dáled ámes shel halóche**)   The four walls of the law

"After his year of globe-trotting, Jerry's decided to go to yeshiva and sit a while within the *daled amot shel halacha*."

An *ama* is literally a "cubit," a measurement of 18 inches or so. *Daled amot*, "four cubits," traditionally expresses a person's own personal space—and any small intimate space in general.
    Daled amot shel halacha, literally "the four cubits of Jewish law," expresses the inward world of *Halacha*, going on so intently behind the walls of the yeshiva.

Said Ulla: Since the day the Temple was destroyed, God has no dwelling in His world save the *daled amot shel halacha* alone.

The Talmud, Berachot

Dati   Orthodox

"Some of these towns are half *dati* and half *chiloni* (secular)."

Dati is the Israeli word (often used by Modern Orthodox Jews in the Diaspora too) for people who keep to traditional Orthodoxy.

Davíd ha-Mélech (Ashkenazi: **Dóvid ha-Mélech**)   King David

"The universal expectation is that the Messiah will be a descendant of *David ha-Melech*."

He was a shepherd boy. He grappled with lions. He was "the sweet singer of Israel." He challenged Goliath and organized an army. He composed scores of psalms giving timeless expression to the religious strivings and stresses of a Jew. But his people have always preferred to know him as *David ha-Melech* —and a direct descendant of this man will, it is fervently believed, be the next king of Israel and the anointed Messiah.

Dávka (Ashkenazi: **Dáfke**)   a. Out of sheer spite (with a verb); b. Of all people, of all things (with a noun)

"That kid—I tell him to stop singing, so he *davka* sings at the top of his voice."

"Would you believe it? She went all the way to Israel to look for a guy and she's marrying her next-door neighbor *davka*."

Most Jews find it well-nigh impossible to translate this word, and I've managed it *davka*.

Dayá le-tsará be-sha'atá! (Ashkenazi: **Dáyo le-tsóro be-sháato!**)
"Don't try to find crises!"

"But while they're fixing the patio, what if they find something wrong with the foundation?"
    "Oh for Heaven's sake, don't start worrying about that! *Daya le-tsara be-sha'ata!*"

Literally "one crisis is enough at a time." This piece of wisdom, perfectly suited to worriers, panickers, and neurotics the world over, actually goes back to Moses—who said it, would you believe it, to God himself, so the Talmud relates. Not because the Almighty was worrying, but in fact because He was intent on reassuring Moses: "Don't you worry. I shall stand by the Israelites in Egypt; and I shall stand by them in all future persecutions."
    To which Moses replied (and was this not, perhaps, the birth of Jewish humor?): "Future persecutions?! Lord of the Universe, *Daya le-tsara be-sha'ata!*"

Dayán, pl. dayaním (Ashkenazi: **Dáyen, pl. dayónim**)   Rabbinical judge

"They've asked *Dayan* Katz for a ruling on surrogate mothers."

See also *Bet Din*, "Jewish court" and *Din*, "Regulation."

To be a *dayan* is to reach the highest rung in practical legal expertise. The traditional *rav* (rabbi) represents an expertise in everyday ritual matters, such as festivals, food, prayer. A very few rabbis go on to become *dayanim* and gain expertise in the intricacies of Jewish family law, business law, medical law, and so on—and to sit on a *Bet Din* (religious court).

When a dayan passes true judgment, he brings the Divine Presence upon Israel.

The Talmud, Sanhedrin

Dérech   Way

"May her grandchildren grow up to continue in her *derech* as good Jews."

"Him, on the other hand . . . I don't like his *derech* one little bit."

Derech is a person's manner, and often by implication the "correct Jewish way." The word *derech*, literally "way, path," forms part of a whole semantic family of words denoting the correct "path" in which to "go." Noah walked "with God," Abraham walked "before Him."

Dérech érets   Good manners, consideration for others

"Come on, show a bit of *derech erets* when an old person gets on the bus."

Literally "way of the world," *derech erets* can mean "worldly occupation"—and *Torah im Derech Erets* (Torah with Worldly Work) has become the slogan and rallying cry of Modern Orthodox Judaism opposed to an exclusively religious education, and associated in the United States with graduates of Yeshiva University in New York. But most commonly *derech erets* simply means good manners, extending to include all those things that spell consideration for other people.

If the Messiah wants to come nicely, gently, with *derech erets*—we'll wait for him.
   If, however, he prefers to come gruffly, with trials and travails—let him be so kind as to wait where he is.

Rabbi Meir of Primishlan

Devár toráh, pl. divréy toráh (Ashkenazi: Dvar tóre, pl. dívrey tóre)
Brief speech on a religious topic

"Chayim, did you bring a *dvar tore* from school? OK, then say it now before dessert."

Traditional Judaism is a *devar torah* culture, an oral way of life as well as a written one. Torah is learned with a view to "telling it over," to acquaintances, to parents, to children. At the center of this are all the *se'udot*, the special meals on Sabbaths, festivals, or other kinds of religious celebration—at which the participants stand up after the meal, between courses, or even during courses, and say a *devar torah*.

– ❧❧ –

Devarím (Ashkenazi: **Devórim**)   The Book of Deuteronomy

Devarim is the fifth and final book of the *Torah*, and takes its name from the first phrase *Ele ha-devarim*, "These are the words. . . ." It records the passing of Moses, and his sermons, songs, and blessings to the Israelites before he died, and is read in synagogues in the summer and early autumn.

The final scene, with Moses allowed one distant glimpse of the Promised Land and then dying in an unknown grave, is moving in the extreme, but custom dictates that the reading of *Bereshit* begin the moment that *Devarim* has ended. Life must go on.

– ❧❧ –

Devarím begó (Ashkenazi: **Dvórim begóh**)   "There's some logic to it"

Literally "there are things in it," *devarim bego* is an ancient rabbinic way of saying that something or other has a logic to it or that it's not as crazy as it sounds.

– ❧❧ –

Devekút (Ashkenazi: **Dvéykes**)   Attachment to God

"He's no run-of-the-mill Chasidic singer; he says the words with real *devekut*."

Devekut is a mystical concept, made familiar by the Chasidic movement, of coming close to God by prayer and contemplation.

There are giants of faith, great souls, whose actual *devekut* is continuous. These men are the pillars of the world.

Rav Kook

– ❧❧ –

Din, pl. diním (Ashkenazi: **Dínim**)   Religious regulation

"You don't learn the *dinim* of mourning until you have to."

To the outsider, the sheer number of *dinim* that a traditional Jew observes is mind-boggling. (And many traditional Jews will tell you that they don't really *know* half the *dinim* that they ought to.) But it's all to do with upbringing—and with the fact that the *dinim* are basically a gigantic system with its own philosophical logic. Rabbis may spend their lives pondering the system. Meanwhile, before every festival comes round, they give refresher courses on the *dinim* of Passover, the *dinim* of *Chanukah*, and so on. And the bookstores in New York are crammed with *dinim* books, *dinim* tapes, *dinim* software.

— ❧ —

Dína de-malchúta dína (Ashkenazi: **Díne de-malchúse díne**)   "The law of the state is the law"

This famous Talmudic maxim (it's actually in Aramaic, rather than Hebrew) established for all times that Jews would accept the civil and criminal laws of their host country as paramount.

— ❧ —

Drash   The applied meaning of a Scriptural text

"Come on now, what's the *drash* of 'You shall not boil a goat in its mother's milk'?"

See also *Peshat*, "The literal meaning."

Drash is central to the ancient rabbis' interpretations of the Bible. Over and above the literal meaning of words (*peshat*), they saw other meanings, often taking their cue from redundant words or letters, from the use of a less common word or phrase, sometimes seeming to voice an alternative unwritten tradition. These meanings are the *drash*.

   Drash sometimes states a law, sometimes fills out a story. It's often very beautiful. Generations of children have learned countless chunks of it in Rashi (the classic Bible commentator) and adored it.

— ❧ —

Drashá (Ashkenazi: **Dróshe**)   Sermon, learned address

"Their son gave a great *drasha* at his *Bar Mitzvah* dinner. I wonder how long it took them to write it for him."

The rabbi usually gives a *drasha* in synagogue midway through the service, following the reading of the Torah. I knew a rabbi who gave his *drasha* just before the end of the service, but that was soon the end of him. The *drasha* is usually about the weekly Torah portion, except when there's a *Bar Mitzvah* boy, in which case the *drasha* is about him, his parents, his extended family, and of course the weekly Torah portion.

In Orthodox circles, the *Bar Mitzvah* boy will probably give a *drasha* of his own at the *Bar Mitzvah* dinner, a time-hallowed rite of passage demonstrating his religious learning.

As the rabbi's *drasha* dragged on, a rhythmic snoring suddenly floated through the synagogue—ever so gentle, but enough to divert all minds and all eyes. The rabbi turned red and glared at the *shamash*.

"Shamash!" he hissed. "Wake this man up and send him home!"

"Why should I have to wake him up?" the *shamash* retorted. "It was you that put him to sleep, so you wake him up!"

Dúchen   Recite the priestly blessing

"Jonathan's a *kohen* so once he's *Bar Mitzvah* he'll be able to *duchen* in synagogue."

See *Birkat Kohanim*, "Priestly blessing."

To *duchen* is to utter the *Birkat Kohanim* (priestly blessing) on the platform in front of the Holy Ark. *Duchan* is "platform" in Hebrew, and the Yiddishized or Anglicized forms "to *duchen*" and "*duchening*" have become the customary words for the ceremony among Ashkenazi Jews.

Echá (Ashkenazi: **Éycho**)   The Book of Lamentations

"All the campers sat on the ground and read *Echa* by flashlight."

The word *echa* literally only means "how," but it is nonetheless a word that evokes stress, suffering, and gloom. It is the first word of the biblical Book of Lamentations, depicting the Babylonian destruction of the great city of Jerusalem and the exile of its population.

The Book of *Echa* is chanted to a doleful melody, sitting on the ground in dimmed synagogues, on the gloomiest night of the year—the night of the fast of *Tisha be-Av* that memorializes the calamity.

How [echa] *solitary sitteth the city, once so full of people!*
Once great among peoples, now become a widow—
Once princess among nations, now put to forced labor!

The opening words of the Book of *Echa* (Lamentations)

As the night of *Tisha-be-Av* set in, dim figures sat on the bare floor of the darkened synagogue, candles in their hands, lamenting the ruined Temple. The reader unrolled the scroll of *Echa* and began: "*Eycho yoshvo bodod . . .* [how solitary sitteth . . .]" And the fitures in turn intoned: *Eycho yoshvo bodod . . .*

But alone among them, Rabbi Avrohom the "Angel" exclaimed, "*Eycho . . .*" and fell silent, his head between his knees. Hours later, long after the elegies had faded away and the worshippers had trailed off home, Rabbi Abraham still sat where he sat, his head between his knees. And that was how they found him when they came the following morning, and it is said that he did not rise that whole day until he had drained the cup of destruction to the bitter end.

— ✣ —

Echád ba-peh ve-echád ba-lev (Ashkenazi: **Échod ba-peh ve-échod ba-leyv**)   "He or she speaks with forked tongue"

This Talmudic expression is a nice blunt description of a hypocrite or anyone else who speaks with forked tongue. Literally "One thing in the mouth, another thing in the heart."

— ✣ —

Égged   Egged (Israeli bus cooperative)

It might appear somewhat capricious to include an Israeli bus cooperative in such company as *Echa* and *Eliyahu ha-Navi*. But like *kibbutzim* and *falafel*, the bus company that enjoys a near monopoly of Israel's public transportation leaves a deep mark on anyone who has set foot in the country and can't afford limos.

The dashing *Egged* driver, fingering his debonair mustache with one hand while he takes money and punches out change with the other, is reported to laugh all the way to Bank Leumi. But the public love him, recalling how *Egged* responded to the military call-up for the Six Day War by mobilizing every bus to ferry troops to the fighting. And how many bus cooperatives can say that their name was designed for them by the national poet (Chaim Nachman Bialik)? If I go on so long, it is because, as Ephraim Kishon has observed, Israel is the only country in the world that is run by a bus cooperative.

. . . And some children have daddies who are Egged *drivers.*
They have a bus parked outside their house.

From an Israeli children's song by Yonatan Gefen

— ✣ —

El Malé Rachamím (Ashkenazi: **El Móley Ráchamim**)　*El Male Rachamim* memorial prayer

"Could you please say an *El Male Rachamim* for my brother?"

El Male Rachamim is the short poignant memorial prayer recited by the cantor on behalf of congregants who have lost a close relative. It is said in the synagogue on the anniversary of a death, in the *Yizkor* service, and at the burial or stone setting itself. The world has sadly grown accustomed to images of military chaplains intoning *El Male Rachamim* at the funeral of soldiers or random victims of terror in the Holy Land.

Merciful God [*El Male Rachamim*] in heaven, grant perfect repose beneath the wings of the Divine Presence, in the ranks of the holy and pure, radiant as the firmament, to the soul of ＿＿＿ who has passed to the World eternal. May her soul rest in Paradise. May the Merciful One protect her forever, and bind her soul in the bond of life. The Lord is her heritage. May her resting place be peace; and let us say *Amen.*

Translation of the *El Male Rachamim* prayer for a woman

– ৽৽৽ –

Eliyáhu ha-Naví (Ashkenazi: **Eliyóhu ha-Nóvi**)　The prophet Elijah

"Come on, we just can't leave the problem till *Eliyahu ha-Navi* comes and solves it!"

Eliyahu ha-Navi is the Jewish people's troubleshooter. The fierce, uncompromising biblical prophet, taken up to Heaven in a fiery chariot, is due to return to announce the Messiah—but meanwhile pays lightning visits to scholars and saints; and the front door is opened for him on Passover night, just in case. One day he will even solve outstanding problems in Jewish law. Jewish folklore adores him.

Eliyahu ha-Navi,
Eliyahu ha-Tishbi [*the man from Tishbe*]
Eliyahu ha-Giladi [*the man from Gilead*]
Soon may he come to us
With the Messiah, son of David.

Opening words of a popular Hebrew hymn marking the end of the Sabbath

– ৽৽৽ –

Élu va-élu divréy elokím chayím (Ashkenazi: **Éylu vo-éylu dívrey elóhkim cháyim**)　"Both are the words of the Living God"

This Talmudic maxim is the bedrock of Torah study: In all the debate and disagreement in the Talmud—about how to keep the laws, about what the Torah is saying—there is in practice no right and wrong. The sages each had their reasons, and by virtue of the power of interpretation vested in them, one can say *elu va-elu divrey elokim chayim.*

And often, in listening to workaday rows and debates, Jews find themselves saying *elu va-elu* . . . "I think you're both right."

Rabbi Yisroel of Rizhyn was holding court. It was the eve of *Shavuot*, the festival commemorating the Revelation of the Torah. Suddenly the rabbi spoke:

"My ancestor Dov Ber, the holy *Maggid* of Mezeritch, would often teach his disciples Torah over the meal—but then, somehow, on their way back home, they always discovered that they each remembered his words differently, and each of them was adamant that Rabbi Dov Ber had meant it this way and this way alone, even though what they said was often totally contradictory. You might have thought that they would simply go back to the *Maggid* and ask him, but when they did he only repeated: *Eylu vo-eylu divrey elokim chayim.*

"And yet again they thought it through, and this time it all made sense. Yes, the Torah is at root one Torah. And yes, in the physical world, *shivim ponim la-torah* (the Torah shows us seventy faces). But if you are able to contemplate one of these faces, you no longer need words of explanation—it is the eternal face that is talking to you, directly and visually."

— ❧ —

Elúl (Ashkenazi: **Élul**)   The month of Elul

Elul is the sixth month of the Jewish year, and coincides roughly with August-September. There are no festivals, but instead *Elul* is the traditional time of preparation—physical and spiritual—for the High Holy Days and the season of repentance.

— ❧ —

(The) Émek   The Jezreel Valley

The *Emek*—or, to use its full name, the *Emek Yizre'el*—is the agricultural heartland of Israel, and an emotional heartland too. Once a vast malarial swamp stretching across the country from Mt. Carmel in the West to the edge of the Jordan Valley in the East, the *Emek* was purchased and turned into a sea of villages, whose names (Ein Charod, Bet Alpha, Nahalal) have become the stuff of song and legend.

The arm ploughs,
The blood gushes,
The rainbow's colors have gone up in flames.
Light, light, light, light,
The whole Emek *is drunk,*
Gilboa and Tabor are locked in embrace! . . .

From a 1930s rhapsody to the *Emek*

— ❧ —

Emét me-érets titsmách (Ashkenazi: **Émes me-érets títsmach**)   "The truth will out"

The Eighty-fifth Psalm provides the vivid proverb *Emet me-erets titsmach*, literally "truth sprouts from the ground"—and there's no known agent that can kill it.

— ✺ —

Emuná (Ashkenazi: **Emúne**)   Belief (in God and the Torah)

"What his family had to go through was enough to try anyone's *emuna*."

Emuna is the foundation stone of Judaism. It is often said that Judaism is a religion of deed rather than belief. But *emuna* is crucial—as a premise upon which the Torah is built: the first two of the Ten Commandments ("I am the Lord your God . . . " and "You shall have no other gods . . . ") are a preamble to "Remember the Sabbath Day," "Thou shalt not steal," and the rest.

From the same root, Hebrew forms the most universal Hebrew word of all, *amen*.

The word *emuna* was on the lips of the masses as they went to their death in the gas chambers. They sang a Hebrew lament to these words:
"I believe with perfect *emuna* in the coming of the *Mashiach* [Messiah], and though he tarry I shall await him." [The thirteenth and last of Maimonides's Principles of Faith].

— ✺ —

En brerá   "There's no alternative"

En brera verges on being the national slogan of Israel—a nation forced into armed struggle, but constantly in need of convincing that there is indeed no *brera*.

— ✺ —

En chadásh táchat ha-shámesh (Ashkenazi: **Eyn chódosh táchas ha-shómesh**)   "There is nothing new under the sun"

It's a mark of the influence that the Bible once had that this verse from *Kohelet* (Ecclesiastes) is widely familiar in English. Jewish tradition depicts King Solomon, the author of *Kohelet*, as an aging man who has seen everything and studied everything—and developed a cynicism to match. Whatever the philosophers may claim to be new, whatever the followers of fashion may think is new, he's seen it all before.

All things are wearisome; no man can speak of them all.
Has the eye not seen enough, has the ear not heard enough?
What was is what will be,
And what has been done will be done again,
And there is nothing new under the sun [en chadash tachat ha-shamesh].

Book of Kohelet (Ecclesiastes)

– ❧ –

En me'arvín simchá be-simchá (Ashkenazi: **Eyn me'árvin símcho be-símcho**)   "One should not mix one celebration with another"

"What, honey, you got a raise too? That calls for double celebrations! But let's go out again tomorrow to celebrate it—*En me'arvin simcha be-simcha.*"

Life has few enough occasions for *simcha* (joy, celebration) as it is, so the Talmud advises us to eke them out, and not to celebrate them all at once. Thus Jews do not wed on *Shabbat* or on festivals.

– ❧ –

Érets Yisraél, also spelled **Éretz Yisraél** (Ashkenazi: **Érets Yisróel**)
The Land of Israel

"Yitzhak isn't here, he's in *Erets Yisroel* for his sister's wedding."

For over 2,000 years, since the close of Bible times, *Erets Yisrael* was the name by which Jews the world over knew their tiny land, or plain *Erets.* Names like Palestina were alien. In 1948, after hurried consultations (funny how people leave things to the last minute), it was decided to name the newborn Jewish State *Medinat Yisrael,* "the State of Israel"—but to this day, many Ultraorthodox Jews in the United States and elsewhere, whether out of custom or out of objection to Israeli secularism, still call it *Erets Yisroel.*

And why *Yisrael*? Because *Yisrael,* meaning "overcoming a mighty force," was the name given to Jacob following his struggle with an angel—and his descendants, from the outset, were called *Bnei Yisrael* "children of Israel" or simply *Yisrael,* "Israel."

When *Yisrael* [the Jewish People] are worthy, the land is called *Erets Yisrael;* when they are unworthy, it is called *Erets Kenaan* [The Land of Canaan].

The Zohar

Erets Yisrael is not something apart from the soul of the Jewish people; it is no mere national possession, serving as a means of unifying our people and buttressing its material, or even its spiritual, survival. *Erets Yisrael* is part of the very essence of our nationhood; it is bound organically to its very time and inner being. Human reason, even at its most sublime, cannot begin to understand the unique holiness of *Erets Yisrael*.

Rav Kook

– ❧ –

Érev   Eve of

"Don't forget that the buses will stop running early on *Erev Pesach*."

Eve of any festival or Sabbath is called *erev*. As the Sabbath or festival always starts just before sundown, *erev* anything is a bit hectic, especially in Israel. Buses and trains stop early, and before they stop they'll have filled up with crowds of people trying at the last moment to get to their Uncle Moshe and Aunt Sonia at the other end of the country.

– ❧ –

Érev Shabbát (Ashkenazi: **Érev Shábes**)   Friday up until sundown

"Look, today's *Erev Shabbat* so how can I possibly take the car in to be fixed?"

In a traditional household, *Erev Shabbat* is something like D day minus one: At some point on Friday—it may be 4:36, it may be 7:55—*Shabbat* will commence. It never seems to matter how long *Erev Shabbat* is or how short. All the food will have to have been cooked, all the rooms cleaned, all the necessary clothes ironed, all time switches set. Then, ignition: The *Shabbat* candles will be lit, the men and children will leave for synagogue, and the homemaker will sink into her armchair. She has got through another *Erev Shabbat*.

Those *Erev Shabbat* afternoons were nicer than all other days of the week. On all other days a child is bound to his books, and his heart and eyes are not his own; if he as much as raises his head from the book, he gets the big stick. On *Erev Shabbat* after midday, he is free from studies. He can do whatever he fancies, and no one will stop him. Were there not such a thing as lunch, the world would be one big Paradise.

S. Y. Agnon

– ❧ –

Erúv (Ashkenazi: **Éruv**)   Area in which a token enclosure enables one to carry on the Sabbath

"I don't know if you can walk over to them with the baby carriage. The *eruv* may not extend that far."

Had someone—it is traditionally said to have been King Solomon, and I can well believe it—not invented the *eruv*, Orthodox Jews would find themselves sitting indoors on the Sabbath, never able to take their babies out for a walk or to take anything to a friend. For nothing may be carried in the public domain on the Sabbath. The ingenious answer was to turn public space into shared private space, enabling everyone to carry. How? By creating a token enclosure, using overhead wires and the like. The whole Jewish neighborhood in places like Antwerp, Manhattan, and Jerusalem has been made into an *eruv*.

Seen on bumper stickers in an Orthodox London neighborhood:
  We want an Eruv *now!*

– ✿ –

Éshet cháyil (Ashkenazi: **Éyshes cháyil**)   Superwoman

"You know, Morry, you really have an *eshet chayil* there."

Literally "woman of value (or valor)." It's a compliment. There may be an equivalent compliment that women can apply to men, but I can't think of it at the moment. (A hunk is normally referred to in Israel as a *gever*, but it's not quite the same thing.)
  In some Orthodox communities, a pale equivalent of the Bar Mitzvah celebration has evolved, called *Eshet Chayil*.

An *eshet chayil* who can find, for her value is far beyond rubies!
The Bible, Proverbs

– ✿ –

Et chata'áy ani mazkír hayóm (Ashkenazi: **Es chatóay áni mázkir hayóhm**)   "At the risk of reminding you of my past blunders"; "I have a confession to make . . ."

If you want to own up to something, or confess it once again—particularly in lighthearted vein—there's nothing so endearing as to use the very words of Pharoah's chief butler in the Book of Genesis (remember? Pharoah threw him in the dungeon): "I make mention of my sins this day . . ."

– ✿ –

Et sefód ve-et rekód (Ashkenazi: **Eys sefóhd ve-eys rekóhd**)   "There's a time to mourn and a time to dance"

Familiar lines from the biblical Book of Kohelet (Ecclesiastes)—do not mix moods. Where there's rejoicing, rejoice; where there's mourning, mourn.

– ✿ –

Etróg (Ashkenazi: **Ésreg**)   The citron fruit

"Larry, hold the *etrog* in your left hand, and all the others in your right, and shake them."

It's rather daft, I'll admit, to translate *etrog* as citron fruit, as no one who hasn't seen an *etrog* will know what a citron fruit is either. It looks like something between a lemon and a lime, but it comes from special localities like Israel or Morocco, smells out of this world, and can easily cost $40. The *etrog* is one of the four special species (*arba minim*) that are waved in the synagogue on the festival of *Sukkot*. Among other things, *Sukkot* is a water festival, and the *etrog* tree is nothing if not thirsty.

Not to mention the respect we Jews have there. No people are as honored and exalted there as the Jew. A Jew's a big shot there. It's a mark of distinction to be a Jew. On *Sukot* you can meet Jews carrying *etrogim* and *lulavim* even on Fifth Avenue. And they're not even afraid of being arrested . . .

Sholom Aleichem

– ✿ –

Etsá (Ashkenazi: **Éytse**)   A piece of advice, a suggestion

"My car won't start first thing. Can you give me an *etsa*?"

To give an *etsa* is as much a good deed as to give *tsedaka* (charity). That's probably why, for so many centuries, the Hebrew word *etsa* figured in Yiddish, and now in English—it's a Jewish value word.

The more *etsa*, the more *tevuna* [sense].

The Talmud, Avot

It is easier to give an *etsa* to others than to oneself.

Rabbi Nachman of Bratzlav

– ✿ –

Ézehu chachám? Ha-loméd mi-kol adám (Ashkenazi: **Éyzehu chóchom? Ha-lóhmed mi-kol ódom**)   "The wise learn from everyone"

Literally "Who is wise? Someone who learns from everyone." This Talmudic maxim is a reminder that the wise and learned, though in many ways the Jewish elite, cannot live apart from the community. Wisdom is with the people.

— ❧ —

Ezrát nashím (Ashkenazi: **Ézras nóshim**)   Women's section in a synagogue

"I take it that the lady waving down to you from the *ezrat nashim* is your wife."

The main difference between Orthodox synagogues and all others is the *ezrat nashim*. The former have it; the latter don't.

The basic idea is that women at prayer should be physically separated from men. This can take the form of a simple low partition (see *mechitsa*), although in many older synagogues there is a women's gallery. Some communities believe in making women not only inaccessible but also invisible, by means of netting, lattices, and so on. In Chasidic prayer houses (*shtiebls*), they sit in a separate room, making them inaudible too.

— ❧ —

Faláfel   Falafel (chick-pea croquettes)

"So we'll meet by the *falafel* bar at 2:30."

Until the pizza invasion, *falafel* was the sizzling king of the Israeli street. I won't go into whether it's made from beans or peas or peanuts and of what color precisely—although one falafel boss swore to me that making it from beans will turn your blood to water—but it's there to be stuffed into your *pitta* bread and to make you think you're eating something vaguely healthy between meals. (That's the *techina*.)

— ❧ —

Fráyer [rhymes with "higher"], pl. **fráyerim**   Sucker

"When I first arrived here, I must admit I was a bit of a *frayer*. Now I wouldn't let myself be taken in by the realtors."

The only Hebrew word in this book to begin with *f* (apart from *falafel*). But is it Hebrew? Yes. The Israelis inherited *frayer* from Yiddish and there isn't a schoolchild in Israel—Sephardi, Ashkenazi, Yemenite, or Ethiopian—who doesn't know the word.

Frayerim range from anyone who believes that the price tag in the Israeli store window is the storekeeper's final word to anyone who has faith in the United Nations.

Question: Why did the chicken refuse to cross the road?
Answer: Because he wasn't a fr[a]yer.

Yaacov Kirschen

Gabáy (Ashkenazi: **Gábe**)   Synagogue official

"Son, a rabbi's no job for a Jewish boy—be a *gabay*."

The *gabay* is a kind of master of ceremonies in the synagogue: making announcements, deciding who to call to the reading of the Torah, and perhaps who to invite to be reader, shaking hands with them all, perhaps frowning or tut-tutting here or there.

In British synagogues, the *gabay* is commonly styled "warden" and frequently wears ("sports" might be the mot juste) a black top hat, taller than the rabbi's and probably deliberately so.

Galách, pl. **galachím** (Ashkenazi: **Gálech,** pl. **galóchim**)   Christian priest

"Did you hear the one about the rabbi, the *galach*, and the commissar?"

The Torah forbids Jews to shave their sideburns off, leaving a circular hairline. The hairline of medieval priests and their tonsure (remember Friar Tuck?) just cried out for the name *galach*, "shaven one." Hairlines change, but the word is still with us today.

(The) Galíl   The Galilee

The northern hill country of Israel is called the *Galil*. Rain-drenched, green, and mercifully rural, it manages to conjure up images of Kabbalists of Tsefat and quaint Druze villages—but also brutal gun battles in which many early settlers perished, among them the legendary Yosef Trumpeldor.

Upon a hill,
There in the Galil,
Sits a watchman,

In his mouth a flute.
He plays a shepherd's song
To the lamb, to the kid,
To the wandering foal . . .

From a Hebrew ballad extolling the death of Yosef Trumpeldor

— ✿ —

Galút (Ashkenazi: **Góles**)   Exile (from the Land of Israel)

"There are so many kosher stores here that it's hard to remember you're in *Galut*."

Galut is a rare case of something that is absolutely meaningless unless you don't want it. It is the sense that for Jews to be living all around the world is abnormal, and that they should be back in their land and living by *their* laws. Many Zionists use the word *Galut* in a secular sense; but this, to religious Jews, is precisely the worst form of *Galut*.

Galut is nowhere near as bad as the spirit of *Galut*.

Yehuda Ha-Levi

Whether or not it is aware of it, this people is always living on ground that may at any moment give way beneath its feet. Every symbiosis it enters upon is treacherous. Every alliance in its history contains an invisible terminating clause; every union with other civilizations is informed with a secret divisive force. It is this inescapable sense of insecurity which we have in mind when we designate the Jewish Diaspora as *Galut*.

Martin Buber

— ✿ —

Gam zu le-tová (Ashkenazi: **Gam zu le-tóhve**)   "It's all for the best"

"So someone else got the job then? Well, don't worry yourself over it, *gam zu le-tova*."

Rabbi Akiva was once on a journey. Reaching a certain town, he asked around for a place to lodge, but no one would take him in. "Oh well," he said to himself, "Everything the Lord does is for the best." And he made to bed down in the fields. With him, he had a donkey, a rooster to wake him at dawn, and a lamp to study by. But a gust of wind blew out the lamp. Then a cat gobbled up the rooster. And the poor ass fell victim to a lion.

"Oh well," said Rabbi Akiva to himself, "Everything the Lord does is for the best."

That night, troops came and took the townsfolk captive.

"Well, well," said Rabbi Akiva. "Everything the Lord does is indeed for the best. Had the lamp been burning, or had the rooster crowed, or had the donkey brayed, would not I have been discovered and captured too?"

The Talmud, Berachot

— ❧ —

Gan Éden (Ashkenazi: **Gan Éydn**)   Heaven; the Garden of Eden

"Great-grandma's not here anymore. She's in *Gan Eden*."

Gan Eden seems to be in two places: It's spoken of as the physical place where humankind started its career. It's also the spiritual place in which the saintly and hopefully the less-than-saintly find eternal peace—*Olam ha-Ba*, "the World to Come," in other words.

When I am called to the World of Truth, I shall prefer *Gehinom* [Hell] to *Gan Eden*. *Gehinom* is where the sufferers are.

Rabbi Moshe Leib of Sasov

— ❧ —

Ganáv, pl. **ganavím** (Ashkenazi: **Gánev**, pl. **ganóvim**)   Thief
Genevá (Ashkenazi: **Genéyve**)   Theft

"Take your hands out of the cookie jar, you little *ganav*."

"I don't feel right about using the firm's phone like this—it's kind of *geneva*."

From the sound of things, the Ten Commandments have placed theft and murder on an equal footing: *lo tirtsach*, "you shall not murder" and *lo tignov*, "you shall not steal." But in fact, the Talmud teaches, the context makes it plain that theft here means a capital offense, namely kidnapping. Ordinary *geneva* was a bad thing, but no one got the chop for it.

It isn't the rodent that's the *ganav*, it's the hole that's the *ganav*.

The Talmud, Gittin

Even as he breaks in, the *ganav* prays for help from on high.

The Talmud, Berachot

If a *ganav* kisses you, count your teeth.

The Talmud, Chullin

There are seven things we can learn from a *ganav*:
   A *ganav* works late into the night.
   What a *ganav* can't do one night, he will attempt again the next.
   Ganavim love one another.
   A *ganav* will risk his life for the merest bagatelle.

A *ganav* will sell even costly things for next to nothing.
A *ganav* will suffer untold beatings for his thieving while denying all
    knowledge.
A *ganav* wouldn't exchange his profession for any other.

Rabbi Dov Ber of Mezeritch

– ❧ –

Gaón (Ashkenazi: Góen)   Genius

"I remember his father at *yeshiva*. Now he was a real *gaon* . . ."

To be called a *gaon* once meant not just that you had a brilliant mind but
that you had used it to acquire a phenomenal command of the Torah.
The *gaon* who towered above all *gaonim* was the late eighteenth century
uncrowned king of Ashkenazi Jewry, Rabbi Elijah, the "Vilna Gaon."

Nowadays, in Israel, the word has been secularized. You only have
to be a "genius." With tens of thousands of Russian academics and
unemployed chess masters flooding into the country, one might say "a
mere *gaon*."

– ❧ –

Gariním   Seeds (especially sunflower seeds)

"Hey, someone's been cracking *garinim* everywhere!"

Some Israelis sleep better because of their *tilim gariniim* (nuclear mis-
siles). But what keeps most of them calm is their *garinim*. You buy
them by the thousands and crack them into millions, in Egged buses,
in cinemas, in the street, and in the privacy of your own home.

Garinim are really, really healthy too—a symbol of the new Levan-
tine Jew.

Bilingual sign in all Egged buses:
The English: *No dropping litter*
The Hebrew: *lo lefatseach garinim* [no seed cracking]

– ❧ –

Gashmiút (Ashkenazi: Gáshmies)   Material pleasure; plushness, materialism

"They've built it up into a beautiful *kibbutz*, I know, but there's a little
bit too much *gashmiut* for my liking."

For *gashmiut*, see what I say about *ruchniut* (spirituality). The important thing is that Judaism and Jews have generally liked a bit of
both—and why not?

If you know a little bit of Hebrew and you also know what the climate in Israel is like, you might think *gashmiut* has something to do with *geshem* (rain). In fact, it doesn't.

There is no *gashmiut* that does not contain sparks of *ruchniut* [spirituality].

Rabbi Elimelech of Lizhensk

From an invitation for *Shabbat* dinner that I once received:
You bring the ruchniut, *we'll provide the* gashmiut.

– ❧ –

Gazlán, pl. gazlaním (Ashkenazi: **Gázlen, pl. gazlónim**)   Robber

"Don't use that travel agency anymore. They're real *gazlanim*."

Who's worse, asks the ancient Midrash, the *gazlan* (robber), who takes by force, or the *ganav* (thief), who takes by stealth? The answer is the *ganav*. In taking by stealth, he clearly fears the eyes of man more than he fears the eyes of God. Whereas the *gazlan*, bless him, at least fears the two of them equally little.

A luckless Jew once heard that one could make a living as a *gazlan*. He decided, "I'll be a *gazlan* too." He donned coarse sacking, took a hatchet and his *tallit* and *tefilin*, and made for the woods. The day wore on, and nobody came. Before the sun set, he decided to say *Mincha* (afternoon prayers)—and suddenly along came another Jew. Not wishing to halt his prayers, he motioned to the other to wait. The other, seeing a Jew in sacking at prayer, naturally obliged. Finishing his prayers, the *gazlan* shouted, "I'm a *gazlan*! Your money or your life!"
    "Are you crazy?" said the other. I'm a poor man, with a wife and kids. Take one rouble." The would-be *gazlan* reflected upon this.
    "OK, gimme one rouble then."
    "A whole rouble?" said the other. "Do you take me for a Rothschild?"
    "OK, a cigarette."
    "Firstly, I don't smoke. Second, where shall I find a cigarette in a forest?"
    "Some snuff, then?" pleaded the *gazlan*.
    "OK, snuff I'll give you." And off he ambled, leaving the *gazlan* to reconsider his decision.

– ❧ –

Gehinóm (Ashkenazi: **Gehínem**)   Hell

"These people who smoke in front of their kids, they should all go to *Gehinem*!"

See *Gan Eden*.

Although it would be nice to report that Hell is a very different place than *Gehinom*, I must confess that they seem to be on the same street.

The Talmud talks of the fires of *Gehinom* where the souls of the wicked are smelted, some of them forever, while the souls of the righteous or semirighteous go to *Gan Eden*.

Said Chizkiya: "The wicked are condemned to twelve months in *Gehinom*: six months of heat and six months of cold."

The Midrash on Genesis

To speak obscenities is to dig *Gehinom* deeper.

The Talmud, Shabbat

The Rizhyner Rebbe said, "They can't punish me with anything. Because if God says to me to go to *Gehinem*, I will do it. So they just can't punish me with anything."

Gelilá (Ashkenazi: **Glíle**)   Binding and bedecking of the Torah scroll

"Excuse me, Mr. Stein, could you do *gelila*, please?"

Ashkenazi Jews have the parchment of the *Sefer Torah* (Torah scroll) mounted on two stout wooden rollers. After reading from it, they tie it tightly with a sash, and cover the whole thing with an artfully embroidered cloth.

The honor of tying and dressing the *Sefer Torah* after the reading is called *gelila*. It calls for deft hands and nimble footwork—and yet, for some reason I've never been able to fathom, *gelila* is typically given to kids.

Sephardim, by contrast, keep the *Sefer Torah* permanently housed in a solid box, even when reading from it.

Gemár chatimá tová! (Ashkenazi: **Gmar chasíme tóhve!**)   "A good final sealing!" (greeting between *Rosh Hashanah* and *Yom Kippur*)

"Have an easy fast, Michael, and *gemar chatima tova!*"

Literally "a good final sealing," this is a traditional greeting still used by Orthodox Jews from *Rosh Hashanah* (the New Year and Day of Judgment) up until *Yom Kippur* (the day on which the Divine verdict for the coming year is sealed).

Gemará (Ashkenazi: **Gmóre**)   Another name for the Talmud

"If your son's twelve, he should be starting *Gemara* soon."

See also *Talmud* and *Shas*.

The *Gemara* is the usual traditional name for that vast anthology of Jewish law and lore otherwise known as the *Talmud* (see entry).

Studying *Gemara* is a lifetime's task. It has no end—and any outsider faced with a page of *Gemara* with no vowel marks, no paragraphs, and no commas or periods would say that it couldn't possibly have a beginning either. And yet they study it (or as the expression goes, "learn" it), the swaying, chanting ten-year-olds in Jerusalem or Borough Park—arguing over such timeless issues as whether an ox that gores has to be put to death (for ox, read pit-bull terrier) and whether rival claimants to lost property need to make a sworn affidavit.

And what seemed impossible fifty years ago is happening. In the most unlikely places, like Israeli army bases and Manhattan board rooms, teenagers and adults are rediscovering their roots in it. And prestigious international publishers are bringing it out in deluxe Hebrew-English versions.

Gemara is the ultimate mind-expander.

Gemátria   System for calculating the numerical value of Hebrew words

"Quiet! I'm working out the *gematria* of the bride and bridegroom's names."

As with ghosts, you can't remain indifferent to *Gematria*—either it takes you or it irritates you. *Gematria* is an ancient mystical system of assigning numerical values to Hebrew words in various ways—for example, the first letter of the alphabet, *alef*, counts as 1, the second letter *bet* counts as 2, and so on—and then taking the sum total, finding another word that has the same total, and deriving some significance from this.

A famous example from the Talmud is the word for pregnancy, *herayon*. Its *gematria* value is 271, and that, remarkably, is the average duration (in days) of a pregnancy!

Some people, by no means mystics, seem to spend all their time playing around with *gematria*. And during the Gulf War, it was duly noted that the *gematria* of Saddam Hussein (spelled in Hebrew, of course) is equivalent to "Amalekite."

Gemilút Chasadím (Ashkenazi: **Gemílus Chasódim**)   Good deeds

"Every Sunday they go to do *gemilut chasadim* for senior citizens in the Bronx."

The word *chasadim*, "kindnesses," comes from the same root as *Chasidim*.

"What's more important?" asked the ancient rabbis, "Doing *gemilut chasadim* (good deeds) or giving *tsedaka* (monetary charity)?" Surely *gemilut chasadim*, which everyone, rich or poor, can do by giving of their time. And the modern world surely makes us more stingy with our time than with our money.

Many know the duty of *tsedaka* and its rewards but do not know the greatness of *gemilut chasadim*. There are four kinds of *gemilut chasadim*: (a) To speak warmly to the poor and cheer them up, (b) to lend them money, (c) to give them advice, (d) to encourage the public to do likewise.

Rabbi Yonah of Gerondi

Upon three things the World stands: Torah study, worship, and *gemilut chasadim*.

The Talmud, Avot

— ❧❧ —

Genevá.   See **Ganáv**.

— ❧❧ —

Ger, pl. gerím; fem. Giyóret (Ashkenazi: **Giyóres**)   A convert to Judaism

"Is it Rachel's friend from college who's studying with the rabbi to become a *giyoret*?"

You can go a long time without hearing the words *ger* or *giyoret*. There are very few, despite the fact that there were once hundreds of thousands, and some of the most famous figures were descended from *gerim*—Rabbi Akiva, for instance. For many centuries, Jews have been exceedingly wary about seeming to encourage *gerim*. It has so often spelled death at the stake. And old fears die hard.

Nowadays, unfortunately, *giyur* ("conversion") is controversial for a quite different reason: There is traditional Orthodox *giyur* and there is now non-Orthodox *giyur*. While the State of Israel vacillates about whether officially to accept both, protestors in the streets of Jerusalem brandish banners insisting "*Giyur ka-Halacha!*" (Orthodox conversion).

Gerim are beloved to God.

The Midrash

Abraham and Sarah were the first *gerim*. For this reason, all male *gerim* are called Abraham and all female *gerim* are called Sarah.

Rabbi Chaim ben Attar

— 🙢🙠 —

Get   Deed of Divorce

"Did he give her a *get*, or is he making problems?"

For a couple to divorce, Jewish Law requires that he give her a document called a *get*, written to a traditional formula. No evidence of wrongdoing or marital breakdown is required, but the regulations surrounding the *get* itself are very stringent. Remarkably, the two letters, *gimel* and *tet*, of the word *get* never appear together in the Torah.

A septuagenarian came to a rabbi: "Rabbi, I want to give my wife a *get*."
　The rabbi couldn't believe it. "After so many years, all of a sudden?"
　"Rabbi, it's like this. A week after the wedding I wanted to give her a *get*, but my in-laws said: 'It'll shame us all—give it a few weeks.'
　"I did, but she gets pregnant. My in-laws say: 'Don't give her a *get* now, wait till the birth.'
　"I did, and waited till she weaned. But then she was pregnant again! And again and again. When that was over, they said: 'Don't give her a *get* now, you have daughters to marry off.' Well, I had quite a few daughters, so that took a while—but yesterday I married the last one off.
　"So now wish me *Mazel tov!* . . . and write me out a *get*."

— 🙢🙠 —

Ge'ulá (Ashkenazi: Ge'úle)   Redemption

". . . and may we all be spared to see the *Ge'ula* speedily in our own days."

The *Ge'ula* is the final, Messianic redemption of the Jewish People from dispersion and aversion, and their wholehearted return to the ways of the Torah.

We trust that in this *zechus* [merit] we will soon all merit the *Geula Shelema*.

Conclusion of a letter asking for charitable donations

Lord of the Universe!
I beg of You, send Ge'ula to the Jewish People.
And if You do not so wish, then at least send Ge'ula to the Nations.

Rabbi Yisroel of Koznitz

— —

Gírsa de-yankúta (Ashkenazi: **Gírse de-yánkuse**)   Knowledge acquired in one's youth

Trying to recall the *girsa de-yankuta* that you got from math and history lessons in school, you may wonder what it's all worth. But *girsa de-yankuta* is highly prized when it is the knowledge of Torah acquired in one's youth through an intensive traditional education. *Girsa de-yankuta* stays with you. It is deemed by the Talmud to be more solid than the knowledge gained in adulthood, let alone old age—like ink on clean paper as against ink on erased paper.

— ✿✿✿ —

Golá   Diaspora

"There are estimated to be half a million Israelis living in the *Gola*."

The word *Gola* is at the core of the Zionist worldview. The biblical word for exile, it has come to denote the Jewish Diaspora seen as something abnormal waiting to be restored to its homeland. Israeli emissaries use it a lot. When planning a trip to London or L.A., however, ordinary Israelis prefer to say *chuts la-arets*, "overseas."

There is another word for exile, *galut*. But this is typically charged with religious overtones, connoting exile from the Divine Presence.

— ✿✿✿ —

Gólem (literally "raw, embryonic")   Artificial human created by mystics; imbecile

"I give up on him—he's a complete and utter *golem*."

The poor *golem* has led a schizoid existence. On the one hand, he's the real-life human (without spirit or speech) materialized or envisioned by medieval mystics, and by legend summoned up from clay to defend the Jews of Prague (as so beautifully retold by Elie Wiesel and Bashevis Singer) but liable to turn on his creator.

On the other, he's a dufus, an imbecile, a *shlemiel*.

At the Weizmann Institute in Israel, there's another *golem*—a mainframe computer.

They told the Chasidic leader, Rabbi Menachem Mendl of Kotzk, about a wonder worker who knew how to make a *golem*.

"Ah," he said, "but does he know how to make a *Chasid*?"

I am not exaggerating when I say that the *Golem* story appears less obsolete today than it seemed 100 years ago. What are the computers and robots of our time if not *golems?*

Isaac Bashevis Singer

There are seven qualities in a *golem* [idiot] and seven qualities in a *chacham* [wise man]:

The *chacham* doesn't speak where there is someone wiser than he, doesn't interrupt others nor answer hastily, asks and answers correctly and to the point, speaks to each point in order, and where he has not learned he says, "I have not learned." The *golem* does precisely the opposite.

The Talmud, Avot

— ✿ —

Goy, pl. Goyím (Ashkenazi: pl. **Góyim**)   Gentile

"His father was a *Goy* and his mother's Jewish? Then he's Jewish."

Goy is not a word that a Jew will readily use in Gentile company. It isn't exactly complimentary—but nor is it a term of abuse hurled at other people (or else I wouldn't have it here). It just represents the coolness that has accumulated over the centuries.

A warmer word is *non-Jew*. Interestingly, the word *Gentile* is little used by Jews.

It is not important what the *Goyim* are saying but what Jews are doing.

David Ben-Gurion, first prime minister of Israel

— ✿ —

Hachnasát kalá (Ashkenazi: **Hachnóses kále**)   Support for poor girls to get married

"Good evening. I've come for *hachnasat kala* for girls in Israel."

A traditional part of giving *tsedaka* (charity) is giving toward *hachnasat kala*, literally "marrying off a bride." To get Jewish girls married off has always been at the top of the agenda—and for girls without means, that involves raising money for the trousseau, and perhaps for a bit more besides. In Orthodox circles today, appeals are always coming in and *meshulachim* (fund-raisers) always going out for *hachnasat kala*.

— ✿ —

Hachnasát orchím (Ashkenazi: **Hachnóses órchim**)   Hospitality

"We were in this synagogue in Athens, and at least five people came up to offer us *hachnasat orchim*."

Every first grader in Jewish school probably knows the story of Abraham sitting out in the noonday sun to find passersby to accept his *hachnasat orchim*. On a *Shabbat* evening in the old days, when you looked around the synagogue, you would always see some stranger, some traveller miles from home—and you'd rejoice that you and your wife and children could now perform *hachnasat orchim* (literally "bringing in guests"). Even today, the mark of a real Jewish home is surely the readiness to do *hachnasat orchim* for all comers.

Hachnasat orchim is greater than receiving the *Shechina* [Divine Presence].

The Talmud, Shevuot

Hadasím (Ashkenazi: **Hadásim**)   Myrtle twigs

"Be careful not to handle the *hadasim*—I don't want the leaves to fall off."

See *arba minim*, "Four Species."

The *hadasim* are the third of the Four Species (*arba minim*) traditionally waved during the prayers on the harvest festival of *Sukkot*. Why myrtle? Well, there are many possible reasons (as so often with Jewish laws and customs, there is no one official reason), but what counts is that the *hadasim* should be physically *kosher*, with the leaves twining in triplets along the twig.

Haftará (Ashkenazi: **Haftóre**)   Weekly recitation from the Prophets

"Oh Bettie, your Norman read his *Haftore* so beautifully!"

See *Maftir*.

To the regular synagogue goer, *Haftara* has entirely different associations than to those who go only for *Bar Mitzvahs* or other special days.

The regulars will be aware that readings from the Torah are rounded off with a relevant chapter or two from the Prophets—the *Haftara*. You don't have to be a professional to read the *Haftara*, as it's normal to read from a regular Bible, with the vowels and singing notes provided. Anyone may be invited to do it.

To others, however, the *Haftara* connotes a *Bar Mitzvah*, and the *Bar Mitzvah* boy's performance of a lifetime. He will probably (if he's up to it) have spent a full six months on the wording and chanting, and his father and mother will by this time probably know the whole *Haftara* by heart too. Very nice.

Hagadá , commonly spelled **Haggadah** (Ashkenazi: **Hagóde**)   (Book of the) Passover story

"Every year, I seem to get more stains on my *Haggadah*—if it's not wine, it's *charoset*."

Haggadah essentially meant "narration." Today it refers to the Passover story, par excellence, as set down in the time-hallowed blend of narrative, commentary, song, and prayer that is called the *Haggadah*. No other Hebrew book has been published in so many forms and with such rich illustration. You can read it in Hebrew or in any language you wish, but the old Hebrew words of songs like *Adir Hu* and *Chad Gadya* continue to exert a fascination. And of course there's *Ma Nishtana*, the Four Questions.

Who but fools would not think of Hitler and Stalin as they read the verse in the *Hagada*, "Pour out Thy wrath upon the nations that knew Thee not!"

Emanuel Rackman

— ❧ —

Hagbahá (Ashkenazi: **Hágbe**)   Raising aloft of the Torah scroll

"He's a massive man—the sort that always gets asked to do *hagbe*."

After the *kriat ha-Torah* (reading of the Torah), the scroll is opened again and lifted briefly aloft for all to see. This is called *hagbaha*, and it's an honor for whomever is invited to do it, a struggle if his biceps and deltoids aren't in good shape (a Torah scroll can be extremely heavy), and a fleeting excitement for the congregation who are hoping against hope that he won't drop it. Custom requires the entire congregation to fast if ever a Torah scroll is dropped, *chas ve-shalom*.
    N.B.: Sephardim do *hagbaha* before *kriat ha-Torah*.

— ❧ —

Ha-Kadósh Barúch Hu (Ashkenazi: **Ha-Kódesh Bórchu**)   The Almighty

"*Ha-Kodesh Borchu* must have been watching over me . . ."

There are many sacred names of God that religious Jews only use in prayer or study. But there are also many "nonsacred" alternatives. One of the most popular is *Ha-Kadosh Baruch Hu*, literally "The Holy One, Blessed Be He," in use for at least 2,000 years. (See also *ha-Shem* and *Ribono shel Olam*.)

"Where does *Ha-Kadosh Baruch Hu* dwell?" the Rebbe of Kotzk once asked some visitors.

"The whole universe is full of His glory!" they replied.

"No, no," he explained. "*Ha-Kadosh Baruch Hu* dwells just where you let Him in."

— ❧ —

Hakafót (Ashkenazi: **Hakófes**)   Circle dancing on Simchat Torah

"We went to *Hakafot* in three different synagogues—and look how many candies I got!"

On the evening of the *Simchat Torah* festival, synagogues fill with young people, old people, toddlers under foot, for the *Hakafot*—the dancing with the Torah scrolls. Seven times they circle the synagogue, officially, singing ancient words of praise. But they'll make at least a hundred extra circuits, singing or yelling every Hebrew song they know. Children may wave little flags with apples or the remains of apples stuck on top. The whole affair is repeated the following morning.

In the old Soviet Union of Khrushchev and Brezhnev, the *Simchat Torah Hakafot* at Moscow's Arkhipova Street synagogue was for years the one occasion when young Jews dared to demonstrate their Jewishness.

— ❧ —

Halachá (Ashkenazi: **Halóche**)   Jewish law

"Look, Liz, the *Halacha* doesn't say that we have to make a big *Bar Mitzvah*!"

The *Halacha*, literally "the way," is the vast body of Jewish law—covering everything from prayer to child custody—laid down in the Torah and by subsequent generations of rabbis. Together with the *Agada*, the philosophical teachings, it makes up what we know as Judaism.

Alongside *Halacha* there are also many *minhagim*, local variations and later customs.

The word *Halacha* sometimes makes the headlines—see the entry *ger*, "convert."

The *Halacha* is not at all concerned with a transcendent world. The world to come is a tranquil, quiet world that is wholly good, wholly everlasting, and wholly eternal, wherein a man will receive the reward for the commandments which he performed in this world. However, the receiving of a reward is not a religious act; therefore, halachic man prefers the real world to a transcendent existence because here, in this world, a man is given the opportunity to create, act, accomplish. . . .

Joseph B. Soloveitchik

Halacha is the string, *Agada* is the bow. When the string is tight, the bow will evoke a melody.

Abraham Joshua Heschel

— ❧ —

Halél (Ashkenazi: **Hálel**) Psalms of praise

"The cantor sang such a beautiful tune during *Halel*."

Some parts of the service are introspective, some are cerebral. *Halel* is joy. These exuberant chapters from the Book of Psalms are sung in the synagogue on almost every festival, and around the family table during the *Seder* service. They are also widely sung on two modern-day festivals, *Yom ha-Atsma'ut* (Israeli Independence Day) and *Yom Yerushalayim* (Jerusalem Liberation Day).

— ❧ —

Haleváy! [rhymes with "sigh"] "I just wish!"

"I'll be happy if he just finds a nice girl and settles down."
   "*Halevay!*"

Halevay! has been doing the rounds for two **millenia,** and it still distills the force of any wish or prayer. Might it be some special quality in that combination of vowels and consonants? *Ay . . . Vay . . . Levay . . .* Of the combinatory powers of the Hebrew letters, here is not the place to talk.

— ❧ —

Ha-motsí me-chaveró aláv ha-raayá (Ashkenazi: **Ha-móhtsi me-chavéyro ólov ha-ráayo**) "He who would extract something from his fellow must furnish the proof"

This classic principle in Jewish Law is reminiscent of the English maxim "Possession is nine-tenths of the law." In a case of dispute, it is the person holding something who can be assumed to be the owner, unless there are witnesses or documents to prove otherwise.

— ❧ —

Har ha-Báyit (Ashkenazi: **Har ha-Báyis**)   The Temple Mount

"From their apartment in the Old City they have a wonderful view of *Har ha-Bayit*."

It is the most sacred site of Orthodox Judaism, yet no Orthodox Jews tread upon it, only Gentiles; on it once stood one of the most spectacular edifices of antiquity, the *Bet ha-Mikdash* (the Temple), yet it has always been called simply *Har ha-Bayit*, "the Mount of the House," meaning the House of God.

Today, Orthodox Jews still await the messianic age when the rites of purification will be reintroduced that will allow them to tread upon the sacred site of Solomon's Temple. How the *Bet ha-Mikdash* will be rebuilt on *Har ha-Bayit* if two mosques occupy the site, only a prophet can say.

— ৪৫ —

Har Sináy (Ashkenazi: **Har Sínay**)   Mt. Sinai

On *Har Sinay* the Torah was revealed to Moses during forty days and forty nights. From *Har Sinay* he brought down the Ten Commandments in stone and the scroll of the Torah. But very soon, *Har Sinay* slipped back into anonymity, just like the grave of Moses.

There are a lot of people out there who think they know where *Har Sinay* is, but that's simply because it suits the pilgrimage industry to locate it in the huge peaks of central Sinai. Jewish tradition holds that *Har Sinay* was puny and utterly unmemorable. Possible meaning of the name: "low bush," "hated."

When the Almighty came to give the Torah on Sinai, the mountains struggled and quarreled with one another. Each said, "The Torah should be given upon *me*." Mt. Tabor came from Bet-Elim and Mt. Carmel from Aspamya. Each said, "I have been summoned." Said God, "All of you have had idolatry performed upon you; Sinai, upon which no idolatry has been performed, is the one that God desires to dwell upon."

The Midrash on Genesis

— ৪৫ —

Hararím hatluyím be-saará (Ashkenazi: **Harórim hatlúyim be-sáaro**)
Castles in the air

Literally "mountains hanging by a hair," *hararim hatluyim be-saara* is a Mishnaic metaphor for any elaborate ideas that have little grounding in concrete reality.

— ৪৫ —

Hashavát avedá (Ashkenazi: **Hashóves avéyde**)   Returning lost property

"I haven't given up hope of finding that ring—someone might do *hashavat aveda*"

Hashavat aveda is one of those things that modern Western law never dreams of imposing on the individual—enough if you don't steal. Biblical and Talmudic law take a quite different view of responsibility for others: You *have* to make elementary attempts to return or announce lost property. And the Talmud is full of zany tales of people who took *hashavat aveda* extraseriously—like Rabbi Chanina who found a few lost chickens, cared for them till his backyard was bursting with them, sold them, and invested the owner's money in goats and . . . years later, discovered the owner of the original chickens.

Two Jews shared a room at an inn. While they were taking an evening stroll, one of them accidentally let slip his wallet—and the other, noticing, leaped to perform *hashoves aveyde*. But the next morning, the wallet was gone—stolen. The victim called in the local constable, who did a bit of rummaging, and up popped the wallet in the other one's backpack! The victim was almost speechless.
   "But yesterday you did *hashoves aveyde* with my wallet! How could you go and steal it . . ."
   "Why are you surprised?" answered the other. "*Hashoves aveyde* is a *mitzve* [good deed], but stealing is my livelihood!"

— ❧ —

Ha-Shém   God

"Can it be a coincidence that *Ha-Shem* allowed the Gulf War to finish on a Jewish festival?"

Among the Orthodox today, English-speaking or Hebrew-speaking, *Ha-Shem* is the regular word for God in everyday conversation. Literally it means "the name," and is an ancient substitute for more sacred names for God. In writing there is particular reluctance in pious circles to write Divine names, even foreign words such as "God" and "Dieu," for fear that they may ultimately end up in some incinerator or shredder. So hyphenated forms like "G-d" are regularly used.

— ❧ —

Hashgachá (Ashkenazi: **Hashgóche**)   a. Divine Providence; b. Supervision, that is, rabbinic supervision of *kosher* food.

"That was real *hashgacha*—a second later and he would have hit us head on . . ."

"Is that new Vietnamese *kosher* restaurant in Brookline under *hash-gacha*?"

See also *Hechsher*, "Rabbinic seal of approval."

Hashgacha is a word that leads a double life: It is charged with the philosophical meaning of "Divine Providence," which already makes it complicated enough. But to most Jews who aren't philosophers, *hashgacha* denotes first and foremost "supervision of *kosher* food," and in Jewish life today, there are few things that are more complicated. There is *hashgacha* by this body and that body, by this town's rabbi and that town's rabbi—some cheaper and some more expensive, some less stringent and some more stringent, some acceptable to some groups and some to others. And, thank Heavens, a few appear to be acceptable to more or less everyone.

A *Chasid* had just passed on. While he lined up to have his good deeds weighed, the angels motioned him to a cold buffet. The *Chasid* hesitated.
   "Who . . . who set out all the food?" he asked.
   "Oh, Miriam the prophetess," said an angel.
   The *Chasid* still hesitated. "But who's the *kosher* supervisor here?"
   "Oh, Moses," said another angel.
   The *Chasid* reflected. "But whose is the *hashgacha* for all the cold cuts?"
   "Oh," said an angel, looking upward in awe, "the Almighty Himself."
   The *Chasid* wrung his hands and thought again. "You know what? I'll stick to dairy."

— ❧ —

Hashkafá, pl. hashkafót (Ashkenazi: **Hashkófe, pl. hashkófes**)
Outlook, philosophy of life

"We get along well, even though we don't share the same *hashkafa*."

It used to be said that it doesn't matter what a Jew's *hashkafa* is, as long as he keeps the same set of *mitzvot* (commandments): There were Chasidic or mystically inclined *hashkafot* and more rationalistic *hashkafot*, modernistic *hashkafot* and traditionalistic *hashkafot*.
   The Jewish world has become mighty complicated in the meantime—*hashkafot* without *mitzvot*, *hashkafot* with *mitzvot* that look the same but are different, and *hashkafot* with *mitzvot* that look different but are essentially the same.

— ❧ —

Ha-shomér achí anóchi? (Ashkenazi: **Ha-shóhmer áchi onóhchi?**)
"Am I my brother's keeper?"

"Why are you blaming me for her speeding? *Ha-shomer achi anochi?*"

This universally known saying goes back to the Book of Genesis 4:9. Having murdered his brother Abel, Cain is confronted by the Almighty, but responds with the earliest recorded instance of *chutzpah*: "*Ha-shomer achi anochi?*"

It's a bit like the thief who stole some articles in the night without being caught. The next day, the watchman nabbed him.
"Why did you steal these things?" he asked him.
"I'm a thief," he retorted, "and I was at least doing my job. But you? Your job is to keep watch at the gate, so why weren't you doing just that?"
So too with Cain:
"OK, I killed him," said Cain to God, "but You created the evil impulse in me. You watch over everything, so why did You let me kill him!? In fact it was really *You* that killed him!"

The Midrash on Genesis

— ✿ —

Haskalá (Ashkenazi: **Haskólo**)　Jewish enlightenment movement

"I have an aunt who insists that Yiddish is a bastard language. She talks like she's right out of the *Haskala* . . ."

Few Jews today have probably even heard of the *Haskala*, certainly far fewer than have heard of *Yetsiat Mitsrayim*. But three or four generations ago, the *Haskala* movement commanded widespread respect among Jews in Europe, holding out the prospect that they might "modernize" themselves, become good Germans or Poles or Englishmen of "Mosaic persuasion," and drop overboard such disgusting habits as speaking Yiddish, growing sidelocks, and frequenting the *mikveh*.

A lot of things have meanwhile happened, Zionism among them. Apart from students of culture, the only people who do care much about the *Haskala* are probably the Ultraorthodox, who still revile it heartily.

The word *haskala* is from the same root as *sechel*, "sense."

A central paradox of the *Haskala* was that its critical, sometimes aggressive stance to the tradition blinded it to certain assumptions on which *Haskala* itself rested. The *Haskala* drew on an Enlightenment that brooked no claim on behalf of particular heritages (least of all Judaism) . . .

Robert Seltzer

— ✿ —

Ha-Tíkvah   Israeli national anthem

"The fundraising meeting concluded with everyone present singing *Ha-Tikvah*."

So many national anthems seem outdated these days. By its sentiments, its Central European folk melody, and the very un-Israeli rhythm of its words, *Ha-Tikvah* is a living relic of the old-time Zionism. In fact, the words were composed about 100 years ago by a wandering Hebrew poet, Naftali Herz Imber, who eventually died in the United States. But every time I hear the strains of *Ha-Tikvah*, when Israel Radio closes down for the night, it makes me want to cry; and I'm not sure why.

As long as a Jewish soul stirs
Deep within the heart,
And eastward, to the Orient,
Eyes look to Zion,
Our hope is not yet lost,
The hope [ha-tikvah] of two thousand years,
To be a free people in our land,
In the land of Zion and Jerusalem.

Translation of *Ha-Tikvah*

— ✿ —

Hatslócho Rábo!   Good luck!

"*Hatslocho Rabo* with your exams!"

This is a traditional Ashkenazi formula for wishing success. Israelis usually say *Be-hatslacha!* You even find it printed at the bottom of university examination papers.

— ✿ —

Háva Nagíla   Popular Israeli folk song

"The guests danced the *Hava Nagila* long into the night."

The tune of *Hava Nagila* started life as a simple tune of Chasidim, the words are simple words of brotherhood (with a hint of the mystical), the dance is a simple Balkan *hora*—but no song of Israel is so well-known around the globe. It's a must at Jewish weddings.

Come let us rejoice and be happy,
Come let us exult,
Awake, brothers, with a joyous heart.

Translation of *Hava Nagila*

— ✿ —

Havdalá (Ashkenazi: **Havdóle**)   Ceremony at the end of Sabbaths and festivals

"Bring me the wine and spices, so we can make *Havdala*."

To make *Havdala* is to mark the end of *Shabbat* or a festival in the home. *Havdala* means "separation." With the goblet of wine that must be overflowing, the smell of *besamim* (spices)—I always burn some juniper wood—and the plaited candle burning in the dark, the ceremony has all the stuff of fantasy. A pity it's not widely practiced outside the Orthodox fold.

He who maketh a distinction between holy and profane—
May He forgive our sins,
Make our offspring and assets as countless as the sand
And as the stars in the night . . .

From a traditional Hebrew *Havdala* song

My soul yearns for the candle and the besamim.
If only you would hand me a havdala *cup of wine.*
Build me roads, clear the way for the bewildered one,
Open me the gates, all you angels on high.
I shall lift up my eyes to God with a pining heart,
Setting out my needs day and night.
Give me all I lack from your bountiful treasures,
For your kindness knows no end or bound.
Renew my joy, my food and happiness,
Banish my woes, aching and dark.
Behold, the working week always starts anew—
May peace and goodness start anew, selah.

Se'adya (Yemen, late Middle Ages)

– ❧ –

Hechshér (Ashkenazi: **Héchsher**)   Rabbinic seal of approval on food; any seal of approval

"Does that pumpernickel bread have an Orthodox *hechsher* or just a *K*?"

"They've knocked a couple of feet off the plans for the extension, but they still can't get a *hechsher* to build."

For processed food to be deemed *kosher*, it ordinarily needs to display a *hechsher*, indicating that it has received *hashgacha* (supervision) by a rabbi. But that's not necessarily the end of it. Non-Orthodox rabbis and their *hechsherim* are not recognized by the Orthodox, and Orthodox *hechsherim* are not always recognized by the Ultraorthodox. And even if you've decided your level, you'll have to be able to identify the letters and symbols used as a *hechsher* in the various parts of the United

States—the Chicago Board of Rabbis has one symbol, in Boston they have another, and then there's that *K* symbol . . .

But things are getting better all the time. The day that Entenmann's cakes appeared with a *hechsher*, there were gastric celebrations across the States. Now they're waiting for Nabisco.

– ❧ –

Hefkér (Ashkenazi: **Héfker**)   Disorganized; ownerless

"I don't like their courses. There's no reading list or curriculum—it's so *hefker*."

"You can take any of these used cassettes here. They're *hefker*."

Originally a legal term for ownerless property, and still used in that sense, *hefker* is a glorious word conjuring up a scenario of total abandon. It's so much more than just a *balagan* ("a mess"). You can have a bit of a *balagan* but there's no such thing as a bit of *hefker*.

– ❧ –

Hespéd (Ashkenazi: **Hésped**)   Funeral oration

"Don't make a whole *hesped* over him—he's not dead yet."

Since biblical times, orations have been said in praise of the dead, either in the house of mourning or at the cemetery. The *hesped* is considered one of the most important elements in paying respect to the dead, a supreme Jewish value.

Chaim Zofnik, editor of a party newspaper and something of a Hebrew author, received an urgent delegation. A party member had died, and could he say a *hesped* at the graveside in the name of the party.

Zofnik exploded; "Do you think I can just draw *hespedim* out of a hat? In future you'll have to give me at least one week's notice . . ."

– ❧ –

Hetsíts ve-nifgá (Ashkenazi: **Héytsits ve-nífga**)   "He courted danger and got harmed"

Hetsits ve-nifga literally means "he peeped and was hurt." It is used to describe any kind of risk taking, but it has its origins in one of the most intriguing stories in the Talmud: Four scholars entered *Pardes*, the inner recesses of Jewish mysticism. Ben Azai peered at the Divine Presence and perished. Ben Zoma peered and was struck with madness. Of the two others, one lost his faith, and just one, Rabbi Akiva, emerged unscathed.

— ❧ —

Hidúr mitzváh (Ashkenazi: **Híder mítsve**)   Putting extra effort and style into a *mitzvah* (observance), or into anything

"This year I want us to make the *sukkah* with real *hidur mitzvah*."

"I wish your son could put a bit more *hidur mitzvah* into the way he cleans his teeth."

Whoever imagines there is no aesthetics in Judaism is not aware of *hidur mitzvah*, the tradition of putting as much time (and resources) as you can into a *mitzvah* or *mitzvot* of your choice—if you like, giving *mitzvot* some individual style.

Some people put tremendous *hidur mitzvah* into the *arba minim* (four species of plant) that they purchase for *sukkot* and into the *tefilin* that they give their sons for their *Bar Mitzvah*. And perhaps some communities put a wee bit too much of it into their synagogues.

— ❧ —

Híllel   Jewish student center

"Are you coming to that talk at *Hillel* after the anatomy class?"

On many, if not most, American college campuses there is a *Hillel*, a center for Jewish students to meet, eat, pray, take courses, and so forth, generally under the supervision of a *Hillel* rabbi-counsellor.

The Talmudic sage, Hillel, would probably have been proud that these centers bear his name. He was a byword for outreach, humor, and patience (see the entry *al regel achat*).

— ❧ —

Hirhuréy averá kashím me-averá (Ashkenazi: **Hirhúrey avéyre kóshim me-avéyre**)   "Thoughts of sin are more grievous than sin itself"

This saying from the Talmud means that the urges and passions are fiercer in the *hirhurim*, the contemplations of sin, than in the act itself.

Hirhurey avera kashim me-avera: If someone comes to *hirhurey avera* (contemplations of sin), it is a sure sign that they have done that sin, for without sin there is no thought of sin.

Rabbi Dov Ber of Mezeritch

— ❧ —

Hosháana Rabá (Ashkenazi: **Hosháano Rábo**)   The day of Hoshaana Raba

"Come round for a final drink in the *sukkah* on *Hoshaana Raba*."

Hoshaana Raba is the name of the seventh and last day of *Sukkot*, and the occasion for a remarkable sight in the synagogue. The name means "the great 'Save, We Beg'" because on this day seven Torah scrolls are brought out of the ark and seven prayers of *hoshaanot* (see entry) are uttered as worshippers circle the synagogue seven times, *lulav* in hand, begging for rain. Finally, the *aravot* (willow twigs) are beaten till the leaves fall off. On this day, the world is handed down its judgment for rain.

– ❧ –

Hoshaanót (Ashkenazi: **Hoshánes**)   Prayers said while circling with the *lulav* on *Sukkot*; willow twigs used on *Sukkot*

"There were so many people doing *hoshaanot* that the circle hardly moved."

"Take some *hoshaanot* home for Mommy and Grandma to beat."

The word *hoshaana* was taken up by the Church as *hosanna* but treated as a word of adulation ("Glory be!") rather than prayer.

Every day of the festival of *Sukkot*, the prayers reach a climax with all the worshippers walking in a circle, holding their *lulav* and *etrog* and chanting *hoshaanot*, prayers for the Land of Israel and Jerusalem—for fertility and for rain. The prayer for each day begins with the word *Hoshaana*, which means "save, we beg." On the last day of *Sukkot* not one but seven such circles and *hoshaanot* are made—for this last day is the great day of *Hoshaana Raba* (see entry).

The word *hoshaanot* has also been transferred to the *aravot* (see entry), the willow twigs that are beaten on *Hoshaana Raba*.

Hoshaana [save, we beg] the soil from curse, the cattle from sterility, the threshing floor from locust, the corn from fire, the resources from mishap, the food from destruction, the olives from windfall, the wheat from the grasshopper . . .
From the Hebrew *Hoshaana* for the sixth circuit

Hoshaanot must surely be mysterious, strange, exciting to those little ones who peek out from under their father's *tallit*. And for those who watch them.
Blu Greenberg

Ikár (Ashkenazi: **Íker**)   Main thing

"Forget all the details, just tell us the *iker*."

The whole world is a very narrow bridge. And the *ikar* is to have no fear whatsoever.

Rabbi Nachman of Bratzlav

– ❀ –

Ikvót meshícha (Ashkenazi: **Íkves meshíche**)   The prelude to the Messiah

"You shouldn't let yourself get so depressed; we may be seeing the *ikvot meshicha!*"

Some say the *ikvot meshicha* (literally "the footsteps of the Messiah") are happening right now and that the *Mashiach* is round the corner. Some say they've been happening for hundreds of years, some for the last two thousand. And some refuse even to think about the subject.

But if our times aren't in fact the *ikvot meshicha*, I for one wonder how long we can avoid some madman blowing up the world, or more likely just poisoning it ourselves.

In the *ikvot meshicha*, arrogance will increase, costs will skyrocket, the vines will yield wine but the price will soar, government will fall prey to nonbelievers, and none will remonstrate . . .

The Mishna, Sota

The Sadigora Rebbe once sat glumly over his meal. The afternoon shadows lengthened. No one present dared speak. Several times, his sister approached to search out what was troubling him. At length, he sighed:
    ". . . our people in Russia . . "
    She replied: "Maybe what they are going through are the birth pangs of the *ikvot meshicha*."
    The Rebbe shook his head. "Maybe," he said, "but each time the suffering comes to a head, our people cry out to the Almighty and He, in His mercy, hears them, and relieves their suffering—and so the *Mashiach* is put off once again . . ."

– ❀ –

Ilúy, pl. iluyím (Ashkenazi: **Íluy, pl. ilúyim**)   Child prodigy

"Their second son's an *iluy*. I heard he knows half of *Shas* already."

An *iluy* is like a *gaon* (Torah genius), except that he's a child. Jewish folklore is densely populated with *iluyim*. In fact, you sometimes can't help thinking that if a person did *not* know half the Talmud by the time he was eleven there was something wrong with him. To be an *iluy* brought with it more than just spiritual benefits; the *iluy* got his gal.

They say there aren't too many *iluyim* around nowadays (in Chaim Potok there are a few), but that's surely because they're mostly playing baseball or locked onto a computer screen.

– 🙐🙑 –

Im ba laharogchá, hashkém lehorgó (Ashkenazi: **Im bo laharógcho, háshkem lehórgo**)   "If he comes to kill you, kill him first."

This Talmudic maxim expresses a whole philosophy of self-defense. It may be harrowing to kill another human being, but the Torah makes the use of reasonable force not merely a right but a duty.

– 🙐🙑 –

Im eshkachéch yerushaláyim, tishkách yeminí (Ashkenazi: **Im eshkóchech yerusholáyim, tíshkach yemíni**)   "If I forget thee, O Jerusalem, may my right hand lose its cunning."

These words from Psalm 137, the psalm that describes the Israelite exiles hanging up their harps by the rivers of Babylon, are among the most compelling words ever written to express the bond with Zion. Look at the yellowing photographs of Zionist conferences and congresses of yesteryear and you'll see these words emblazoned somewhere in the background. Read the speeches, and they're everywhere.

– 🙐🙑 –

Im yirtséh hashém (Ashkenazi: **Im yírts-ashém**)   "God willing"

"So I'll see you next week, then, Liz, *im yirtseh hashem* . . ."

Literally "if God wills." *Im yirtseh hashem* is very common among Orthodox Jews when they're talking about doing something, whether in the near or the distant future. I was once at a synagogue service when they announced that *Mincha* (the afternoon prayers) would be at 5 P.M. that day *im yirtseh hashem*," but to most Orthodox Jews that would sound paranoid.

Dayan Chanoch Ehrentreu, *shlita* [long may he live], will *IYH* [guess what that stands for] give a *shiur* [class] on Wednesday December 11 . . .
> From a small ad in a London Jewish newspaper

– 🙐🙑 –

Inyán, pl. inyaním (Ashkenazi: **Ínyen, pl. inyónim**)   Topic

"That was an interesting *inyan* that the rabbi brought up, wasn't it?"

Inyan comes from the vocabulary of Talmud study, and it generally has something scholarly or at least intellectual about it. You write or discuss or argue about an *inyan*.

— ❧ —

Ípcha mistábra (Ashkenazi: **Ípche mistábre**)   "Quite the contrary!"

They say "two Jews, three opinions," and traditional Hebrew brims with debating expressions, derived of course from the Talmud. This one (it's Aramaic in fact but it's part of Hebrew in the same way as Latin "i.e." and "e.g." are part of English) is used when you're having a discussion and want to argue precisely to the contrary.

— ❧ —

Ísru Chag   The day after a festival

"Does school start on *Isru Chag* or the next day?"

Once they get into a happy headspace, Jews are reluctant to let go. *Shabbat* is allowed to go on a bit longer. Saturday night is a time for a *melave malka* party. And the day after the festivals of *Pesach, Shavuot*, and *Sukkot*—called *Isru Chag*—everyday life returns to normal, but in traditional circles there is a touch of festivity: more eating and drinking, fewer sad prayers, and, most important to certain people, no school.

— ❧ —

Isúr, pl. isurím (Ashkenazi: **Íser, pl. isúrim**)   Forbidden act

"Most rabbis say that taking up smoking is a serious *isur*."

Related to *isur* is the word *asur*, "forbidden."

Any kind of forbidden act is an *isur*. Some *isurim* go right back to the Bible; others are precautionary *isurim* laid down over the ages.

There is an additional aspect in the matter of forbidden foods. The reason they are called *isur* [chained] is that even in the case of one who has unwittingly eaten a forbidden food intending it to give him strength to serve God . . . , the vitality contained therein does not ascend and become clothed in the words of the Torah or prayer, as is the case with permitted foods, by reason of its being held captive in the power of the *sitra achra* [the side of nonholiness].

Rabbi Shneur Zalman of Liadi, "Tanya"

— ❧ —

Ivrít   The (modern) Hebrew language

"Daddy, how do you say *bagel* in *Ivrit*?"

What exactly is *Ivrit*? A time-hallowed name for Hebrew (it's there in the Talmud), it nevertheless seems to mean *modern* Hebrew to most Diaspora Jews. They call traditional Hebrew simply Hebrew or, particularly if they're Ultraorthodox, *loshn kodesh*, "the Holy tongue."

For this we must thank the secular Zionists, early this century, who began calling themselves *Ivri* (a biblical word for a Hebrew) because the word *Yehudi*, "Jew" sounded too religious. And it all rubbed off on the word *Ivrit*, which now became modernistic and radical.

As far as I'm concerned, *Ivrit* is *Ivrit* is *Ivrit*—and it's all *loshn kodesh*, whether it was written by Amos the Prophet or, *lehavdil*, by Amos Oz.

— ❦ —

Iyár (Ashkenazi: **Íyer**)   The month of Iyar

The second month of the Jewish year, *Iyar* falls in April-May. This is the time of semi-mourning known as the *Sefira*, but also the time of *Yom ha-Atsma'ut* (Israel Independence Day), and the feasts of *Lag ba-Omer* and *Yom Yerushalayim*.

— ❦ —

Iyóv (Ashkenazi: **Íyov**)   The Book of Job

Iyov is probably the hardest book of the Bible. The language is obscure, the theme—why do good people suffer—is mind-boggling. So it is hardly surprising that *Iyov* as a whole is not recited at any particular time, nor is it (nowadays) widely studied. But subtle allusions to it and straight quotations from it abound in the prayers. In a way, *Iyov* is everywhere.

God's response to *Iyov* related to the desire to understand the *why* of evil. His answer to the Prophets related to the issue of *how* to abolish evil. There is no human solution to God's problem, and God's only answer is the promise of messianic redemption.

Abraham Joshua Heschel

— ❦ —

Juk [rhymes with "nook"], pl. **júkim**   Israeli cockroach

"You'd better not leave crumbs or we'll have huge *jukim*."

One of the Israeli sights that tourists don't usually get a chance to see are *jukim*. Red, plump, visually crunchy, and reportedly fond of uncovered feet, they make no distinction between one-star and two-star hotels, but hesitate at three stars.

— ✣ —

Kabalá, also spelled **Kabbaláh** (Ashkenazi: **Kabóle**)   Kabbalah

"Why do they walk seven times round the bride?"
    "It's all to do with *Kabala*"

See *Mekubal*, "kabbalist" and *Zohar*.

Kabala is Jewish mysticism—the search for an "inner spiritual meaning" to the Torah and its commandments.

Time was when *Kabala* was studied and practiced in secret, amid esoteric chanting and visualizations. In the late Middle Ages, it spread across the Jewish intelligentsia via books like the *Zohar*. Finally, through the teachings of the eighteenth- and nineteenth-century *Chasidim*, it has now become the intellectual property of the masses, although many Jews are still highly suspicious of it and there is dark talk of what happens to you if you study *Kabala* before the age of forty.

Others, however, are convinced that the slow steady revelation of the esoteric is all a preparation for the coming of the Messiah.

Kabbalah means literally "tradition," in itself an excellent example of the paradoxical nature of mysticism. . . . The very doctrine which centres about the immediate personal contact with the Divine, that is to say, a highly personal and intimate form of knowledge, is conceived as traditional wisdom. The fact is, however, that the idea of Jewish mysticism from the start combined the conception of a knowledge which by its very nature is difficult to impart and therefore secret, with that of a knowledge which is the secret tradition of chosen spirits or adepts. Jewish mysticism, therefore, is a secret doctrine in a double sense. . . .

Gershom Scholem

— ✣ —

Kabalát Shabbát (Ashkenazi: **Kabóles Shábes**)   Prayers welcoming the Sabbath

"*Kabalat Shabbat* in our synagogue always begins fifteen minutes after *Shabbat* comes in."

The mystics of the *Kabbalah*, with their ability to personify and to create metaphor, always visualized the Sabbath as a queen or as a ravishing bride. Welcoming her meant finding the right words—and this is *Kabalat Shabbat*, literally "welcoming *Shabbat*," a sequence of psalms and poems leading in to the Friday evening prayers. Synagogues everywhere are a-sway with the melodies.

— ✣ —

Kabdéhu ve-chashdéhu "Respect him and suspect him"

"I know he can be a helpful neighbor, but take my advice: *Kabdehu ve-chashdehu*"

A useful Talmudic expression for anyone—or anything—that requires a certain distant respect, such as certain computer programs, certain lawyers, certain employers . . .

— ❧ —

Kaddísh (Ashkenazi: **Káddish**) Literally "sanctification." A prayer customarily recited by mourners.

"He gets up at six every morning for synagogue, to say *Kaddish* for his mother."

Kaddish is an old and revered prayer of hope that God's kingdom comes in one's lifetime. Mourners are given the honor of reciting the final *Kaddish* in every service, hence its association with mourning. It is also recited at the graveside—and for eleven months after the loss of a parent.

Magnified and sanctified be His great name
Throughout the World that He created as He wished,
May He establish His kingdom
In your lifetime, in your days,
And in the lifetime of the whole House of Israel,
Speedily, imminently,
And say Amen . . .

Translation of the first words of the *Kaddish*

While the parents still live, unobservant children obscurely feel that the religion is still being carried on by the old folks, and they go about their secularized lives with relative peace of mind. Then death strikes. The children stare at the broken end of the chain of the generations, swinging free. It is a hard sight. The punctilious reciting of the *Kaddish*, linked so directly with the vanished parents, is a symbolic retrieving of the ancient chain.

Herman Wouk

For three years the rabbi had been giving the boy private Hebrew lessons at the temple, but he still couldn't read a line from the prayer book. In desperation, he began teaching the boy the *Kaddish*.

When the boy's parents heard, they first of all had a fit. Then they called the temple.

"With all respect, Rabbi," said the boy's father, "we have no plans to die in the near future. Why should the boy know the *Kaddish*?"

"Don't panic," said the rabbi. "You should both live till 120 and you can rest assured that your dear son will still not know how to say *Kaddish* . . .

— ✂ —

Kalá (Ashkenazi: Kále)   Bride

"The *kala* says you should all make a circle around her and dance."

A beautiful word. And much used by poets and mystics for expressing the love of God for Israel, of Israel for the *Shabbat* and so on.

Go, my beloved, to meet the kala.
Let us welcome the Sabbath . . .

> Opening of the Hebrew song "Lecha Dodi" for the Sabbath eve

How do we dance in front of the kala?
"Lovely kala, *lovely, charming* kala!"

> A Hebrew song sung today at traditional weddings

— ✂ —

Káshe, pl. káshes   Challenging question

"I have a *kashe* to ask you on what you just said."

Kashe is classically a Talmudic term: *yeshiva* students vie with each other to test their teachers, by asking *kashes* on whatever they are studying. If anything was responsible for the development of Jewish brains, it was the *kashe*.

— ✂ —

Kashér (Ashkenazi: Kósher, Kóhsher)   Conforming to Jewish dietary law

"Do you see an *OU* anywhere on this can? I'm not sure if it's *kosher*."

"Their children go to Jewish school so they're trying to keep *kosher*."

See also *Kashrut*.

There are *kosher* and non-*kosher* animals, birds, and fish. There are *kosher* and non-*kosher* parts of a *kosher* animal or bird. There are foods that are always *kosher*, such as water, fruit, vegetables. And there is food that becomes non-*kosher*: dairy products mixed with meat. There are people who "are *kosher*," meaning not that observant Jews will eat them but that they only eat *kosher* food. And, thank Heavens in this age of a hundred ingredients per item and a thousand new products per month, there are agreed symbols on cans and wrappers indicating that a particular food has been certified *kosher.*

A Russian count was entertaining a Jewish merchant. Came evening, and a dazzling array of sizzling roasts and vintage wines was brought in. The count offered his guest some meat, but he declined.

"So kind of you, but the meat isn't *kosher,*" he explained. His host pressed him to take wine, but again: "Thank you, your excellency, but the wine isn't *kosher.*"

The count shook his head in disbelief. "But what if you were starving, and this were the only food and drink to be had?"

"Oh, that would be different," said the Jew. "If it's life or death, we can eat anything."

Suddenly, the count seized a pistol, leveled it at the Jew, and screamed: "Drink the wine!"

Trembling, his guest drank—whereupon the count tossed the gun away, roaring with laughter.

"It was just a joke, my friend!" he said. "I hope you're not angry."

"Angry? I'm livid!" said the Jew. "Why didn't you play the same joke on me with those roasts?!"

— ❧ —

Kashrút (Ashkenazi: **Káshres**)   *Kosher*-hood

"Most of the immigrants know nothing about *kashrut.*"

Kashrut denotes being *kosher* or the whole system of keeping *kosher.* They say that when life was simpler, *kashrut* was simpler. *Kashrut* is now a big business, in more ways than one.

— ❧ —

Kavaná (Ashkenazi: **Kavóne**)   Intense concentration

"When we say these holy words, let us try to have *kavana* for what we are saying."

When one reads that the ancient Chasidim used to spend an hour in *kavana* before prayer and an hour in *kavana* after it, one is reluctant to talk about *kavana* nowadays at all. The high points of *kavana* are the beginning of the *Shema* and *Amida.* Not only is one meant to block out all other thoughts, one is also meant to project oneself to the Temple Mount in Jerusalem. Modern-day Chasidim recite special meditations, called *kavanot,* before performing all kinds of *mitzvot.*

Kavana comes into being with the deed. Actions teach.

Abraham Joshua Heschel

— ❧ —

Kavód (Ashkenazi: **Kóved**) Honor, respect, dignity

"*Koved, Koved*, that's all she ever seems to care about."

"Even college kids should show a bit of *kavod* to the faculty."

See *Kibud av va-em*, "Respect for parents."

Apart from basic *kavod* to others, Judaism demands special *kavod* to parents, to grandparents, to elder siblings, to teachers and rabbis . . . and to the dead.

Let your fellow man's *kavod* be as dear to you as your own.

The Talmud, Avot

In Hebrew, the noun *kavod*, dignity, and the noun *koved*, weight, *gravitas*, stem from the same root. The man of dignity is a weighty person. The people who surround him feel his impact. Hence, dignity is measured not by the inner worth of the in-depth-personality, but by the accomplishments of the surface-personality. No matter how fine, noble, and gifted one may be, he cannot command respect or be appreciated by others if he has not succeeded in realizing his talents and communicating his message to society through the medium of the creative majestic gesture.

Joseph B. Soloveitchik

Whenever people run after *kavod*, *kavod* runs away from them.

The Midrash

— ❧ —

Kedushá (Ashkenazi: **Kedúshe**) Sanctity

"When you meet one of these great rabbis, you feel an aura of *kedusha* about them."

"Don't leave the *tallit* [prayer shawl] on the floor—it has *kedusha*!"

The Jewish world is a finely textured world. All kinds of things have *kedusha*, with different degrees of intrinsic *kedusha* and *kedusha*-by-association: Religious writings have *kedusha*, above all a *Sefer Torah* (Torah scroll). They are not destroyed but given religious burial. Other objects such as a *tallit* or an *etrog* fruit, when discarded, are meant to be wrapped with care and not just tossed into the garbage. Places: Synagogues have *kedusha*; so, too, the Land of Israel. The *Kotel* (Western Wall in Jerusalem) has a high *kedusha*, and the Temple Mount the highest of all. Times, too, have *kedusha*—the Sabbath, for example. And language: Hebrew was traditionally called *leshon ha-kodesh*, "the Holy Tongue," each letter and each word having a real or potential *kedusha*—perhaps even some words in this book.

— ❧ —

Kehilá (Ashkenazi: **Kehíle**)   Jewish community

"They're in South Bend, Indiana? Is that a large *kehila*?"

Kehila once signified a community with all its own institutions—giving many Jews in the Old Country a real sense of autonomy: their own school system, their own welfare, their own laws and enforcement officers, and (this is the bad news) their own taxation.

Nowadays, of course, the *kehila* (this word is generally used by the Orthodox) revolves around the synagogue, which sometimes has its own school or Y. And where there is more than one synagogue—and there usually is—there is in a sense more than one *kehila*.

— ✿ —

Ken yirbú! (Ashkenazi: **Ken yírbu!**)   "May there be many more!"

"Shoshana's had another baby? Her third? *Mazel tov! Ken yirbu!*"

Literally "may they multiply even more." Said particularly on news of a birth, this phrase is rich in echoes of a time when Jewish parenting was a crime: The biblical Book of Exodus, recounting the Egyptian assault on the Israelite birth rate, records that the more they were oppressed "the more they multiplied" (*ken yirbu*)—an ambiguous phrase, for it also means "may they multiply even more." And the ancient *Midrash* comments that these words were God's own blessing to the people.

— ✿ —

Keréach mi-kan u-mi-kan   To lose both ways

"Don't be overambitious or you'll end up *kereach mi-kan u-mi-kan*."

Literally "bald on both sides," *kereach mi-kan u-mi-kan* is the Talmud's vivid way of describing what happens when someone goes for two things and loses both ways. It comes from the story of a man who took two wives, one a young girl and the other a mature matriarch. The young girl proceeded to pluck out all his white hairs to make him look young, while the older woman plucked out all the fellow's black hairs to make him look old. The result was a bald man.

— ✿ —

Keriá (Ashkenazi: **Kríe**)   Rending of a garment

"Before the burial, the close mourners stood and did *keria*."

No mourning custom creates such a bond with the Jewish past as *keria*, the mourners' rending of their garment from the collar downward. Jacob rent his clothes on being told that his son Joseph was dead, so did David on the death of King Saul, and Mordechai at the news of Haman's impending genocide.

After a few simple prayers the immediate family performed the act of *keria*, the tearing of one's clothes. . . . Though this was only a symbolic act, it served as a potent physical and emotional release of sorrow and anger at precisely the needed moment. Whatever we wore during the following week was torn slightly, serving as a blatant reminder of our grief.

Deborah Lipstadt

— 🙠 —

Ketivá ve-chatimá tová! (Ashkenazi: **Ksíve ve-chasíme tóhve!**) "Happy New Year!"

"If I don't see you in *shul*, Debbie, *ksive ve-chasime tohve*, and we should only all be well.
   "*Omeyn!* [Amen]."

This New Year's greeting (for *Rosh Hashanah*, of course, not for January 1) is quite a mouthful, which may explain why only the Orthodox generally use it, but it's a beautiful greeting. Literally "a good writing and sealing," that is, may God inscribe you and seal you in the Book of Life. *Rosh Hashanah* is the Day of Divine Judgment for behavior in the outgoing year, but with a stay of verdict until *Yom Kippur* ten days later, and so *ketiva ve-chatima tova* is said until *Rosh Hashanah*. From *Rosh Hashanah* to *Yom Kippur* a different greeting is used, *gmar chatima tova* (see entry).

— 🙠 —

Ketubá (Ashkenazi: **Ksúbe**)   Marriage contract

"Did you see that gorgeous *ketuba* hanging on their living room wall?"

I wonder how many cultures take a long-winded and long-worded legal contract written in a language they don't understand, add all kinds of fantastic illustrations, and hang it up in their living rooms?

   That is what many Jews, particularly Spanish and Italian, did with their *ketuba*. And recent years have seen a return to the old traditions of *ketuba* ornamentation. The text of the *ketuba* itself is a pledge by the groom to maintain the bride and to set aside a sum of money for her if he dies or divorces her. The *ketuba* is read out by the rabbi at the wedding, and presented, signed and witnessed, to the bride—to be kept in a very safe place.

— ❧ —

Kéver avót (Ashkenazi: Kéver óves)   Visiting a parent's grave

"My father takes my uncle every year to do *kever avot*."

It is customary to do *kever avot*, that is, to visit the graves of parents, shortly before the *Yamim Noraim* (High Holy Days). One says *Tehilim* (Psalms) and tends the grave. Pebbles are commonly placed on the tomb to commemorate a visit.

— ❧ —

Kibúd av va-em (Ashkenazi: kíbud av vo-eym)   Respect for parents

"He asked his mother if he could get divorced? Now that's real *kibud av va-em*."

Respect for parents is the fifth of the Ten Commandments. What is "fear of parents," asks the Talmud: Not to sit in their place, to talk in their turn, to contradict what they say. And what is "respect for parents": To feed them and clothe them, to walk them in and walk them out (if they are infirm).

In Ashkelon lived a Gentile named Dama, who possessed a gem that was needed for the High Priest's breastplate. The Sages offered him 100 dinars. He went for the keys to the chest—and found his father asleep with them clasped in his fingers. No sale, he told them. Thinking he was bargaining, the Sages offered 200, and finally 1000. When eventually his father awoke, Dama would only accept 100. "I do not wish to make money out of *kibud av*," he said.

The Jerusalem Talmud, Pe'ah

A father once wanted a drink of water. His children, all seven of them, promptly began squabbling for the honor of doing the *mitzvah* of *kibud av*. Finally, the eldest son announced he would pay them two roubles for the honor. But the next son bid five roubles, and the next seven. "Then I'll give ten roubles," said the eldest, "and that's that."

Then he thought for a moment and announced: "You know what? If it's such a great *mitzvah*, let's give our father the honor of fetching the water himself . . ."

— ❧ —

Kibbútz, pl. **kibbutzím** Kibbutz

"Tanya's on *kibbutz* this year, working in the laundry."

Despite the demise of international communism, the commune dream is alive and well (or kind of) in the Israeli *kibbutz*.

The very word means "collective"—the first *kibbutz* was set up in 1909 by Russian-Jewish revolutionaries near Lake Kinneret. Nowadays, true, not everything is shared; and as state subsidies to *kibbutzim* become a memory, outside employees, incentive bonuses, and other trappings of capitalism are becoming the usual thing. But a *kibbutz* is still unlike anywhere else on earth.

Kiddúsh (Ashkenazi: **Kíddesh**) Blessings marking the Sabbath in the home; buffet after Sabbath morning prayers

"Come on, Jack, make *kiddush* already. I'm hungry."

"Someone was leaving for Israel, so the synagogue laid on a *kiddush* for him."

Kiddush is the ceremonial way of marking the Sabbath in the home, involving a benediction over wine and two *chalot* (Sabbath loaves) on *Shabbat* evening, and again over wine or liquor and *chalot* or cakes the following day. In the children's eyes, *Kiddush* is the father's big moment, just as lighting the candles is the mother's. The literal meaning of *kiddush* is "sanctification."

As the *Shabbat* morning service lasts two to three hours, *kiddush* is often held at the synagogue—with a scrumptious buffet. Human nature being what it is, the buffet itself is also called *kiddush*.

Rabbi Yisochor Ber of Radoshitz had a disciple who could imitate his way of saying *kiddush* so perfectly that anyone might have thought it was the rabbi himself. One day the disciple received a summons to Rabbi Yisochor Ber:

"I hear you can say *kiddush* exactly like me. Do it, please."

"But I don't want to offend you . . .," said the disciple.

"Have no fear," said the rabbi.

And the disciple proceeded to make *kiddush* with precisely the same intonations and inflexions and gestures. But upon reaching a certain phrase, he paused, froze—and then mumbled his way to the end as best he could.

"What happened?" asked the rabbi.

The disciple took a deep breath: "When you come to that phrase, you dedicate your whole being to the Almighty. It's not for me to do that."

Kiddúsh ha-Shém (Ashkenazi: **Kíddesh ha-Shém**)   Bringing honor to God; martyrdom

"I always treat my staff generously. It's a *kiddush ha-Shem*."

"Here is a mass grave of some of the Jews who did *kiddush ha-Shem* in Belsen."

Kiddush ha-Shem, literally "sanctification of the Name," is an ultimate value. To obey God's injunctions for their own sake, unquestioningly, neither out of fear nor for gain, is to do *kiddush ha-Shem*. The word also applies to anything that serves to give Judaism greater repute in the world at large.

To sacrifice one's life rather than be forced into idolatry, immorality, or unjustified homicide is the ultimate *kiddush ha-Shem*.

Our Father, our King, act for the sake of those who went through fire and water for *kiddush ha-Shem*.

> From the High Holy Day *Avinu Malkenu* prayer

In the Warsaw ghetto Rabbi Isaac Nissenbaum, a famous and respected Orthodox rabbi, made the statement—much quoted by Jews of all persuasions in their desperate efforts to defend, preserve, and hallow Jewish life against an enemy sworn to destroy it all—that this was a time not for *kiddush ha-Shem* [martyrdom] but rather for *kiddush ha-chayim* [the sanctification of life]. It is a time for *kiddush ha-chayim* still. The Jewish people have passed through the Nazi antiworld of death; thereafter, by any standard, religious or secular, Jewish life ranks higher than Jewish death, even if it is for the sake of the divine name.

> Emil Fackenheim

. . . The sum-total of all that I have written is that I want you to perform the *mitzvah* of *kiddush ha-Shem*—sanctifying God's name in everything that you do. The essence of that *mitzvah* is not martyrdom, although it sometimes calls for that. However, our sages define it differently. "So act," they enjoin us, "that all who behold you will say: 'Blessed is that man's God.'"

It is thus that I pray you will act. And you and we shall rejoice.

> Love, Dad.
>
> Rabbi Emanuel Rackman, letter to
> his son on going away to college

– 🙙🙘 –

Kiddúsh levaná (Ashkenazi: **Kíddesh levóne**)   Sanctification of the moon

"It's cloudy again tonight—no way can we do *kiddush levana*."

Once a month, in synagogue yards, in the moonlight, people gather after evening prayers to do the custom of *kiddush levana*. Peering up at the thin sliver of the new moon, they bless God for "renewing the month," and for renewing the Jewish people time after time—for the moon is a symbol of Jewish destiny.

Kilachár yad (Ashkenazi: **Kilácher yad**)   Nonchalantly, perfunctorily

"The teacher just checks my work *kilachar yad*—without really looking at it."

Kilachar yad means literally "with the back of the hand." That was how donkey drivers used to hold the reins if they really got bored on the job. It's still the perfect description for the way some people I know drive their Toyotas. But *kilachar yad* has long ago been extended to the performance of any task uncaringly or even carelessly.

Kiná, pl. **kinót** (Ashkenazi: **Kíne**, pl. **kínes**)   Poem of lament

"They're sitting on the floor saying *kinot*."

On the fast of *Tisha be-Av*, people sit on the synagogue floor or on low chairs, evening and morning, and recite a long series of *kinot*, poems of lament. The *kinot* are medieval, some of them intricate and erudite and others, particularly those by the prince of Spanish Hebrew poetry, Yehuda Halevi, simple, direct, and extremely moving. They are a mix of the historical and the existential, lamenting the desolation of Zion and the demise of a people and yearning for its rebirth.

Zion, lament your house burned down,
Scream bitterly at the ruins of your vines.
Zion, be roused like a widow
Enslaved to every passerby for a plethora of sins.
Upon the hills raise a kina *and dirge and*
Loud wailing for your masses that were killed . . .

           Translation of a sixteenth-century *kina*

If we really believed with perfect faith in the coming of the Messiah, not one of us would be putting away the *Kinot* book to use on next *Tisha be-Av*.

           Rabbi Mordechai of Lechovitz

Kipá   Yarmulke (skullcap)

"If you're going to wear the crocheted *kipa*, put another clip in it so it doesn't fly away."

Orthodox Jewish men (and boys) are required to cover their heads. In Israel you can more or less tell a person's politics from the *kipa* he wears: crocheted means Nationalist-Zionist Orthodox; the bigger the *kipa*, the "more" Orthodox, or at least that's what the wearer thinks. Black means non-Zionist Orthodox (and you'll only wear it indoors; outside you'll wear a black hat). A velvet *kipa* probably means you've just arrived from an American *Bar Mitzvah*. A black paper *kipa* means you've just arrived from a funeral.

In the United States, the very word *kipa* is "modernistic" or Zionist (it's Israeli). The Yiddish word *yarmulke* is still widely used.

— ❧ —

Kisé shel eliyáhu   Elijah's chair

At a *brit mila*, the *mohel* (circumcisor) proclaims in Hebrew, "This is the *kise shel eliyahu* of blessed memory," and the baby is placed briefly on a chair designated as *kise shel eliyahu*, Elijah's chair, before being placed on the lap of the *sandek* for the circumcision to take place. The *kise shel eliyahu* embodies the tradition that the prophet Elijah is present at every *brit mila*. Elijah, the Jews' own most fiery critic, is there to acknowledge, however grudgingly, that his wayward people still keep the *brit mila* religiously.

— ❧ —

Kislév (Ashkenazi: **Kíslev**)   The month of Kislev

Kislev (around November-December) is the ninth month of the Jewish year—a month with short days and long nights, but with the special lights of *Chanukah*.

— ❧ —

Kitsúr Shulchán Arúch (Ashkenazi: **Kítser Shúlchen Órech**)   Name of a code of Jewish laws

For 100 years, the standard digest of Ashkenazi Jewish laws and customs has been the *Kitsur Shulchan Aruch*—based ultimately on the great sixteenth-century code, the *Shulchan Aruch* (see entry), but shorter and a lot livelier. The *Kitsur*, as it is popularly dubbed, has been translated into umpteen languages. Two English versions were renamed "Laws and Customs of Israel" and "The Jew and his Duties."

It's one of those books that all Jewish households used to have, even if they may only have opened it to study the customs of mourning. I remember giving someone one for a *Bar Mitzvah* gift, and discovering that it was the fourteenth copy he had received.

— ❦ —

Klal Yisraél (Ashkenazi: **Klal Yisróel**)   The Jewish people

"These have been years of major significance for *Klal Yisrael*."

So accustomed have we become to *Yisrael* as the name of the Jewish state that it can come as a surprise to hear that *Yisrael* was traditionally the name of the Jewish people—going right back to biblical times. They derived this profound and poetic name, meaning "overcoming a mighty force," from their ancestor Jacob, whom God renamed *Yisrael*, "Israel."

Nowadays this use of *Yisrael* lives on in the expression *Klal Yisrael*.

— ❦ —

Knésset   Israel's parliament

"There were protests by *Knesset* members of all parties at the orchestra's decision to play Wagner."

The name *Knesset* recalls the last independent Jewish constituent assembly over 2,000 years ago, the *Knesset ha-Gdola*. It is celebrated for its multitude of parties.

— ❦ —

Kóach   Strength

"You won't be able to make a skirt out of this material—it has no *koach* to it."

"Guys, take five. I just have no *koach*."

Not by might and not by *koach*, but by my spirit, saith the Lord.
The Bible, Zechariah

— ❦ —

Kohélet (Ashkenazi: **Kohéles**)   The Book of Ecclesiastes

Tucked away in the Bible is the short Book of *Kohelet*, a sobering, worldly wise philosophy of life ascribed to King Solomon in his old age—the name *Kohelet* has been explained as "the preacher" or "the encyclopedic mind."

It is traditionally recited during the harvest festival of *Sukkot*, often from a special parchment scroll. *Kohelet* is the source of all manner of wonderful sayings that everyone knows, such as "there is nothing new under the sun."

The words of Kohelet *son of David, king in Jerusalem.*
Vanity of vanities, says Kohelet, *vanity of vanities, all is vanity.*
What advantage does a person derive from all his labor which he performs under the sun?

Opening words of the Book of Kohelet

— ❧ —

Kohén, pl. **kohaním** (Ashkenazi: **Kóen**, pl. **kohánim**)   Priest

"He can't go into a cemetery, can he, if he's a *kohen*."

A *kohen* these days is not what most people think of when you say "priest." He is not a minister, nor need he be a scholar or rabbi. Rather, he is entrusted with a very few, but major, religious responsibilities: to bless the congregation with the biblical *Birkat Kohanim* (priestly blessing), to be called first to the Recital of the Torah, to conduct the *Pidyon ha-Ben* (firstborn redemption) ceremony—and to avoid contact with the dead. These are all that survives of the *Kohen*'s ancient role of temple priest.

Although Cohen is a well-known Jewish name, there are actually very few *kohanim*. And of these, even fewer actually care to perform these responsibilities.

— ❧ —

Kol ishá (Ashkenazi: **Kol ísho**)   A woman's (singing) voice

"We can't have any fathers at the girls' concert because of *kol isha*."

Jewish men are traditionally not supposed to listen to *kol isha*, the singing of a woman (literally "a woman's voice"), or at least not solo singing. In Ultraorthodox circles, this stops men (perhaps "excuses men" would be more correct) from going to hear the local ladies' charity performance of *Fiddler on the Roof* or a mixed klezmer band.

— ❧ —

Kol ha-kavód!   "Well done!"

"Meet Vivienne. She just finished her Ph.D."
  "Oh wow, *kol ha-kavod!*"

This is a modern Israeli form of congratulation and verbal back slap-ping. It literally means "all honor!" A popular song after the Six Day War was *Kol ha-Kavod le-Tsahal* ("Well done, Israel Defense Forces!").

Don't use it for wedding, birth, and *Bar Mitzvah* congratulations—there you say *Mazel tov!*

— ❧ —

Kol ha-mosíf goréa (Ashkenazi: **Kol ha-móhsif gohréa**)   "To add is to detract"

"Don't start adding anything to the drawing. It's fine. *Kol ha-mosif gorea.*"

Originally a legal maxim, designed to stop any tampering or adding to the Mosaic law, *kol ha-mosif gorea* is now appropriate to any sphere.

— ❧ —

Kol kevudá bat mélech peníma (Ashkenazi: **Kol kvúdo bas mélech pnímo**)   "All the glory of a princess is within"

These words from Psalm 45 may actually have been talking about some-thing entirely different (*kevuda* means "paraphernalia, trousseau")—but they have come to be widely used as a proof text for the idea that the Jewish woman's place is in the home. If I wished to propound the idea, I'd feel much happier with the Psalmist's way of saying it.

— ❧ —

Kol Nidréy (Ashkenazi: **Kol Nídre**)   The *Kol Nidrey* service

"Every time I hear *Kol Nidrey* I have to cry."

Kol Nidrey unleashes the emotional power of *Yom Kippur*. It is the first service of this holiest of days, or more exactly the first prayer. In the gathering dusk, the synagogue fills; then silence, and the cantor intones, three times over, a plaintive melody that has become almost synonymous with *Kol Nidrey*. Is it the melody that does it, or is it the words, which seem to say that all human resolutions are but breath?

All vows [*kol nidrey*], oaths, and resolutions of any kind [between us and God] that we will have made between this *Yom Kippur* and the next we hereby renounce and declare null and void. Our vows shall be nonvows, our oaths nonoaths, and our resolutions nonresolutions.

Loose translation of the *Kol Nidrey* declaration

— ❧ —

Kol tuv! "All the best!"

"I have a call on the other line, so call me back in an hour. *Kol tuv!*"

Literally "all good," *kol tuv* is a charming oldtime way of closing a friendly letter, conversation, or phone call. The other person can also respond *kol tuv*. Israelis and traditional Diaspora Jews both use it. Yet I have never seen the slightest mention of it in a Hebrew textbook.

– ҈ –

Kol yisraél arevím ze ba-ze (Ashkenazi: **Kol yisróel oréyvim ze bo-ze**) "All Jews are responsible for one another"

This Talmudic saying expresses a collective responsibility to prevent wrongdoing and to spread the word. No one dare say, "It is not my affair."

– ҈ –

Kol yisraél chaverím (Ashkenazi: **Kol yisróel chavéyrim**)　"All Jews are friends"

Another Talmudic saying—or would *wish* be a better word? Familiar to synagogue attenders from the Blessing for the New Month.

I met a girl. I used to see her every evening. Sweet moonlit nights, sweet dreams! How happy she made me! How happy I was when the *chazan* said the Blessing for the New Moon, *kol yisroel chaveyrim*. Do you realize what it means to have seven or eight million brothers and sisters—and dear Miriam was one of them! That made me feel strong and proud.

Yitzchak Leib Peretz

– ҈ –

Kolél (Ashkenazi: **Kóhlel, kóylel**)　Talmudic seminary for married men

"Her husband's in *kolel*, so they really need the second income."

Wherever Ultraorthodox Jews reside in large numbers, the *kolel* is on the rise—and controversially. Traditionally, a highly gifted minority of *yeshiva* graduates went on, after marriage, to a *kolel* to train as rabbis and jurists. Nowadays, increasing numbers of married men are *kolel-niks*, studying full time at *kolel*, supported by donations and by their wives' incomes. There has been a desperate desire to thus repair the devastation done to traditional Jewish scholarship by the Nazis and the Bolsheviks. In Israel, however, many voices are being raised, Orthodox ones included, against the refusal of many *kolelniks* to do any military service or to enter the labor force.

— ✤ —

Kosher. See **Kasher.**

— ✤ —

(The) **Kótel** (Ashkenazi: [The] **Kóhsl**)   The Western Wall

"Joan said they're having the *Bar Mitzvah* at the *Kotel*—isn't that great?"

The one surviving wall of the ancient Temple compound in Jerusalem has always been called the *Kotel Maaravi*, "the Western Wall." (The name Wailing Wall is an insensitive appellation by outsiders.) Nowadays, Israelis generally call it simply *ha-Kotel*, "the Wall." Even the nonreligious treat it with some kind of transmuted reverence, a symbol of the Jewish state.

The *Shechina* [Divine Presence] never departs from the *Kotel Maaravi*.

The Midrash

— ✤ —

Kotsó shel yud (Ashkenazi: **Kútso shel yud**)   The tiniest thing, a minutia

"I can't work with him. He won't allow you to change a *kotso shel yud*."

The tiniest letter of the Hebrew *alef-bet* is the *yud*. And atop the *yud* is a tiny scribal stroke, called a *kots*. Hardly surprising, then, that *kotso shel yud* has come to signify the tiniest thing (just like the Greek letter iota, in fact).

— ✤ —

Kóva témbel   Floppy Israeli hat

If one were to design an Israeli national costume, to rival the Japanese kimono, Mexican sombrero, or British bowler hat, pin-striped suit, and umbrella, it would have to start with the *kova tembel*, literally "imbecile hat." The high floppy khaki cotton hat was something that many *kibbutznikim* and laborers used to wear, and would probably still be wearing if it weren't impossible to find a *kova tembel* that didn't say "I love Tel Aviv" or "1986 Hadassah Fact-finding Mission."

Fortunately, the *kova tembel* has been immortalized by the Israeli cartoonist Dosh in the wonderful image of Israel as a wide-eyed kid in shorts with a *kova tembel* on his head. And factories in Taiwan will continue to turn them out for years to come.

Kriát ha-Toráh (Ashkenazi: **Kríes ha-Tóhre**)   Reading of the Law in the synagogue

"As there's a *Bar Mitzvah* today, there'll be quite a few uncles and cousins to call up for *Kriat ha-Torah*."

See *Baal Kore*, "Torah reader" and *Aliyah*, "Calling up to the Torah."

Every Sabbath and feast or fast day, and on Mondays and Thursdays too, the Torah scroll is brought forth and read in the synagogue. This is *Kriat ha-Torah* (popularly known in America by the Yiddish word *leyning*).

The reading is traditionally in Hebrew, with a complicated chant that takes endless hours to learn. Meanwhile, the congregation follow the reading from a book, though if you know Hebrew and the *baal kore* (reader) doesn't mumble, it's a joy to sit back, close your eyes, and just listen.

Kriát Shemá (Ashkenazi: **Kríes Shma** or **Kríshme**)   The reading of the Shema

"Before I call them, I must say *Kriat Shema*."

See *Shema* for details.

Kriat Shema, reading the *Shema* declaration early in the morning and in the evening, is one of the basic duties for Jewish men—and one of the first things that all children, boys as well as girls, are taught. The *Shema* itself is popularly called *Kries Shma* or *Krishme* by Ashkenazim, hence "to say *Kries Shma*."

Kriát Yam-Súf (Ashkenazi: **Kríes Yám-Suf**)   The parting of the Red Sea

"It was an absolutely stupendous miracle, just like *Kriat Yam-Suf.*"

This word *kriat* has nothing to do with *kriat* in *kriat shema*. They're spelled differently in Hebrew.

Kriat Yam-Suf—when the Red Sea parted for the Israelites to march through on dry soil, only for the Egyptian armies to drown—has become synonymous with the sort of thing that seems natural but in reality wrenches Nature asunder.

Getting enough to eat is as hard as *Kriat Yam-Suf.*

The Talmud, Pesachim

Finding Jewish people their right partners in life is as hard as *Kriat Yam-Suf.*

The Midrash

Labriút!   "Bless you!" (literally, "to health!", said when someone sneezes)

Labriut is a modern Israeli expression. It isn't only for when someone sneezes. It's also what you say when, ever so gently, you want to get someone out of your hair.

Lag ba-Ómer (Ashkenazi: **Lag bo-Óhmer**)   Lag Ba-Omer festival

"I just have to buy a new dress—we have three weddings to go to on *Lag ba-Omer.*"

In the month of May, thirty-three days through the period of semi-mourning called the *Omer* (see entry) comes a mini-festival: *Lag ba-Omer* (literally 33rd of the *Omer*). *Lag ba-Omer* is not about what you *have* to do but what you *can* do: you *can* get married—and couples get married in the thousands. You *can* have a haircut—and on Mount Meron in the Galilee throngs of people bring their three-year-old sons for their first haircut. And you can generally have a good time; *Lag ba-Omer* is a day for school outings, campfires, and baked potatoes.

Our bows are on our shoulders,
Our flags are held up high,
To our friendly forest

We're heading young and old.
Today's Lag ba-Omer! *Today's* Lag ba-Omer!

From a popular Israeli children's *Lag ba-Omer* song

Lámed-vav tsadikím (Ashkenazi: **Lámed-vov tsadíkim**)   The thirty-six hidden saints

"Never refuse a beggar—he may be one of the *Lamed-vav tsadikim*."

Tradition teaches that the survival of the world revolves around thirty-six *tsadikim* (saints) alive in each generation—and that their identity is a mystery. It might be that beggar over there sleeping and it might be your unassuming next-door neighbor.

Said Abaye: The world contains at least *lamed-vav tsadikim* that receive the Divine Presence every day.

The Talmud, Sukkah

Lébn   Sort of very low-fat sour yogurt

Lebn seems to be going the same way as *kibbutzim* and *moshavim*. This relative of yogurt was once a pioneer's breakfast, lunch, and probably dinner—cool, thirst-quenching, and excitingly Middle Eastern. I still see it in the store on the corner, but one has increasingly to search for it among the twelve-packs of fruit yogurts and pseudo yogurts that all my Israeli neighbors seem to live on.

Le-cháyim   "To life!" (said when making a toast); a strong drink

"Do you want a *le-chayim*? Or are you driving?"

Le-chayim is the universal and age-old Jewish toast—said on wine or liquor. One "makes a *le-chayim*." People often respond *le-chayim u-le-shalom* "to life and to peace."

By extension, *le-chayim* is the drink itself. You "drink a *le-chayim*."

After morning prayers, the rabbi of Pitev always used to join his flock in drinking a *le-chayim*. One day, however, he took off his *tefilin* before prayers were over, made his way to the vodka, and began drinking all by himself. People stared in amazement.

Later that day, someone plucked up courage to ask the rabbi why he had drunk a *le-chayim* before prayers were over.

The rabbi grinned. "For the simple reason that yesterday I waited till the end of the service and there wasn't a single drop of the stuff left!"

— ✣ —

Lech la-azazél   "Get lost!" (literally "Go to Azazel")

"Lois, here's that guy again who was pestering us. Hey you, *lech la-azazel!*"

Lech la-azazel does the job in modern Hebrew of "go to hell!", but it's so much more aesthetic. In fact, *lech la-azazel* is just bursting with Jewish heritage. And the phrase was used in pious literature long before bus drivers began losing their tempers in the heat of Tel Aviv.

Azazel was a vague place of cliffs and crags, somewhere in the Judean Desert, to which a sacrificial goat was led, every Yom Kippur in ancient times, to atone for the sins of the people. The word seems to mean might, power; even the sound of it is vaguely forbidding. The nearest I could get to it in English is "get lost!" Or perhaps, "You get my goat"?

— ✣ —

Lechá Dodí (Ashkenazi: Lechó Dóhdi)   The Sabbath song *Lecha Dodi*

"I love that new Israeli tune for *Lecha Dodi.*"

Lecha Dodi is the song that welcomes the Sabbath in synagogues everywhere at Friday dusk. A romance with a hint of lament, *Lecha Dodi* embodies the profound imprint of Kabbalah mysticism on Jewish prayer. It would take forty years of Sabbaths for all known *Lecha Dodi* melodies to be sung.

Come in peace, crown to your husband,
Joyfully, exultantly,
Among the faithful of the precious people,
Come, bride—come, bride!
Come, my beloved [lecha dodi], *to meet the bride.*
Let us welcome the Sabbath.

The final stanza of *Lecha Dodi*

The worshippers unconsciously respond to the broad themes, the real essence of the prayer which, like the moon obscured behind the clouds, exerts a hidden but inexorable influence upon the ebb and tide of their religious experience. . . . So does the secret of the success of *Lecha Dodi* lie in the magnificent sweep of its esoteric Unity theme.

Norman Lamm

— ✣ —

Léchem mishnéh (Ashkenazi: **Léchem míshne**)   Twin Sabbath loaves

"Are there enough rolls for all the guests to have *lechem mishneh*?"

Literally "double bread." Tradition requires the *Shabbat* meals to begin with a blessing over two loaves (or rolls, *matzo*, or the like). This commemorates the double portion of manna that the Israelites were granted for *Shabbat* in the wilderness—and also symbolizes the heightened spirituality-within-materiality of the Sabbath Day.

Lehavdíl (Ashkenazi: **Lehávdil**)   "If you'll pardon the comparison"

"As for this idea of the unborn child knowing the Torah, I recall something similar in Plato, *lehavdil*."

Lehavdil, literally "to make a distinction," is one of the joys of Hebrew— a delightful device that allows you to get away with mentioning the sacred and the profane in the same breath, and then promptly to apologize for it.

In principle, the distance between Jewishness and the culture of the environment was signified by the expression *lehavdil*.

Max Weinreich

Lehitraót   "Au revoir"

". . . and *Lehitraot* and *Mazel tov* to Miss Rabinowitz on her forthcoming marriage. The whole school looks forward to having her back with us soon."

Lehitraot is modern Hebrew's version of *au revoir, dasvedanya, auf Wiedersehen*. It means, quite simply, "to see each other soon." I know no one ever said it in the Bible and I know there is something to be said for keeping up the old biblical ways of greeting, but I love the sound of *lehitraot*, and even the slangy *lehit!* (see ya!) With a bit of an effort, I can just imagine Adam saying it to Eve.

What I'm sure Adam didn't say is this ghastly *lehitraot bye!* or *lehitraot bye bye!*

Le-shaná ha-baá birushaláyim! (Ashkenazi: **Le-shóno ha-bó birusholáyim!**)　"Next year in Jerusalem!"

This wish and prayer for messianic redemption is the way Jews the world over round off their *Seder* night prayers—and the fast of *Yom Kippur.*

Passover was around the corner, and a group of Chasidim were in the court-yard drawing water to make the dough to bake the *matzo*; and as they heaved, they exclaimed back and forth: "*Le-shono ha-bo birusholayim!*"
　　Rabbi Shalom of Belz heard them and frowned. "Why *next* year in Jerusalem?" he asked. "With this water we are drawing, may we bake *matzo* tomorrow in Jerusalem redeemed and eat it in the company of the Messiah."

The ram's horn was blown, everyone trembled, and then came a mighty roar: "*Le-shono ha-bo birusholayim!*"
　　The riffraff were already picking the wax candle drippings off the table, and the week-day reader was already standing at the desk and reading the weekday Evening Prayer in a weekday chant.

Yitzchak Leib Peretz

– ৡৢ৾ঌ –

Leshém shamáyim (Ashkenazi: **Le-shém shomáyim**)　For pure motives (literally "for the sake of Heaven")

". . . She was a really good teacher. And she didn't ask for any money. It was *leshem shamayim* . . ."

All who labor for the *tsibur* [the public] should labor *leshem shamayim.*

The Talmud, Avot

– ৡৢ৾ঌ –

Leshón ha-Kódesh (Ashkenazi: **Lóshn Kóhdesh**)　The Holy Tongue (i.e., Hebrew)

"When my grandfather wrote home to his father, it was always in *Loshn Kohdesh.*"

Don't think for a moment that *Leshon ha-Kodesh* only means biblical Hebrew or prayer book Hebrew. *Leshon ha-Kodesh* is Hebrew, period. It's one of the most ancient names known for the language, and was the standard name until the rise of secular Zionism made *Ivrit* (liter-ally "language of the Hebrews") a more fashionable label. In response, some Ultraorthodox circles today would like to draw a clear divide between "sacred" Hebrew (*Loshn Kohdesh*) and "profane" Hebrew (*Ivrit*)—but such a divide never existed in history.

History, however, moves on; and today Hebrew is almost universally called *Ivrit*.

When the child begins to speak, his father talks *Leshon ha-Kodesh* with him and teaches him Torah.

The Midrash on Deuteronomy

Leshón ha-rá (Ashkenazi: **Lóshn hóre**)   Disparaging talk, gossip (literally "evil language")

"What I'm saying about her isn't *loshn hore*—it's true."
    "Well, that makes it even worse *loshn hore!*"

Jewish Law (Halacha) defines *leshon ha-ra* as any talk about other people that serves no positive purpose—whether or not it is intended maliciously.

The famed Polish sage, Rabbi Israel Meir Ha-Cohen, popularly known as the Chafetz Chayim, wrote whole books against the practice of *leshon ha-ra*. Once, the story goes, a woman came to him to buy his latest book about *leshon ha-ra*.
    "Oh thank heavens you have it in stock," she said. "My neighbor could really do with it. She talks such *loshn hore* . . ."

Said Rabbi Shemuel bar Nachman: Why is *leshon ha-ra* called "the triple tongue"?
    Because it kills in triplicate: It kills the person who says it, and the person who receives it, and the person who is the subject of it.

The Talmud, Arachin

Levayá (Ashkenazi: **Leváye/Levóye**)   Funeral

"So many people came to the *levaya* that they jammed all the roads around the house."

The dead are not just buried. They are "accompanied" (the basic meaning of *levaya*) on their last journey. As the hearse moves off slowly, people may walk behind it for a few yards. At the cemetery, they again accompany the body to its resting place, and take turns shoveling earth into the grave. Then the *kaddish* is said, followed by *nichum avel*.

Out of respect, the *levaya* is traditionally held as soon as possible, in Israel usually on the same day—and there black-bordered posters hastily appear on walls and trees, announcing the time of the *levaya*.

Leví, pl. leviyím (Ashkenazi: **Léyvi, pl. leviyim**)   Levite

"Are you a *Levi*, a *Kohen*, or a *Yisra'el*?"

The Jewish last name Levy (or Levine, Lewin, and so on) has a long pedigree.

In biblical times there were twelve tribes of Israel. The only tribal group to survive to this day is that of the *Levi* and the *Kohen*—both of them male-line descendants of the tribe of Levi. All other Jews may conceivably be descended from any other tribe, and are known collectively as *Yisra'el*. The tribe of Levi itself is subdivided into *Kohanim* (see entry) and *Leviyim*, the former descended from the priestly line of Aaron while the latter are all other Levites.

Once a *Levi* might have sung or played in the Jerusalem Temple. Today, he is called second to the recital of the Torah, washes the *kohen*'s hands before the priestly blessing, and that's it.

– ❦ –

Lo alécha ha-melachá ligmór (Ashkenazi: **Lo olécho hamlócho lígmor**)   "It is not up to you to complete the work"

"Look, reorganizing the department is a vast undertaking, so just do what you can. *Lo alecha ha-melacha ligmor.*

This proverb forms part of a philosophy of life by Rabbi Tarphon, a sage of the second century. It is a metaphor in which life is a business and the Almighty the boss.

The day is short, the task is great, the workers are lax, the pay is good, and the Employer is insistent.

It is not up to you to complete the work [*Lo alecha ha-melacha ligmor*], yet you are not free to desist from it. If you have studied much Torah, much reward will be yours, and your Employer is certain to pay you for your work—but be aware that the reward of the righteous is in the World to Come.

The Talmud, Avot

– ❦ –

Lo alénu (Ashkenazi: **Lo oléynu**)   "May it not happen to us"

"If someone's business burns down, *lo alenu*, they ought to call in insurance adjusters."

See also *Rachmana litslan*, "Heaven protect us."

Literally "not upon us." Many Jews adhere to the philosophy (or should one say, mentality?) of *al tiftach peh la-satan*, "Don't open your mouth to the Devil." When you mention something bad, you slip in a hasty *lo alenu*, particularly if it happened to an acquaintance. Perhaps to douse any tiny trace of schadenfreude . . .

— ✿ —

Lo dubím ve-lo yáar! (Ashkenazi: **Lo dúbim ve-lo yáar!**)   "Nothing of the kind!"

"I hear your company's moving."
  "*Lo dubim ve-lo yaar!* We only just moved here."

Lo dubim ve-lo yaar is the way to dismiss any story as groundless. It literally means "no bears and no forest," but it has absolutely nothing to do with Goldilocks. It all goes back to the biblical story of the prophet Elisha who was taunted by a group of youths and cursed them, whereupon two she bears emerged from the forest and mauled them. What was the exact nature of the miracle, the Talmud ponders. Were the bears supernatural? Was the forest supernatural? Or were there no bears, and no forest either?

— ✿ —

Lo hayá ve-lo nivrá! (Ashkenazi: **Lo hóyo ve-lo nívro!**)   "There never was such a thing (or person)!"

"The kind of Gone-with-the-Wind romantic lifestyle you're talking about *lo haya ve-lo nivra.*"

"What, a video lending library in this town? *Lo haya ve-lo nivra!*"

Literally "it (or he or she) never was and was never created," this Talmudic exclamation was used when the ancient academies were discussing who exactly the biblical hero Job was, and when he lived: during the Exodus from Egypt was one opinion; during the Return from Babylon was another. And a third opinion: The Book of Job was one long allegory. As for Job himself, *lo haya ve-lo nivra.*

— ✿ —

Lo mi-duvshách ve-lo mi-uktsách! (Ashkenazi: **Lo mi-dúvshoch ve-lo mi-úktsoch!**)   "Keep your honey and keep your sting!"

There are people whose favors you'll do anything to avoid, because you just don't trust them, or because they've done you such harm that you just can't stand their sight. Like the heathen prophet Balaam who came to give a curse but also offered a blessing, like the corporate raiders who offer the old board a golden handshake, and like the person who has been stung by a bee, you will want to tell them all to keep their honey and keep their sting: In the words of the Midrash, *lo mi-duvshach ve-lo mi-uktsach!*

— ✿ —

Lúach   A Jewish calendar

"Do you have a *luach* handy, Elliot, so I can check when *Yom Kippur* is?"

The *luach* used to be part of the paraphernalia of every Jewish home, a little booklet with the civil dates of Jewish festivals, times for the start and close of the Sabbath around the year, and all manner of other intriguing information. (The Jewish calendar is lunar-based, that is, months begin at each new moon, roughly every twenty-nine days, putting them out of sync with the conventional solar calendar. Thus the civil date for every festival turns out differently every year. The whole thing is so complicated that even a Talmudist would have trouble memorizing it.)

— ✿ —

Luláv, pl. lulavím (Ashkenazi: **Lúlev, pl. lulóvim**)   Palm branch

"Benji, will you stop waving that *lulav* around in people's faces—it's sharp."

See *Sukkot* and *Arba Minim*, "The Four Species."

The *lulav* is one of the *arba minim*, the four species that are waved ceremonially during prayers on the *Sukkot* harvest festival. The *lulav* is actually a palm branch cut in infancy before it can splay out. Waving it is quite an art: You wave it in a particular order in all four directions and heavenward and earthward, contemplating God's hegemony over nature—while never forgetting that you can jab someone else with the end of it. Interestingly, the *lulav* with the *etrog* fruit are reminiscent of the scepter and orb of kings.

This was the custom of the people of Jerusalem:
    A person emerges from his house with his *lulav* in his hand; goes to synagogue with his *lulav* in his hand; recites the *Shema* and *Amida* with his *lulav* in his hand; puts it down to read the Torah and say the priestly blessing; goes to visit the sick and console the mourners with his *lulav* in his hand . . . which shows you how enthusiastically they performed the *mitzvot*.
                                                                                    The Talmud, Sukkah

— ✿ —

Ma Nishtaná (Ashkenazi: **Ma Nishtáne**)   The Four Questions on Passover

"I'm the youngest, so *I* want to say *Ma Nishtana*!"

Ma Nishtana is a popular name for the Four Questions, the prelude to the story of the Exodus as told from the *Haggadah* on the Passover *Seder* night. (The opening words, *ma nishtana*, literally mean "how different.") The *Ma Nishtana* expresses surprise at all the strange things going on at the *Seder* table: the *matzo*, the *maror*, the vegetable dips, the reclining. *Ma Nishtana* is customarily chanted by the youngest person present, and is one of the first things children learn in first grade, over and over again.

How, then, can it all be a surprise? Ah, because on the actual night, what child isn't surprised?

How different [ma nishtana] *this night is from all other nights!*
For on all other nights we may eat chametz *and* matzo,
But this night is all matzo!

Translation of the opening of Ma Nishtana

— ᘓᘓᘓ —

Ma pitóm!   "What are you talking about!"

"To Jerusalem? 95 shekalim, please."
    "*Ma pitom!* Last time we paid 70 shekalim!"

Literally "why suddenly!" *Ma pitom!* is as Israeli as *pitta* and *falafel* (which means that it's probably doing very nicely in New York City and L.A.). As your plane descends toward Ben-Gurion Airport, do mouth exercises and get ready to use *ma pitom!* the moment you're told anything remotely outrageous—like the price of a cab to Jerusalem or the commission for changing dollars into shekalim.

Ma pitom! is even more effective with a hand gesture, which we will supply the moment this book goes into video.

— ᘓᘓᘓ —

Ma'alín ba-kódesh ve-en moridín (Ashkenazi: **Máalin ba-kóhdesh ve-eyn morídin**)   "You can make more holiness but not less"

This Talmudic maxim finds its most familiar expression on the festival of *Chanukah*, with the custom of lighting one light on the first night, two on the second, and so on, until the eighth night. More generally, it means that once something is considered holy it should not be profaned.

— ᘓᘓᘓ —

Ma'arív (Ashkenazi: **Máariv**)   Evening prayers

"Do they wait till after dark before saying *Ma'ariv*?"

Ma'ariv, the third of the group prayers traditionally said every day, is generally recited at the synagogue at dusk.

The prayer *Ma'ariv* should not be confused with the Israeli afternoon mass-circulation newspaper of the same name. Many an unsuspecting Jewish tourist surrounded by vendors yelling *Ma'ariv! Ma'ariv!* and *Idiyot! Idiyot!* (the name of another tabloid) has fancied that, in the Jewish state, you get called idiot to your face if you look like you haven't said *Ma'ariv* prayers.

– ❧❦ –

Ma'asér (Ashkenazi: **Máyser**)   Tithe

"Have they taken *ma'aser* from the grapefruit?"

Ma'aser is a tithe, literally "a tenth." Believe it or not, it is still the practice among the Orthodox to take a tithe from produce grown in Israel. In ancient times, various tithes would have been set aside for priests, Levites, the poor, and others. Nowadays, just the smallest of tithes— technically called *teruma*—is actually taken from produce and disposed of. (Some of it ends up in Israeli zoos.) The Israeli Rabbinate sends teams all over the country to ensure that the population won't be eating *teruma* in its cornflakes or salad bowls.

The whole procedure of taking a tithe is called "taking *ma'aser*," though in fact *ma'aser* (the 10 percent tithe) does not get disposed of but redeemed, and then eaten like normal produce.

– ❧❦ –

Ma'aséy avót simán le-vaním   "The forefathers' lives are a sign to their sons"

"What happened with Saddam reminds me of Saul and the Amalekites— *ma'asey avot siman le-vanim.*"

This proverb reflects the age-old belief that every experience of the biblical "greats" was larger than life, and in some way a harbinger of all future Jewish experiences—especially the experiences of Abraham, Isaac, and Jacob, the *avot* (fathers) par excellence. In Jewish historic consciousness, the past is the present is the future.

– ❧❦ –

Ma'ayán ha-mitgabér (Ashkenazi: **Máayan ha-misgáber**)   A never-ending source of ideas

Literally "an overflowing spring," this was the Talmudic description for the wisdom of Rabbi Elazar ben Arach. It has come to describe the individual with the ideas that just never stop coming, particularly the sort who never stops verbalizing them.

– ৽৽৽ –

Machlóket (Ashkenazi: **Machlóhkes**)   Disagreement

"Look, I don't want to go into the whole *machloket* between Freud and Jung . . ."

Machloket is the spice and ice of Jewish life. *Machloket* is the legal and spiritual disagreement between the sages on virtually every page of the Talmud. In monetary arbitration, who selects the judges? By what hour must one say *Shema*? What kind of lost property must the finder publicize?

There is no greater intellectual enjoyment than to get your teeth into an ancient *machloket*—nay, to discover a hitherto unsuspected *machloket* between two religious authorities. It makes no difference that they may have lived hundreds of miles and hundreds of years apart, it still counts as a *machloket*.

Some people derive equal enjoyment from another sort of *machloket*: the senseless disagreements between next-door neighbors or Uncle Sid and Aunt Rosa. Hence, the following saying.

Better a false peace than a true *machloket*.

The Seer of Lublin

There are famous people whose whole fame rests on *machloket*.

Rabbi Nachman of Bratzlav

– ৽৽৽ –

Machmír (Ashkenazi: **Máchmir**)   Stringent

"Some of the rabbis aren't prepared to recognize the Ethiopian Jews, but perhaps they're being *machmir* about it."

See *Chumra*, "Stringent ruling" and *Mekel*, "Lenient."

Jewish laws and customs allow quite some leeway in interpretation. On a certain issue, one rabbi may be more *machmir* and another more *mekel* (lenient), depending on all sorts of factors, including an individual rabbi's whole philosophy of life.

Some sophisticated observers of the Orthodox Jewish scene would say that since World War II the attitudes of rabbis and their flocks have become perceptibly more *machmir*. Such *chumrot* (stringent rulings) build barriers against the outside world and no doubt compensate for the tragic loss of the heart and soul of European Orthodox Judaism.

— ❧ —

Machzór, pl. machzorím (Ashkenazi: **Máchzer, pl. machzóyrim**)
Festival prayer book

"Didn't you bring your *Pesach machzor*? You won't find all these things in the regular prayer book."

As much a part of the distinctive flavor of a festival as the ceremonies or the food is the special festival prayer book, the *machzor*. To many a child, the special *machzorim* for *Shavuot*, *Yom Kippur*, and the other festivals are a treasure house of mysterious hymns, unheard-of Bible readings, and curious customs. He and she yearn to be proud possessors of their own set of *machzorim*.

"*Ribono shel Olam*! [Almighty God!]," exclaimed Rabbi Hirsh Dinuber with a deep sigh, placing his heavy *machzor* on his desk in the synagogue. "Look, I'm opening my *machzor* at the contents page—I really don't know which prayer to offer You. Please just select whichever prayers please You best . . ."

— ❧ —

Madregá, pl. madregót (Ashkenazi: **Madréyge, pl. madréyges**)   Spiritual level

"People in those days were altogether on a different *madrega*."

See *Yeridat ha-dorot*, "The decline of the generations."

The notion of levels of purity (Moses is said to have reached the forty-ninth—only the fiftieth was beyond him) is popularly expressed in terms of *madregot*, literally "rungs."

It doesn't matter which *madrega* you're on. What matters is whether you're on the way up or on the way down.

Chasidic saying

— ❧ —

Madrích, pl. **madrichím** (fem. **madrichá**, pl. **madrichót**) Youth leader

"When she's eighteen, Melissa wants to be a *madricha* at summer camp."

The *madrich* and *madricha* are at the center of Jewish teenage life in Israel and in the Diaspora, wherever youth groups and camps exist.

— ❧ —

Maftír (Ashkenazi: **Máftir**) Concluding section of the Torah reading

"Is your son reading *maftir* or is he doing the whole *sidra*?"

It's the *mazel* (fortune) of some little things to be treated like they're very big. That has been the *mazel* of the *maftir*, meaning the last three or four verses of the weekly Torah reading (*sidra*). They get repeated as a prologue to what comes next, the *haftara* (the reading from the Prophets)—and precisely because they're short and sweet, they've become the standard *Bar Mitzvah* boy's Torah portion. He may in fact "do *maftir* and *haftara*."

It's the vogue in certain circles nowadays, particularly in Israel, for the *Bar Mitzvah* boy to read the whole *sidra*—but *maftir* is certainly quite respectable too.

Scholars have suggested that *maftir* (and *haftara*) mean "dispensation to talk." In the name of all fathers and mothers of *Bar Mitzvah* boys, I hope not.

— ❧ —

Magén Davíd (Ashkenazi: **Mógn Dóvid**) Star of David

"Who bought you that beautiful *Magen David* you're wearing?"

Literally "shield of David," the *Magen David* is by no means the oldest Jewish symbol, and indeed has no intrinsic sanctity. It "only" dates from medieval times, but like so many other customs this is sufficient to give it deep roots in Jewish life. You find it on synagogue windows and gates, on New Year cards, on necklaces, on all kinds of things, but perhaps most familiar of all: on the flag of Israel.

— ❧ —

Magén Davíd Adóm (Ashkenazi: **Mógn Dóvid Adóm**) Israeli Emergency Medical Service

"We're aiming to sponsor two ambulances for *Magen David Adom*."

The *Magen David Adom* organization runs the Israeli nationwide emergency medical services: ambulances, emergency clinics, and so on.

If you break a leg (*lo alenu*), you dial 101 and soon you are being sped to a hospital by a white ambulance with a red *Magen David* painted on the side, perhaps with some further information such as "Donated by the Sisterhood of Temple B'nai Jeshurun of Sunny Valley, NJ."

The actual choice of the *Magen David Adom* symbol is clearly in reference to the Red Cross and Red Crescent, although the Red Cross has consistently denied *Magen David Adom* recognition.

— ❧ —

Makólet Israeli grocery store

"Run over to the *makolet* and get me two *chalot*, 100 grams of olives, and candles . . . and either the Jerusalem *Post* or *Idiyot*."

The *makolet*, the small Israeli grocery store, is said to be doomed and the supermarket will inherit the land—people want variety, discount food, credit cards, easy parking, long hours.

False. Israelis are pledged to conserve their *makolet*: You can send little Racheli along by herself and without any money and expect her back in five minutes with three liters of milk (the *makolet* lady has a fat book full of all the credit she's always giving people); you can saunter in and have a deep conversation with the *makolet* man while he totally ignores everyone else who's lining up to pay for something; and if you search along the top shelf among the stock that came in long before anyone ever dreamed about "sell-by dates," you can come to an entirely new understanding of the word *metsia* (find, bargain).

— ❧ —

Malách, pl. malachím (Ashkenazi: **Málech, pl. malóchim**)   Angel

"That was a narrow escape—you must have a *malach* looking after you."

The basic biblical meaning of *malach* was "messenger," sent by man or by God. Jewish thought has always been full of *malachim*, and they are all essentially messengers of God. They can be forces of nature; or supernatural (it's hard for a Jew not to think of *malachim* with wings and things, as in Christian art, but in fact these derive from bona fide Jewish biblical visions of *malachim*).

Hebrew names for *malachim* include Michael, Gavriel, and Raphael.

Shalom *upon you, ministering* malachim, malachim *of the Most High*
From the King of Kings, the Holy One Blessed be He.

Come in peace, ministering malachim, malachim *of the Most High,*
From the King of Kings, the Holy One Blessed be He.

> From a Hebrew song sung to the *malachim* that accompany
> a Jew home from the synagogue on Friday night

The Almighty is not short of *malachim*. What He needs is whole and healthy Jews able to perform His will and His *mitzvot*.

> Rabbi Moshe of Kobryn

Malách ha-mávet (Ashkenazi: **Málach ha-móves**)   The Angel of Death

"She looked so white, you'd think she'd just seen the *malach ha-mavet*."

The *malach ha-mavet* has probably retained more hold on the imagination than most other folk beliefs. Tis he that comes to take a person to the Other Side—and many Jews must have in the back of their minds those artists' images of the *malach ha-mavet* as described in the song *Chad Gadya* which rounds off the Passover *Haggadah*.

. . . and the malach ha-mavet *came,*
and slaughtered the slaughterer
That slaughtered the bull
That drank the water
That doused the fire
That burned the stick
That beat the dog
That bit the cat
That ate the little goat
That father bought for two pennies . . .

> From the Aramaic-Hebrew Passover song *Chad Gadya*

It's hard on the *malach ha-mavet* to do the killing himself, so God gave him doctors to help him.

> Rabbi Nachman of Bratzlav

Mamásh (Ashkenazi: **Mámesh**)   Really

". . . and you know, Estelle, it was *mamash* a miracle that no one got killed . . ."

Mamash probably gets the prize for the most used Hebrew word in American Orthodox Jewish circles. But why American Jews whose mother tongue is English and rarely put a Yiddish or Hebrew sentence together should so like the word *mamash* is *mamash* a mystery to me.

Mamzér, pl. mamzerím (Ashkenazi: **Mámzer, pl. mamzérim**)   Offspring of gravely illicit relationship; son of a _____

"If that *mamzer* doesn't come clean, I'll sue him for every cent he has."

To be called *mamzer* used to be a pretty serious thing, though not half as serious as being one: The offspring of adultery, incest, and the like were (and still are) forbidden to marry anyone except another *mamzer*.

But if an Israeli calls you *mamzer*, don't get too alarmed (provided you know him and he's smiling, not snarling). It'll be no more than a joking "you son of a _____!" It can also just mean "shrewd character."

Most *mamzerim* are shrewd.

The Jerusalem Talmud, Kiddushin

– 🙙🙛 –

Maóz Tsur (Ashkenazi: **Móez Tsur**)   The *Chanukah* song *Maoz Tsur*

"Alison already knows all five verses of *Maoz Tsur* by heart."

There can be very few Jewish communities in the world that don't sing *Maoz Tsur* at the lighting of the *Chanukah* lights—and few that don't use the same tune (in a major key, oddly enough, and curiously reminiscent of a German drinking song).

What many who sing *Maoz Tsur* do not realize is that only the fifth stanza has anything explicitly to do with *Chanukah*. Stanzas two and four are actually about the festivals of *Pesach* and *Purim*.

Fortress, rock [maoz tour] *of my salvation,*
To You it is fitting to give praise.
Restore my House of Prayer
And there we shall bring a thanksgiving offering.
When You bring calamity on the baying foe,
I shall complete with song and psalm
The dedication of the altar.

Translation of the first stanza of *Maoz Tsur*

– 🙙🙛 –

Marcheshván (Ashkenazi: **Marchéshven**)   The month of Marcheshvan

Also known simply as *Cheshvan*, this is the eighth month of the Jewish year, coming in October-November. Following nearly four weeks of High Holy Days and jollifications, *Marcheshvan* is a remarkable month, for it has absolutely no festivals or fasts, major or minor, which is probably no accident. It's back-to-work time.

– 🙙🙛 –

Marór (Ashkenazi: **Mórer**)   Bitter herbs

"Don't grate the *maror*—I want it to taste real bitter . . ."

The Bible bids the Israelites and their descendants to eat *maror* at the Passover ceremony, and so they do during the *Seder* night storytelling. But what is *maror*, apart from the fact that the word means "bitter thing"? Some eat long lettuce, some eat horseradish, but the main thing is that it's a bitter root. Every year, people everywhere go red in the face from *maror* in an attempt to enact the bitterness in Egypt.

This *maror* that we eat—why do we do it? Because the Egyptians embittered the lives of our forefathers in Egypt. As it is said, "And the Egyptians embittered the lives of our fathers with hard work in clay and bricks . . ."

From the Haggadah

. . . they're Jews down to the last drop. They observe all the Jewish customs, love all Jewish foods, celebrate all the Jewish holidays, Passover is Passover. *Matzos* are baked all year round. And there's even a separate factory for the *maror* we use during the holiday. Thousands upon thousands of workers sit in that factory and make *maror*. And they even make a living from it. America's nothing to sneeze at!

Sholom Aleichem

Mashál, pl. meshalím (Ashkenazi: **Móshl, pl. meshólim**)   Parable

"You want to know why it's so hard to be a Jew? Let me tell you a *moshl* . . ."

"It's like the king who had an only child . . . It's like the man who lost his knapsack . . ." The *mashal* is a part of Jewish folk culture that still lives on—in traditional circles, especially in schools. The "meaning" behind the *mashal* is called the *nimshal*.

The Dubno Maggid (Preacher of Dubno, one of the greatest *mashal* tellers) was once asked how he was able to find a *mashal* to fit every situation.
    "Let me tell you a *moshl*," he said. "A young nobleman once went to a military academy to study musketry. After five years of learning all about marksmanship that there is to know, he graduated with a gold medal.
    "On his way home, he stopped for a beer at a tavern. And there on a wall he noticed several chalk circles—and bang in the center of each, a bullet hole. Who might the marksman be with such a perfect aim?
    "'You'll find him in Eisenberg's *cheyder* (Jewish school),' they told him. And sure enough, he did: a small Jewish boy, with long side curls and no shoes on his feet.
    "'How did you learn to shoot like that?' asked the nobleman.

"'It's easy,' chuckled the boy. 'Just give me your gun for a moment.' And he fired a shot at the wall, took some chalk out of his pocket, and proceeded to draw circles around the holes.

"And I do just the same," said the Dubno Maggid. "When I hear a good story, I file it away, and sooner or later, I find the right use for it!"

— 🙞❧🙜 —

Mashíach (Ashkenazi: **Meshíach**)   Messiah

"The *Mashiach* will be here before you get any money out of that guy."

"When will the *Mashiach* come? Who will he be? How on earth will he cope?" These are some of the questions that most Jews in history must have asked themselves. The confidence in a golden age to come is fundamental to Judaism (the prophets and the Talmud are full of it), and perhaps fundamental to the Jewish involvement in modern revolutionary movements.

Many Jews believe that the State of Israel is a sign that the *Mashiach* is imminent. Some believe that the Holocaust and the 1991 Gulf War were also a sign. Some believe they know who he is.

> All the prophets have confirmed that the *Mashiach* will redeem Israel, save them, gather their dispersed, and confirm the commandments.
>
> Maimonides

Two Jews meet. They've both had a bit to drink, and they're in a good mood.

Says one, "When the *Meshiach* comes, everything will be wonderful. The Red Sea will be brandy."

Says the other, "Why the Red Sea? Why not the Atlantic? If you're already going to believe in something, why believe in so little?"

> Don't say "I'm waiting for *Mashiach*." Say "*Mashiach* is waiting for me."
>
> Shelomo Riskin

— 🙞❧🙜 —

Mashkéh (Ashkenazi: **Máshkeh**)   Alcoholic drink

"Let's first get out a little *mashkeh* and drink a *Le-chayim*—and then get down to business."

Traditional Judaism and teetotaling don't mix. Wherever there's a *simcha* (celebration) you'll find a little *mashkeh*. The *Shabbat* and the festivals are ushered in with *mashkeh*. As the Psalmist put it, "Wine gladdens the human heart." Even the newborn baby gets a little *mashkeh* at his *brit*. The operative word is "a little."

— 🙞❧🙜 —

Matán Toráh (Ashkenazi: **Máten Tóre**)   The Revelation of the Torah

"The concept of a Sabbath goes right back to before *Matan Torah*."

See *Har Sinai*, "Mt. Sinai."

Matan Torah on Mt. Sinai towers over all other events in Jewish history. There were no cameras at the Revelation, nor have there been any archeologists—for the simple reason that no one knows where Mt Sinai was. Nevertheless, *Matan Torah* seems like yesterday.

— ৡৡ৾ঌ —

Matanót la-evyoním (Ashkenazi: **Matónes lo-evyóhnim**)   Gifts to the needy (on *Purim*)

"I'm putting aside $50 to do *matanot la-evyonim* on Purim."

Among the traditional duties on the festival of *Purim* is the giving of gifts or money to the needy, *matanot la-evyonim*. They are surely as important as the friends and neighbors to whom one is sending gifts with such care and attention. In some neighborhoods in the United States and England, schemes have been set up by which *matanot la-evyonim* donated on *Purim* are instantly passed on to be distributed that same day to the needy in Israel.

— ৡৡ৾ঌ —

Matzá, pl. **matzót**, commonly spelled **matzo**, pl. **matzos** (Ashkenazi: **Mátze** pl. **mátzes**)   Unleavened bread

"What else is there to spread on my *matzo* apart from jam and honey and butter and margarine, Mommy?"

See also *Shmure matze*, "Protected matzo."

The *matzo* that some Jews eat comes precision packed, looks like punched computer cards, and tastes as light as air. Other *matzo* is handbaked, individually packaged, and pockmarked as the moon. All of it, however, is in fulfillment of the ancient law of eating unleavened bread on the festival of *Pesach*.

And you shall sacrifice a *Pesach* offering to the Lord your God from the flock and herd, in the place which the Lord will choose for His name to reside. You shall not eat *chametz* with it; seven days you shall eat with it *matzot*, the bread of affliction, for you left the Land of Egypt in haste . . .

Deuteronomy 16

— ৡৡ৾ঌ —

Matzevá (Ashkenazi: **Matzéyve**)   Tombstone; tombstone ceremony

"She always keeps talking about how she wants a very simple *matzeva*."

"I can't make it next Sunday. I have to go to a *matzeva*."

It is customary to return to the cemetery twelve months after a death—in Israel, one month—to dedicate a *matzeva* perpetuating the name of the dead. It will bear the Hebrew name and Hebrew date of passing, with a prayer that the soul be bound up in the bond of life. An Ashkenazi graveyard looks very different from a Sephardi one: Ashkenazi *matzevot* are vertical; Sephardi *matzevot* lie flat.

With the opening up of eastern Europe, groups of Jews are beginning to journey back to Kraków, Mezeritch, and scores of other fabled places to perform the duty of *kever avot*: to seek out and repair the *matzevot* of great rabbis.

And Rachel died and was buried on the way to Ephrat, which is Bethlehem. And Jacob set up a *matzeva* on her grave, the *matzeva* of Rachel's grave until this day.
Genesis 35

Máyim acharoním (Ashkenazi: **Máyim achróhnim**)   Washing the hands before Grace After Meals

"We'll talk about that later. Let's do *mayim acharonim* and say *Birkat ha-Mazon*."

Many Orthodox families have the custom of doing *mayim acharonim* (literally "latter water") before saying Grace After Meals on festivals and festivities. A tiny pitcher of water is passed around and a little water poured onto the fingers.

Máyim genuvím yimtáku (Ashkenazi: **Máyim gnúvim yimtóku**) "Stolen waters are sweet"

These words from the biblical Book of Proverbs make the wry observation that things seem to be much more fun when they're illicit. (Of course, not everything that's illicit is as harmless as *mayim* . . .)

I for one have always held that the rabbis shouldn't allow synagogues to be used for praying.

A waiter at a wedding whipped a half-finished bottle of sauvignon from the rabbi's seat at the head table. But the rabbi spotted him, and asked him what he was carrying.

"Oh, just a bottle of water," replied the waiter.

"Let me try a little," asked the rabbi. Then, turning to the waiter, he whispered: "Now I know what King Solomon had in mind when he wrote *Mayim genuvim yimtaku . . .*"

— ❧ —

Mazál, commonly spelled **mazel** (Ashkenazi: **Mázl**)　Luck

"We've never had any *mazel* with that Volkswagen . . ."

Some people may tell you that in Judaism there's no such thing as luck. Don't believe them. True, the Almighty watches over the world, rewarding the righteous and smiting the wicked (sometimes, of course, you may have to wait until the Next World). But folk insist that it still leaves room for *mazel*. Hence, at weddings, *Bar Mitzvahs*, and at the drop of a *yarmulke*, the exclamation *mazel tov!* (q.v.)

Interestingly, *mazel* also denotes "a sign of the zodiac," and many of the greatest Jewish philosophers have taken astrology very seriously (while others have damned it).

Said Rabbi Yochanan: There is no *mazal* among Jews.

The Talmud, Shabbat

What use is beauty, if one has no *mazal.*

Moroccan Jewish proverb

To change one's village is to change one's *mazal.*

Ladino proverb

— ❧ —

Mazál tov!, commonly spelled **Mazel tov!** (Ashkenazi: **Mázl tov!**) "Congratulations!"

"Fran's had a baby girl!"
　"*Mazel tov!*"

"Guess what, Debbie's engaged!"
　"Wow, at last! *Mazel tov!*"

Literally "good luck," this is the universal Jewish congratulations, but its uses go much further: You say it not only to the congratulatee but also to the bearer of the good tidings—and in fact to anyone and everyone you see at the *brit mila, bar mitzvah,* wedding, and so on.

Dear Ms. _____ ,
　Your pregnancy test result is positive. *Mazal tov!*

Rough translation of a standard reply sent out
by an Israeli pregnancy testing clinic

— ❧ —

Mazík, pl. mazikín (Ashkenazi: **Mázik, pl. mazíkin**)   Demon or (of a person or animal) mischief maker

"Has that little *mazik* of ours been at the candy again?"

From ancient times down to the very present, Jewish views on demons—authoritative as well as popular—have ranged from apprehension to studied disbelief. And in between, a kind of nervous jokiness . . .

Said Abba Binyamin: "If we could view the *mazikin* with our own eyes, there is none among us that could face them . . ."
Said Rava: "The crush in the lecture halls is their doing . . ."

The Talmud, Berachot

Our rabbis taught: "There are three reasons not to venture into ruins: To avoid suspicion of hanky-panky, to avoid them collapsing on top of you, and to avoid *mazikin*."

The Talmud, Berachot

Rabbi Yaakov Meshulem Orenstein, the Chief Rabbi of Lvov, was frequently seen pacing the streets of Lvov at night. His students were nonplussed.
"Rabbi," they asked, "Didn't our Sages teach that a scholar should not walk alone at night because of *mazikin*?"
"Yes," he said, "but this city's full of *mazikin* who can't even see that I'm a scholar . . ."

– ✳ –

Mechalél shabbát (Ashkenazi: **Mechálel shábes**)   Sabbath-desecrating
Chilúl shabbát (Ashkenazi: **Chílel shábes**)   Desecration of the Sabbath

"Shari writes that she had to move out of the dorms because kids were *mechalel shabbat* all the time."

"They put sticky tape over the light switches to prevent any inadvertent *chilul shabbat* by the children."

To do any of the multitude of acts forbidden on the Sabbath, such as writing, cooking, and sewing, is called *chilul shabbat*. Deliberate and flagrant *chilul shabbat* was always deemed an extremely serious offense, particularly if committed in public. In Israel, *chilul shabbat* by running a business or a state institution on *Shabbat* is largely prohibited by law. Thus El Al does not fly on *Shabbat*, nor do theaters open. But by a peculiar logic, the media broadcast and buses run in Haifa.

– ✳ –

Mecháye   A delight

"Thank goodness you have air conditioning in your car. What a *mechaye*!"

Literally "a resurrection" (from the ancient phrase *mechaye ha-metim*), this lovely Hebrew expression has had all the juices of Yiddish pumped into it.

The logic's impeccable: As the longed-for, prayed-for Resurrection of the Dead will be a great delight—not to say a relief—to everyone, every delight that's a relief is therefore justly called a *mechaye*. Getting out of a girdle is a *mechaye*, a hot bath is always a *mechaye*, and that first cup of coffee after *Yom Kippur* is the *mechaye* of *mechayes*.

– ✿ –

Me-cháyil el cháyil   "From strength to strength"

"Today sees the opening of your new synagogue. May you all go *me-chayil el chayil* and see it grow into a great *kehila* [community] . . ."

See *Eshet chayil*, "Superwoman."

Based on a verse in Psalms, *me-chayil el chayil* is a wish that embodies the importance of material blessings alongside spiritual blessings in Jewish tradition. *Chayil* denotes "might" and "wealth." "May you be a *ben-chayil*" is a common biblical wish. And the greatest compliment to a woman is to call her an *eshet chayil*, "a woman of strength."

– ✿ –

Mechirát chamétz (Ashkenazi: Mechíres chómetz)   Selling of leavened food

"I have to go along to the rabbi tonight to do *mechirat chametz*."

Shortly before the festival of *Pesach*, many people visit their rabbi to do *mechirat chametz*, the selling of their *chametz*. Jewish law does not permit *chametz* (leavened food, such as bread, cookies, whiskey) to be in Jewish possession during the festival of *Pesach*. Fortunately for those with big stocks of whiskey—or with medicines or other things that might contain *chametz*—the law allows them to be locked away and sold to a Gentile for the duration of the festival, a fairly technical transaction conducted through a rabbi.

Mechitsá (Ashkenazi: Mechítse)   Partition separating men and women

"If we don't set up a *mechitsa* in the hall, we can't have any dancing after the meal."

In more than one way, the *mechitsa* divides. It divides men from women, in Orthodox synagogues and at weddings and other occasions on which people let their hair down. It divides Orthodox from non-Orthodox: The latter refuse to have it, period. It can even divide communities: Some feel it should be high enough and opaque enough to deny men the mere sight of a woman; while others feel that a 3-foot-high barrier is ample. Meanwhile, in daily life, in the store, in the subway, Ultraorthodox man still finds himself at close quarters with Ultraorthodox woman. So the *mechitsa* is fundamentally a symbol, challenging the invasion of Eros. The last frontier.

— ❦ —

Mechután, pl. mechutaním (Ashkenazi: **Mechúten, pl. mechutónim**)
Son-in-law's or daughter-in-law's father (in plural: their parents)

"My *mechutanim* are coming all the way from Zurich for the *bris*."

Mechutan is from the same root as chatan, "bridegroom" *and* chatuna, "wedding."

You may feel aggrieved that your husband or wife didn't consult you about their choice of parents, but that's nothing to what you may feel about your children's choice of *mechutanim*. Not to worry: The *mechutanim* are the linchpin of the extended Jewish family known as the *mishpacha*—through them you can acquire a set of relatives that you never dreamed of, including doctors, lawyers, and CPAs far better than any on your own side of the *mishpacha*.

And the best part of the arrangement is that they are probably thinking the same about you.

— ❦ —

(The) Megilá (Ashkenazi: [The] **Megíle**)   The scroll of Esther

"We have that beautiful *Megila* that belonged to your grandfather. You can read from that one on *Purim*."

The *Megila* (or, more fully, *Megilat Ester*) is the name given to one of the best loved Jewish stories: the biblical Book of Esther, telling of the attempted genocide of the Jews of the Persian Empire by the megalomaniac Haman. It is recited annually in synagogues around the globe on the festival of *Purim*, from a handwritten parchment scroll. Hence the popular name *Megila*, "scroll."

— ❦ —

Megíle   Long-winded tale

"OK, OK, I just asked why you're late. I didn't want to hear a whole *megile!*"

I for one have never found the Book of Esther (see the preceding entry) long-winded—perhaps because when I'm not busy getting ready to drown the sound of the wicked Haman's name with my mega-rattle, I'm busy wrestling with my *Megila* scroll, which defies all my efforts to rewind it as we go along.

Be it as it may, the word *megile* is popularly used of any long-winded explanation, account, or tale.

— ❧❧ —

Mekarév (Ashkenazi: **Mekórev**)   Bring back to Judaism

"He wants to be a Hillel rabbi so he can *mekarev* people."

Mekarev literally means "bring closer." It expresses the idea that non-committed Jews are never outside the fold, just at a temporary distance. Perhaps best known for their work in *kiruv* (bringing closer) are the emissaries of the Lubavitcher Rebbe. A legend in his own lifetime was Jerusalem's Rabbi Aryeh Levine, who frequented the prisons in British Palestine to *mekarev* the most downcast and outcast inmates.

— ❧❧ —

Mekél (Ashkenazi: **Méykl**)   Lenient

"If you want to ask a rabbi what you should do, ask Danny's uncle. He's very *meykl.*"

One of the first questions an Orthodox Jew asks on coming to town is "Which rabbis are *meykl?*" The observant are forever asking a rabbi for rulings. There are so many things in Jewish law and custom laypeople don't know, and so many things that aren't clear-cut. A lot also depends on who the questioner is and how well he or she can be counted on to follow what the rabbi suggests to the letter without cutting religious corners.

There are rabbis who are reported to be *meykl* and rabbis who are reported to be *machmir* (strict). This is often based on sheer rumor, but not surprisingly it's the *meykl* rabbis who tend to get the most queries and *she'elot* (questions). I doubt whether the *machmir* rabbis mind. At least they don't get called at 11:30 every night.

My grandfather was known as a *maikil*, a liberal jurist. Wherever it was possible, he took the way of permission, of acquittal. He reconciled many couples who came to him for a divorce; he brought about some divorces in embittered and stalemated cases. With his reputation for liberality in decision, and humanity in judgment, went an extreme personal strictness. His way was to allow others the easy side of a doubt and to construe the law on the hard side for himself.

Herman Wouk

— ❧ —

Mekubál, pl. Mekubalím (Ashkenazi: **Mekúbl, pl. Mekubólim**)
Kabbalist

"They say his great uncle's a *Mekubal* . . ."

See *Kabala*.

Somewhere out there, in the cobbled alleyways of Tsefat or Jerusalem, in the quiet avenues of Bnei Brak or Brooklyn, or where you'd least expect to find them, are *Mekubalim*—men elevated in the intricacies of *Kabala* mysticism.

— ❧ —

Melachá, pl. melachót (Ashkenazi: **Melóche, pl. melóches**)   An act forbidden on the Sabbath

"I couldn't start fixing the chair, because that would be a *melacha*."

Melacha essentially means "craft, creativity." The traditional observance of Sabbaths and festivals has two parameters: enhanced spiritual activity, and concomitant reduction of work—not physical work per se (*avoda*) but work that sets a human stamp on the environment, *melacha*.

The Talmud defines thirty-nine "archetypes" of *melacha* and many, many subtypes—and ever since, philosophers have pondered them, while observant Jews train their families to simply avoid them: planting, writing, cooking, washing, burning, mending, and so forth. Sometimes, the rabbi needs to be consulted. And with every new gadget, a rabbi somewhere will ask: "Will this involve a *melacha*?"

The breakdown of the *melacha* prohibition to thirty-nine separate major categories, into an untold number of *toladot* or minor categories subsumed under them, signifies the fragmented nature of the profane days. The unsanctified days are the real World of Disunity. Man's involvement with nature requires of him to atomize his experience in the various arts and crafts by which he sustains himself physically and economically.

Norman Lamm

— ❧ —

Melámed   Teacher of religion to children

"It's not surprising Moses was the humblest of men—he worked till he was 120 as a *melamed*."

For two words from the same root as *melamed*, see also *talmid chacham* and *Talmud*.

If words had feelings, *melamed* would be the saddest. He may be high on the official rankings of Jewish professions, but if pay and conditions mean anything, he's low. So it's no surprise that when spoken Hebrew was brought back to life in the Land of Israel, *melamed* was one of the Ashkenazi Hebrew words that was buried. The word to use now is *moreh*. Unfortunately, that doesn't mean you get paid more . . .

Usually an elderly man who feared and despised everything he had found in the new world, the *melamed* turned to teaching of children, whom he often also feared and despised, because he had a bit more learning than other immigrants and because he shared with them a need to eat regularly.

Irving Howe

A *melamed*, desperate to improve his lot, decided to sell cooked fish. "Add some horseradish," his wife suggested, "and stand opposite the bank." He did a roaring trade. An old friend, still a *melamed*, came by to ask if he could spare 5 roubles. He really didn't want to, but how could he say no? Then he had a brainwave:

"Listen, Yankl, I'd love to have lent you . . . but it's just your bad *mazl* [luck] that I have an agreement with the bank over there: They won't sell cooked fish and I won't lend money . . ."

— ❧ —

Melaméd zechút (Ashkenazi: **Melámed zechús**)   Speak in someone's defense, give the benefit of the doubt (literally "demonstrate innocence")

"I know he's screwed up, but you have to be *melamed zechut*—it's his first job."

Melamed zechut doesn't really have anything to do with *melamed*, "teacher." But see *zechut*.

— ❧ —

Melavéh malká (Ashkenazi: **Meláve málke**)   Festive meal on the evening following the Sabbath

"You are cordially invited to a musical *melaveh malka* on Saturday, March 11 at 8 P.M."

Literally "accompanying the queen," the *melaveh malka* is a splendid way of starting the week: Instead of waving a cursory goodbye to the "Sabbath Queen" (as *Shabbat* is traditionally known), one accompanies her a little of the way, which translates into the widespread custom of having a further meal, perhaps even a festivity or supper party, on the Saturday evening.

The *Melaveh Malka* was always a happy occasion. White tablecloths on the tables, gleaming cutlery and lovely glasses, as if it was the *seder*, lighted candles and silver candlesticks. The family sat with the visitors, rich and poor together, but men separately and women separately. They all ate and drank, and kept calling out: "*Dovid ha-Melech zochur lo-tov chay ve-kayom!* [David the King, of blessed memory, lives and endures for ever]." And then they danced.

Yitzchak Leib Peretz

– ✤ –

Melíts yósher (Ashkenazi: **Méylits yóhsher**)   Advocate on high

"May the *niftar* [deceased] be a *melits yosher* for us all."

Literally "pleader of righteousness," *melits yosher* has come to denote above all the spiritual beings that "put in a good word" for the living in the Heavenly Court—the angels created by one's good deeds, and the deceased. The tombs of the righteous, such as Rachel's Tomb and the tomb of Shimon Bar Yochai, are crowded with worshippers praying for God to accept the righteous as a *melits yosher.*

– ✤ –

Menoráh (Ashkenazi: **Menóre**)   Chanukah candelabra

"Put another candle in the *menorah*. Tonight we light four lights."

The basic meaning of *menorah* is "lamp."

Chanukah menorah or simply *menorah* is the traditional Ashkenazi name for the candelabra lit on the festival of *Chanukah*. The modern Israeli name for it is *chanukiya* (see entry).

– ✤ –

Meshugá (Ashkenazi: **Meshúge**)   Crazy
pl. **meshugaím** (Ashkenazi: **meshugóim**)   Crazies

"A Passover cruise to Egypt? Are you *meshuga*?"

Why Jews, down the centuries, have kept up the *Hebrew* word for "nuts" in their everyday speech, I have no idea. There's nothing distinctively Jewish about being nuts—and the type of nuts you are if you're *meshuga* is not distinctively Jewish either.

The distinction of being the first person to be called *meshuga* in the Bible is David's. And it was no insult: With a warrant out for his arrest, he was on the run in the land of the Philistines, and pretending to be certified *meshuga*. He did such a good job that the Philistine king uttered the famous one-liner: *Ha-chasar meshugaim ani?* "Am I so short of *meshugaim* here that I need this one?"

— ❧ —

Meshumád (Ashkenazi: **Meshúmed**)   Apostate, that is, a Jew who has espoused another faith

"They have this priest on the radio. . . . From the way he talks, I'm sure he's a *meshumad*."

Meshumad is a word that raises Jewish hackles. Related to the word *mashmid*, "destroyer," it evokes not just lost Jews but also informers, blackmailers, missionary campaigns, and, most frightening of all, the collective memory of Jewish *meshumadim* who turned on their people and unleashed reigns of terror—men like Torquemada, Spain's first inquisitor general, and Lazar Kaganovich, Stalin's right-hand man.

— ❧ —

Mesirút néfesh (Ashkenazi: **Mesíres néfesh**)   Self-sacrifice (metaphorically)

"She's been caring for her parents with such *mesirut nefesh*."

Literally "giving up one's life." *Mesirut nefesh* is a superlative on the Jewish scale of values—there is nothing higher, save actually giving up one's life, which is generally termed *kiddush ha-Shem*. Straining oneself to the physical or mental limit is *mesirut nefesh*. The inmates of Bergen Belsen who contrived to retain their humanity represent *mesirut nefesh*.

A Jew with no *mesirut nefesh* is no Jew.

Rabbi Mordechai of Lachovitch

— ❧ —

Met (Ashkenazi: **Mes**)   Corpse

"You know, they say that the *met* can still hear the *hesped* [funeral eulogy]."

See *Techiyat ha-Metim*.

Jewish Law goes to great lengths to ensure respect for a *met*. It must be buried as soon as possible—and not cremated. In Israel the custom is to bury the *met* in a *tallit* or shroud rather than in a coffin.

Anyone seeing a *met* and failing to accompany it is guilty of mocking the helpless.

Kitsur Shulchan Aruch

– ❧ –

Metapélet, pl. metaplót   Caregiver

"The *metapelet* wants to know if you mind if she tunes in to a Mozart concert."

All hail the *metapelet*, who since the dawn of Israeli society (the 1920s in fact!) has gallantly come in for three, four, five hours a day to free the New Israeli Woman to go to her job, while she, the *metapelet*, gets on with her physics studies (she has her own ambitions) and with minding the New Israeli Woman's babies.

   In their dogged efforts to bring the Israeli economy into line with the United States, Israeli politicians have not so far managed to adjust one key economic phenomenon: Thousands upon thousands of *metaplot* are available to look after the nation's small children without charging either an arm or a leg. How, one wonders, can this possibly go on?

– ❧ –

Metsiá, pl. metsiót (Ashkenazi: Metsíe, pl. metsíos)   A bargain, a good deal

"Yes, I looked in at the book sale, but I didn't find any *metsiot*."

"Don't start finding fault with me—you're no *metsia* yourself!"

This Hebrew word (originally "a find") has had a long career—including many centuries in daily use in Yiddish as "bargain." And although Israelis generally eschew Yiddishized Hebrew, they've made an exception for *metsia*. It's just too much of a *metsia* . . .

– ❧ –

Méyven   Expert, connoisseur

"If you want to know the best buy in amplifiers, ask my brother-in-law—he's a real *meyven*."

There's a *mumche* and there's a *meyven*. They're both experts. They both go to a Rostropovich master class. The *mumche* promptly identifies which piece the master is playing, closely observes the master's every crick of a finger and sleight of the bow, and goes back home even more of a *mumche*. The *meyven* sits with the complete score on his lap, very visibly. Every now and again, he will close his eyes and sigh with delight.

The *mumche* and the *meyven* also like to come with you when you're looking to change cars. If there's anything mechanical to be faulted, rely on the *mumche* to fault it. Meanwhile, the *meyven* will probably also be telling you that when you turn a corner the car just doesn't "feel" good, and that he saw a much nicer interior color combination on the '91 model anyway.

Mezonót (Ashkenazi: **Mezóhnes**)   Cakes, cookies, cereals, and all other grain-based foods (except bread)

"Do you want to eat some *mezonot* before we leave for *shul* [synagogue]?"

See *Birkat ha-Mazon*, "Grace After Meals."

When a chemist is faced with a tableful of food, he probably classifies it mentally into fats, proteins, and carbohydrates. A traditional Jew, faced with the same table, is likely to classify it according to which *bracha* (blessing) is to be said over what: over vegetables, one blessing; over fruit, a different one; over grains, a blessing that concludes with the words *borey miney mezonot*, "who createth varieties of foods"— hence the term *mezonot* for grains in general.

Children will often ask which blessing to say on something: "Daddy, is this cereal *mezonot*?"

Printed message inside a *kosher* airline meal:
   The roll with this meal is mezonot.

> (This means that the roll is made with sweetened dough and thus does not require Ritual Washing of the Hands, a difficult thing to do in the confined facilities of an airliner)

Mezúmen   Prelude to Grace After Meals in a group

"If your son's thirteen, he can be the third person we need for making a *Mezumen*."

A *Mezumen* is a ceremonial "invitation to participate" in saying *Birkat ha-Mazon* (Grace After Meals). The word literally means "invited."

The idea is that a group of three or more adults who have eaten together should not simply say Grace After Meals separately but as a group—group worship is more inspiring, and bonds Jews together.

And so they preface the Grace After Meals with a ceremonial exchange. A *Mezumen* begins like this (translating from the Hebrew):

Opening: "Let us bless."

Response: "May God's name be blessed from now to eternity," and so on.

— ✤ —

Mezuzáh, pl. **mezuzót** (Ashkenazi: **Mezúze**, pl. **mezúzes**)
Untranslatable

"We'll need twelve *mezuzot*—one for each doorway except the bathroom."

You can always recognize a Jewish home (or at any rate, a traditional one) by the *mezuzah* on the doorpost. It's a slim container of metal or wood housing a slim roll of parchment (strictly speaking, this is the *mezuzah*). On the parchment are the first few lines of the *Shema* declaration, meticulously written by a traditional scribe. A *mezuzah* is affixed to every inside doorpost too. The ideal housewarming gift.

And you shall bind them as a sign on your arm and they shall be an emblem midway between your eyes. And you shall write them on the doorposts [*mezuzot*] of your house and on your gates.

The last words of the *Shema* in the *mezuzah*
(the word *mezuzah* originally denoted the doorpost itself)

— ✤ —

Mi she-béyrech   Blessing after being called to the Torah reading; telling-off

"You should have heard the *Mi she-beyrech* she gave me, and I hardly made a mark on her car!"

Mi she-beyrech is a phrase with a smile. The synagogue cantor makes a *Mi she-beyrech* blessing over the people who have just been called to the reading of the Torah, thanking them for donating money in the name of their parents, their siblings, their brother-in-law, their cousins, the rabbi's wife—in short, anyone living who they can think of just at that moment. (The words *Mi she-beyrech* are the first words of the blessing, and literally mean "He who blessed.")

Then along comes Yiddish and lovingly subverts the phrase into "a good telling-off." What's it got to do with the blessing? Simple: They both go on and on and on . . .

– ✣ –

Midá, pl. midót (Ashkenazi: **Míde, pl. mídes**)   Personality trait

"I'm so glad she's going out with him, he has such good *midot.*"

See *Musar.*

Traditional Jewish education (especially for girls) has tended to set aside time for learning "good *midot,*" such as *kibbud av va-em* (respect for parents), *tseniut* (modesty), truthfulness, cleanliness, and so on.

Irascibility too is an exceedingly bad *mida,* and one should work toward the opposite extreme and train oneself not to lose one's temper even for something that merits it.

Maimonides, Laws of Personality

People have to learn to control their midot:
To learn pride, but not to be proud;
To learn anger, but not to be angry;
To learn speech, but not to speak;
To learn silence, but not to be silent.

Rabbi Dov Ber of Mezeritch

– ✣ –

Midá kenéged midá (Ashkenazi: **Míde kenéged míde**)   The punishment fits the crime

Literally "measure for measure," *mida keneged mida* is one of the Almighty's ways of responding to human ways: to tailor the punishment to the crime—and the reward to the good deed. The Torah and Jewish folklore are full of *mida keneged mida*—the Egyptian armies drowning in the Red Sea for the drowning of the babies of the Israelites is just one example.

– ✣ –

Midrásh (Ashkenazi: **Médresh**)   Ancient commentaries on the Bible

"The trouble with Cecil B. de Mille's *The Ten Commandments* is that he didn't check the *Medresh* first."

Midrash is now the rage. This vast, sprawling maze of verse-by-verse explanations and elaborations to the Bible, dating back 1000 to 2000 years, was for so long the "outsider" of modern Judaic studies. It defied the modern taste for the literal, the logical, the historical meaning of the Bible. Much of it has still not been translated into English. But times change. The way the Midrash unfolds every conceivable layer of the text as the rabbis understood it, using every ounce of their linguistic and literary sensitivity, is increasingly appealing to a "postmodern" generation of teachers and students.

Midrash is the profoundest and most indigenously Jewish and hence most authoritative theology ever to emerge within Judaism. What makes it both profound and indigenously Jewish is that it takes the form not of propositions and systems . . . but rather of stories and parables. These never pretend to have all the answers.

Emil Fackenheim

I am, as you know, a trusting person, and I never question God's ways. Whatever He ordains is good. Besides, if you do complain, will it do you any good? That's what I always tell my wife. "Golde," I say, "you're sinning. We have a *medresh*—"
"What do I care about a *medresh*?" she says. "We have a daughter to marry off. And after her, two more are almost ready. And after these two, three more—may the evil eye spare them!"
"Tut," I say. "What's that? Don't you know, Golde, that our sages have thought of that also? There is a *medresh* for that too—"
But she doesn't let me finish. "Daughters to be married off," she says, "are a stiff *medresh* in themselves."
Try to explain something to a woman!

Sholom Aleichem

– ❀ –

Mi-kol melamdáy hiskálti (Ashkenazi: Mi-kol melámday hiskálti)
"I have learned something from everyone"

If you want to assure someone that their advice or suggestion was valuable, even though they don't think so themselves, this is a nice phrase to use.

Actually, it's a play on words. In Psalm 119, from whence it comes, it really means "I have become wiser than anyone"!

– ❀ –

Miktsát shivchó shel adám omrím befanáv (Ashkenazi: Míktsas shívchoh shel ódom ómrim befónov)   "You don't recite all a person's virtues in his or her presence"

To say only *miktsat shivcho shel adam*, "part of a person's virtues" in his or her presence is an old-established Jewish custom. When you introduce someone by the standard "Meet Ms. ___ , who is a ___ ," don't go on to say her whole résumé for her—it's crass flattery as well as embarrassing.

Rabbi Yirmiya, making this point in the Talmud, takes his cue from God's own words to Noah: "I consider you a righteous man" whereas when talking *about* Noah and not to his face, the Bible says, "Noah was the perfect righteous man . . ."

— 🙞🙜 —

Mikvéh or **Mikváh** (Ashkenazi: **Míkve**)   Pool for religious immersion

"On my way to synagogue in the morning, I often run into Reb Dovid coming back from the *mikveh*."

The first building priority of every traditional Jewish community is a *mikveh*, not that you'd notice it on the skyline. In fact, by its very nature it has to be an exceedingly modest, nondescript building. It houses the pool in which brides and married women do religious immersion, in order to be religiously permitted to their husbands.

Not too long ago, the *mikveh* was associated in the modern Jewish mind with the primitive Old Country; now it's likely to be an upscale sort of place—and the whole idea of *taharat ha-mishpacha* (see entry) has begun to appeal to women outside the Orthodox fold.

Many Orthodox men use a *mikveh* too before *Yom Kippur*. And there is a special *kelim* (kitchenware) *mikveh* for the purpose of *tevilat kelim* (purifying new kitchenware).

— 🙞🙜 —

Miluím   Israeli Army reserve service

"I'm sorry, Mr. Katz is in *miluim*. He'll be back on Monday."

Every few months, the Israeli lawyer or electrician you so desperately needed to talk to vanishes. He is no longer a lawyer or electrician but a major or captain, in *miluim*. Had he been in *chuts la-arets* (abroad), a place a bit like heaven where lawyers, carpenters, plumbers, and other high wage earners go, you could at least have cursed. But he is in *miluim*—and doing his sacred duty.

Contrary to what you might think, Israelis are said to thoroughly enjoy spending their annual few weeks in *miluim*, not necessarily because they like yomping down a wadi through the night with half a ton on their back, but because no one else can get through to them, not even their wives.

– ❧ –

Min ha-katséh el ha-katséh (Ashkenazi: **Min ha-kótseh el ha-kótseh**) Radically, from one extreme to the other

"Life in Israel has changed *min ha-katseh el ha-katseh*."

There's nothing particularly poetic or graphic about this biblical phrase. Literally, it means "from extremity to extremity."

– ❧ –

Min ha-shamáyim (Ashkenazi: **Min ha-shomáyim**)   Heaven-sent

"That tax refund was really *min ha-shamayim*!"

Shamayim means both "heaven" (and metaphorically, God) and "sky." But when you say something's *min ha-shamayim*, you usually mean that it's come from heaven. Even the rain always comes from heaven in Israel, though the advent of acid rain may be changing people's conceptions of that.

– ❧ –

Minchá (Ashkenazi: **Mínche**)   Afternoon prayers

"Do you think there'll be enough time between meetings to say *Mincha*?"

Mincha is the shortest of the three group prayers traditionally said every day. It's as if Jews were specifically intended to find some time for God in the thick of the workday. (The word means "tribute, gift.") Ten minutes will do, even five. If there's a *minyan* (quorum of ten), how much the better; but one can just find a quiet spot for one's own private *Mincha*.

Being out and about, how do you find a place to say *Mincha*? Orthodox Jews have become streetwise at it. My grandfather used to favor a public telephone booth—the British ones are completely enclosed, unlike the American pay phones, so only a Hebrew-speaking lip reader could have imagined what he was saying. And I've participated in countless *Minchas* at the back of El Al jumbos in mid-flight.

– ❧ –

Minhág, pl. **minhagím** (Ashkenazi: **Mínhag**, pl. **minhógim**)   Custom

"In our family we have a *minhag* of using olive oil for the Chanukah lights."

Besides the basic practices, Jews from different regions may keep up a variety of *minhagim*, local customs that add both color and confusion to the Jewish way of life.

There is a broad difference in *minhag* between Sephardim, Jews of Mediterranean and Oriental origin, and Ashkenazim. For example, Sephardim keep their Torah scrolls in a solid casing; Ashkenazim use an embroidered cloth. Sephardim will eat rice and beans on Passover; Ashkenazim will not. Ashkenazi *minhag* is to name children after departed relatives; Sephardi, after the living.

Stick to local *minhag*.

The Talmud, Bava Metzia

Minyán, pl. **minyaním** (Ashkenazi: **Mínyen**, pl. **minyónim**)   Prayer quorum

"Can you get to the synagogue? We need just one more for a *minyan*."

Ever since Abraham begged the Almighty to spare Sodom and Gommorah if they contained ten good people, there has been a notion of a community of ten. Praying as a group is the Jewish way, and the *minyan* of ten adults is at the heart of this. Without a *minyan*, no *kaddish*, no *birkat kohanim*, no *kriat ha-torah*. So next time you're walking down a Tel Aviv street in the twilight and someone rushes out of a doorway and tells you "we just need one," look upon it as part of a cosmic quest for Jewish *achdut* (togetherness).

They wanted to say *Mincha* prayers but there were only nine of them, one short of a *minyan*. Once more, the rabbi peered out of the synagogue window—and there he saw a well-known atheist emerging from a pork store.
   "Quick, call him to make the *minyan*!" the rabbi shouted to the *shamash*.
   "What, him?!" said the *shamash*. "An atheist?"
   "Why not?" said the rabbi. "We're nine, so we're only short of one zero."

Mi-she-nichnás Adár, marbím be-simchá (Ashkenazi: **Mí-she-níchnas Óder, márbim be-símcho**)   "When Adar comes in, there's lots more merrymaking"

See *Purim* and *Mishloach manot*.

The month of *Adar*, in February or March, is a time for high spirits: On *Adar* 14 comes the festival of *Purim*, and as the Talmud puts it, *mi-she-nichnas Adar, marbim be-simcha*. Frantic parents start making their kids' *Purim* costumes, kids start planning who their parents should send *mishloach manot* to—and as the month of *Adar* was a time when the luck of the enemy ran out, it's deemed a lucky time to start a lawsuit. Lucky lawyers.

— ❀ —

Mishebeyrach. See **Mi she-beyrech.**

— ❀ —

Mishléy (Ashkenazi: **Míshley**) The Book of Proverbs

The biblical book of *Mishley* is a difficult book but highly influential, and particularly in Israel one can still find people who know it by heart and backward—and bits of it are scattered all around the prayer book.

    Mishley, literally "parables," is one of the three "wisdom books": *Iyov, Mishley, Tehilim* (Job, Proverbs, Psalms). They are called *sifrey emet*, "books of truth," *emet* being the initials of *Iyov, Mishley, Tehilim.* Sephardi Jews in particular have a long tradition of studying them intensively.

— ❀ —

Mishlóach manót (Ashkenazi: **Mishlóach mónes**/ **Shlach mónes**)
Food gifts for Purim

"Be a good girl and take this *shlach mones* round to Mrs. Margulies."

Mishloach manot is one of the duties on the festival of *Purim*, and one of the great pleasures. Literally, it means "sending food." The tradition is to send little, or not so little, packs of ready-to-eat food to friends and neighbors. In Jewish neighborhoods, and Israeli towns and villages, the streets are filled with children, dressed up as Esther, Mordecai, John Wayne, Saddam Hussein, or whichever goodie or baddie is in vogue, delivering their *mishloach manot*. Before the day is out, many of the pretzels and cookies will have been recycled a few times and perhaps handled a few times, but if *mishloach manot* promotes recycling, who can complain?

— ❀ —

Mishná (Ashkenazi: **Míshne**)　The Mishna

"The whole school is learning *Mishna Sukka* in memory of Rabbi Rosen."

To get a bird's-eye, if somewhat skeletal, picture of Jewish law, open the *Mishna*—as do pupils in traditional boys' schools by the age of eight or nine.

The Torah is not just the biblical Five Books of Moses. It is also the so-called Oral Torah, ancient interpretations and elaborations of the former—once handed down orally but later written down in the form of *Mishna* and *Midrash*: *Mishna* in the form of a terse body of legal rulings, one chapter on *Shabbat*, one on *Brachot* (blessings), and so on, and *Midrash* in the form of running commentary on the Bible.

Later came *Gemara*, itself an interpretation of both of these. Later still came interpretations of *Gemara*, and then interpretations of the interpretations . . .

The more genuinely and characteristically Jewish an idea or doctrine is, the more deliberately unsystematic is it. Its principle of construction is not that of a logical system. Even the Mishnah, which comes nearest to presenting an orderly array of thought, reflects this lack of systematization.

Gershom Scholem

(The) **Mishná Brurá** (Ashkenazi: **Míshne Brúre**)　The book *Mishna Brura*

"You don't know where to stand the *Chanukah* lights? Then look it up in the *Mishna Brura*."

You won't find it in the Jewish bestseller lists, but like the Bible, the Talmud, and the prayer book, it sells to virtually every Orthodox Jewish household.

The *Mishna Brura* is the closest one can get to an authoritative Orthodox code of twentieth-century Ashkenazi Jewish law and custom. It was compiled by the spiritual leader of prewar Polish Jewry, Rabbi Yisroel Meir of Radin, known as "the Chofets Chayim." It is not as widely accessible as it once was—fewer Jews, outside Israel, are at home with Hebrew, and the ramifications of things like televisions and plastics were never dreamed of, but user-friendly English-language translations and updates are keeping the *Mishna Brura* in all-round use.

Mishpachá (Ashkenazi: **Mishpóche**)   Extended family; relatives

"Do you really plan on inviting the whole *mishpacha*?"

"We have a lot of *mishpacha* in Jerusalem."

In the Bible, it's a "clan" or "extended family." And that's how *mishpoche* went on being used in the bosom of Yiddish, and still among Jews everywhere today. Even Israelis, who use it for the standard colorless Dad + Mom + 2.2 kids, are wont from time to time to lump uncles, cousins, aunts, and of course the untranslatable *mechutanim* (see entry) into their *mishpacha*.

Funny how ancient words can hang on to their original sense . . .

– ✤ –

Mitóch she-ló lishmá, ba lishmá (Ashkenazi: **Mitóch she-lóh lishmó, bo lishmó**)   "What starts with the wrong motives ends up with the right motives"

"Fine, so they get to see a video for every good book they read—*Mitoch shelo lishma, ba lishma*."

This saying from the Talmud reflects the pragmatic attitude generally characteristic of Judaism down to this day. Best to get people involved in *mitzvoth* and not to query beliefs and opinions too much; best to fling open the doors of the academies to whoever wishes to come and learn.

– ✤ –

Mitzváh, pl. **mitzvót** (Ashkenazi: **Mítzve**, pl. **mítzves**)   Commandment; good deed; special honor at synagogue service

"On our kibbutz, we keep all the agricultural *mitzvot* laid down in the Torah."

". . . and don't forget to call your aunt—it's a big *mitzvah*."

"Mark was called up to the Torah reading on Rosh Hashanah? That's a big *mitzvah*."

See *Bar Mitzvah, Taryag mitzvot*.

A Talmudic tradition states that 613 *mitzvot* were laid down for the Israelites in the Torah (the Five Books of Moses). In addition, at least seven *mitzvot* (the Noahide laws) were laid down for humankind as a whole—among them, bans on robbery, murder, adultery, and blasphemy. Many *mitzvot* are ritual in nature; many are social. Most involve action, and a few involve belief. Taken together, the *mitzvot* are the core of Judaism.

Blessed art Thou, LORD, our God, King of the Universe, who has sanctified us with His *mitzvot* and commanded us to . . .

Opening words of the various blessings
that Jews say before doing a *mitzvah*

To do a *mitzvah* is to outdo oneself, to go beyond one's own needs and to illumine the world.

Abraham Joshua Heschel

God who is worshipped through the *mitzvot* anchors the Jew within the historical and makes him or her understand that God's home lies within the temporal. The revealed commandments constitute a total way of life that must be implemented within the framework of human history.

David Hartman

One *mitzvah* leads to another; and one *avera* [sin] leads to another.

The Talmud, Avot

Mitzvát anashím melumadá (Ashkenazi: **Mítzvas anóshim melumódo**)   A rote action

"His apologies are always just a kind of *mitzvat anashim melumada.*"

Literally "a studiously acquired commandment of men," this phrase from Isaiah is used to describe any rote religiosity—or any action learned by rote.

And the Lord said: Since this people draw near,
Honoring Me with their mouth and their lips
But distancing their heart from Me,
And their fear of Me
Is a mitzvat anashim melumada,
I will therefore again do a marvellous thing with this people,
A marvel and a wonder,
And the wisdom of their wise men shall perish . . .

Isaiah 29

To the Orthodoxy of his time [Samson Raphael Hirsch] referred as *mitzvat anashim melumada*, Judaism inherited but not understood, "without the spirit," "afraid of awakening the spirit," Judaism "carried about on the hands like a holy mummy."

Eliezer Berkovits

Mizrách (Ashkenazi: **Mízrach**)   East

"If we stand over there by the window, we'll be facing *mizrach*."

Jews at prayer have always faced Jerusalem, site of Solomon's Temple. For those in the western Diaspora, this has meant facing east. In synagogues, the Holy Ark has been set in the eastern wall; in homes, the custom arose of fixing a sign on an east-facing wall, with the word *mizrach*.

My heart is in the East [mizrach], and I in the uttermost West—
How can I find savor in food? How shall it be sweet to me?
How shall I render my vows and my bonds, while yet
Zion lieth beneath the fetter of Edom, and I in Arab chains?
A light thing would it seem to me to leave all the good things of Spain—
Seeing how precious it is in mine eyes to behold the dust of the desolate Sanctuary.

Yehudah Ha-Levi

Modéh Aní (Ashkenazi: **Móhdeh Áni**)   *Modeh Ani* prayer upon waking

"Up you get! But first say *Modeh Ani*."

After the *Shema*, the first prayer that most Jewish children learn is *Modeh Ani*, said immediately upon waking.
   In translation, it says:

I thank You [modeh ani], living, eternal King,
For restoring my soul to me in mercy.
Great is Your trustiness.

In the service of the Almighty the point of departure is *Modeh Ani*.

Rabbi Sholom Dov Ber of Lubavitch

Mohél, pl. **mohalím** (Ashkenazi: **Móel**, pl. **móelim**)   Circumcisor

"Sergei's uncle was an underground *mohel* in the Ukraine until Stalin put an end to it."

See *Brit mila*.

The *mohel*, like Clark Kent, is prepared to fly anywhere, anytime, to bring Jewish infants into the covenant of Abraham. He is highly trained medically and religiously to perform *brit mila* (circumcision) the Jewish way, in many places without charging a fee. Aside from being the oldest Jewish profession, it can be the most dangerous, as the *mohalim* of the Reich and the former USSR discovered. It can also be prestigious: The British Royal Family brought in a *mohel* on the birth of Prince Charles. Rule Brit-annia!

That's my boy, that's my little boy,
With the rabbis all around him,
That's my boy.
Eight days old, only eight days old,
With the Rabbis and the Mohel,
That's my boy.
We make a kiddush *on the wine*
And we say a little prayer
And we pray to God to keep him safe from harm . . .

From a song by Moshe Yess

Mosád   The Israeli Secret Service

"Mommy, Ruthie says her Daddy works for *Mosad*. What's that?"

Feared by the bad, loved by the good, the *Mosad* has the distinction of being the most universally known Hebrew word after *amen*.

I had a cleaning lady in Haifa who, when she'd finished sponging my floors, scuttled off to do the cleaning for the "*mosad*" up the street. As *mosad* literally means "institution" (commonly housing the disabled or the orphaned), the opportunities for ambiguity, counterambiguity, and double identities would appear to be endless.

Mosháv, pl. **moshavím**   Israeli cooperative village

"They have a farm with horses and chickens on a *moshav* near Natanya."

Unlike the *kibbutzniks*, the *moshavniks* own their own homes and farm their own land, while sharing the burden of investment, marketing, and planning with the other members of the *moshav*. The *moshav* is as much part of the Zionist success story as the *kibbutz*. It is, however, a threatened species: The declining economics of small-time farming, coupled with the steady withdrawal of state support, have driven many *moshavim* to the wall.

Moshé Rabbénu (Ashkenazi: **Móhshe Rabbéynu**) "Moses our Teacher"

"You can't help losing your temper with them—it even happened once in a while to *Moshe Rabbenu* . . ."

Moses is traditionally known by the affectionate title *Moshe Rabbenu*, "Moses our Teacher"; he is remembered above all as the man who patiently taught the entire Torah to the Israelites during forty frustrating years of wandering in the wilderness. Never will there be anyone like him.

I believe with perfect faith that the prophecy of *Moshe Rabbenu*, peace be upon him, was true; and that he was the supreme among prophets, whether before him or after him.

I believe with perfect faith that all the Torah now in our hands is that given to *Moshe Rabbenu*, peace be upon him.

Translation of the seventh and eighth of
Maimonides's Thirteen Principles of Faith

— ❧ —

Motsaéy Shabbát (Ashkenazi: **Motsóey Shábes**) Saturday evening after *Shabbat*

"If *Motsaey Shabbat* doesn't begin too late, we can go to a movie."

With the end of *Shabbat* on Saturday night (you can look for three stars of medium magnitude, but you'd do better to check the time in a Jewish newspaper), *Motsaey Shabbat* begins. It's like the mirror image of *Erev Shabbat* (Friday before *Shabbat*): You have this exhilarating feeling of not having to prepare for anything. The new week has technically begun, but who cares—*Motsaey Shabbat* is a time for parties, movies, dates. True, there are piles of dishes to wash, but maybe *Mashiach* will come.

— ❧ —

Motsí (Ashkenazi: **Móhtsi**) Blessing over bread

"The rabbi is now going to recite the *Motsi* over the bread."

The blessing for bread concludes with *ha-motsi lechem min ha-arets*, "who brings forth bread from the ground," hence its popular name *motsi*. This blessing is said by traditional Jews whenever they are about to eat bread. But many Jews never hear it except on such occasions as the Passover meal and wedding feasts.

— ❧ —

Mótek   Sweetheart

"Careful, come away from the edge, *motek*."

Wherever you find Israelis—and you'll find them everywhere, as Israeli Defense Minister Moshe Arens discovered to his irritation when an Israeli tourist recognized him on a secret visit to China—you'll hear the word *motek*. The wife is a *motek*, hubby is a *motek*, the kids are all *motek*. Literally "sweetness."

Muát ha-machzík et hamrubéh (Ashkenazi: **Múet ha-máchzik es hamrúbe**)   "There's not much of it, but what there is, is good"

Literally "a little that holds a lot," *muat ha-machzik et hamrubeh* might be used of anything that's small but enormously important or influential: a document like the United States Constitution or a formula like $E = mc^2$ or a building or even a person. Or a country like Israel.

Muktséh (Ashkenazi: **Múktse**)   Things not to be handled on the Sabbath

"Leave the radio where it is. It's *muktseh*."

If some object is not meant to be used on the Sabbath—say, a ballpoint or a spade or a coin—then, in Jewish Law, it is to all intents and purposes out of bounds, and is not to be handled. It is *muktseh*.

Mumchéh, pl. mumchím (Ashkenazi: **Múmche, pl. múmchim**) Expert

"If you want to know about Russian music, don't go asking Mrs. Ashkenazi. She's no *mumcheh*!"

What a *mumcheh* is, an "expert" is. If it's more than a *mumcheh* you want, you may need a *meyven*—turn back.

Musáf (Ashkenazi: **Músef**)   The Additional Prayer on Sabbaths and festivals

"The rabbi's going to speak before *Musaf*, so if you want you can go out now."

The *Musaf* prayer is said on Sabbaths and festivals. It forms the third part of the morning service, following the *Shacharit* prayer and the reading of the Torah. The whole service commonly begins around 9 A.M. and lasts two to three hours, depending on whether there is a *Bar Mitzvah*, a sermon, and a *chazan* (cantor) in good voice.

Musaf is *chazan* territory. By this time, the synagogue has filled up, and the *chazan* knows it. Generations of melody writers have made *Musaf* rich in tunes and dramatic possibilities, and in the good old days the entire congregation would sing along, cry along, and wish that *Musaf* would go on forever.

— ৡৼৡ —

Musár (Ashkenazi: **Múser**)   Ethical training; a talking-to

"If he goes on driving your car like that, you'll have to give him some *musar.*"

One of the most influential intellectual movements in late nineteenth- and early twentieth-century Jewish history was the *Musar* movement, an attempt to make ethical training a central part of a young man's *yeshiva* education—a reaction to the overintellectualization that dogged the *yeshiva* world. The most famous *musarnik* was Rabbi Yisrael Salanter; commonly studied *musar* authors are Moshe Chaim Luzatto and Eliahu Dessler; and perhaps the best known description of the world of these *musar-niks* is Chaim Grade's novel *The Yeshivah.*

There are few among our people who would eat a meal without washing their hands, even though they may be utterly famished or distressed. However, with the far more serious offense of *leshon ha-ra* [evil talk], they will so easily do wrong even without having a particular passion for it. And now it becomes plain that the prime means of protecting ourselves from an *avera* (sin) is to make it our second nature to avoid it, in other words our energies must be channeled into *musar*, into avoiding *leshon ha-ra* with our senses and our thoughts . . .

Rabbi Yisrael Salanter

— ৡৼৡ —

Náchat (Ashkenazi: **Náches**)   Fulfillment

"Edit that video, will you, and give your grandma some *naches.*"

I translated *nachat* as fulfillment. I shouldn't have. There is by definition no foreign word for the *nachat* that Jewish parents can get from their children, Jewish grandparents from their grandchildren, Israel from new *olim*, and God from *baaley teshuva*. Fulfillment you can get from writing poetry, but it's not *nachat*.

A beggar at the Tel Aviv *Tachana Merkazit* [Central Bus Station] had the perfect system.

To those who gave, he wished "*parnasa* [livelihood], and *nachat* from your children."

To those who didn't, he wished "*nachat*, and *parnasa* from your children."

— ✤ —

Naé dorésh ve-naé mekayém (Ashkenazi: **Nóe dóhresh ve-nóe mekáyem**)   Someone who practices what he or she preaches

Literally "expounds properly and practices properly," *nae doresh ve-nae mekayem* is what most voters fondly imagine their candidate to be. Like the wise men of the Talmud expounding each letter of the *Torah*, politicians spend endless time expounding their programs or explaining away what they were quoted as saying—but the similarity ends there.

— ✤ —

Nána   Mint

"Can I offer you another cup of tea with *nana*?"

The leaves of the *nana*, the common or garden mint, make a delicious tea, as is known to every Arab and Turk—and to every Israeli. There is no sense in tourists complaining about the taste of the instant coffee or the size of the tea bags. Israel is *nana* country.

— ✤ —

Naví, pl. nevi'ím (Ashkenazi: **Nóvi, pl. neví'im**)   Prophet

"Don't ask me where it will all end. I'm no *navi*."

See *Nevua*, "Prophecy" and *Eliyahu ha-Navi*, "Elijah the Prophet."

The *nevi'im* have been central figures in Jewish history—but to call them prophets in the normal English sense of the word would be highly misleading. Jewish thinkers have been at pains to point out that the *navi* communicated what God wanted humanity to do, and particularly what not to do.

Navi (and its feminine form *nevi'a*) refers to people like Abraham, Leah, Moses, Aaron, Miriam, Samuel—and a whole line of people whose prophecies are collected as separate books of the Bible, under the cover name of *Nevi'im Acharonim* ("latter prophets"): Isaiah, Jeremiah, Ezekiel, and the authors of twelve short books from Amos to Malachi (termed *Trei Asar*, "the twelve"). *Nevi'im Rishonim*, "first prophets," is a cover name for the books Joshua, Judges, Samuel, and Kings.

— ❧ —

Nechbá el ha-kelím (Ashkenazi: **Néchbo el ha-kéylim**)   Self-effacing

Literally "hiding among the equipment," this expression for anyone who shuns the limelight actually harks back to one of the great limelight shunners of all time, the humble Saul, first King of Israel. When they wished to proclaim him king, he was nowhere to be found—he was literally *nechba el ha-kelim*, hiding among the equipment.

— ❧ —

Nedavá, pl. nedavót (Ashkenazi: **Nedóve, pl. nedóves**)   Donation (to a synagogue)

"What kind of *nedava* should I give for being called to the Torah? Twenty dollars? Fifty dollars?"

In many, if not most, synagogues, it is customary to give a *nedava* on being called to the Torah reading, or to mark a birth, wedding anniversary or the like. A *nedava* is often $18 or multiples of $18—the number eighteen having the same *gematria* (numerical value) as the Hebrew word for life, *chay* (see entry).

— ❧ —

(The) **Négev**   The Negev Desert

The *Negev*, literally "the dryland," is the desert stretching south from Beersheba to the Red Sea at Eilat. Once hailed by Israel's first premier David Ben-Gurion as the land of tomorrow, the *Negev*'s tomorrow seems to have been indefinitely postponed. With the exception of Beersheba, a couple of other towns, and some rather sensitive military installations, it is still virtually uninhabited and untouched. Perhaps it always should be.

In the Negev *flatlands glistens the dew.*
In the Negev *flatlands a defender has fallen.*
The boy is not breathing and the heart is still,
And a forelock of hair is caressed by the wind.

From a Hebrew ballad of the 1950s

— ❧ —

Ne'ilá (Ashkenazi: **Ne'íle**)   Final Prayer on *Yom Kippur*

"During *Ne'ila* you just don't want to think about anything except life and death . . ."

Literally "closing" (of the prayers), *Ne'ila* probably evokes in most people's minds the closing of the gates of Heaven at the end of *Yom Kippur*, holiest day in the year. *Ne'ila* is the fifth and final service of the day. The future of all humankind has come before God for judgment—and now, as the *Ne'ila* prayers begin and the dusk thickens, just a last few minutes remain for a last desperate plea for a sweet New Year.

Then the *aron kodesh* (holy ark) is closed, the *Kaddish* is sung, and *Ne'ila* is over—till next year.

Ner tamíd (Ashkenazi: **Ner tómid**)   Permanent synagogue light

In front of the *aron kodesh* (holy ark), at the focal end of the synagogue, is the *ner tamid*, literally "constant lamp." Like so many other objects in the synagogue, it keeps alive the memory of the way things were in the ancient Temple, in which the *menorah* (candelabra) was unceasingly kept burning. Nowadays, synagogues generally have a permanent electric *ner tamid*. Once, the *ner tamid* was simply a lamp or candle that was lit during prayers.

Nes, pl. nisím (Ashkenazi: **Nes, pl. nísim**)   Miracle

"I don't know what's the bigger *nes*—the Scuds not exploding or the Patriots not exploding."

There are two sorts of *nes*: the "big ones" that everyone's heard of (from Sarah giving birth at ninety, through the Ten Plagues and the Parting of the Red Sea, down to the Story of *Chanukah*) and the "little ones." After the Six Day War, Israeli bookshops were full of catalogs of the "little" *nisim* of the war. After the Gulf War, there seems to be no need to catalog them.

The *baal ha-nes* [beneficiary of the miracle] doesn't notice the *nes*.

The Talmud, Nida

A *Chasid* once journeyed to the big city to see a certain rabbi, of whose saintliness he'd heard so much. There, he met a disciple of the rabbi.
    "Tell me, what *nisim* has your rabbi done?" the Chasid asked him.
    "Oh, there are all different sorts of *nisim*," the disciple answered. "For

instance, to the people of your town it would be a *nes* if the Almighty were to do what your rabbi desires. To us, on the other hand, it would be an equal *nes* if our rabbi were to do what the Almighty desires . . . You can't rely on a *nes*."

The Talmud, Pesachim

— ❧ —

Neshamá (Ashkenazi: Neshóme)   Soul

"OK, he's a real jerk, but he has a good *neshama*."

Related to the verb *nasham*, "to breathe," the *neshama* is deemed to be the divine spark "breathed" into Adam. The philosophy of Kabbala and *Chasidut* (Chasidism) is much concerned with the *neshama*, and with such questions as what the *neshama* is, what it might imply about the purpose of life, and whether it migrates after death from one person to another.

I thank Thee, everlasting King, for mercifully returning my *neshama* to me . . .

The first Hebrew words that a Jew says on waking

God, the *neshama* that Thou gavest to me is pure . . . Blessed art Thou, O Lord, who restorest *neshamot* to dead bodies.

From the prelude to the Morning Prayers

The *neshama* descends to the body and cries "woe, woe, woe!"

Chasidic saying

— ❧ —

Neshamá yeterá (Ashkenazi: Neshóme yeséyro)   Heightened Sabbath soul

"Perk up, Joel, have you lost your *neshama yetera* already?"

The Almighty gives one a *neshama yetera* [heightened soul] on Friday evening, and at the end of the Sabbath it is taken back.

The Talmud, Betsa

During the week everyone has a *neshama*. But on *Shabbat* we receive a *neshama yetera*. This suggests that there is some kind of undeveloped facet of personality, a spiritual dimension, of which we remain unaware in the normal course of events.

Norman Lamm

— ❧ —

Nesiá tová!   "Have a safe journey! Bon voyage!"

Nesia tova! is the way Israelis usually send you on your way. It is a modern expression, and like many modern expressions it lacks—to my mind—the beauty of the oldtime *lech le-shalom,* "go in peace" or (my favorite) *lech le-shalom va-chazor le-shalom,* "go in peace and return in peace."

— ✥ —

Netilát yadáyim (Ashkenazi: **Netíles yedáyim**)   Ritual Washing of the Hands

"Waiter! Do you have a place here for *Netilat yadayim*?"

Netilat yadayim is one of those archetypal ancient customs: Before breaking bread, Orthodox Jews take a cup and pour water over each hand, then making a benediction and drying each hand carefully, a practice that goes back to ancient purity laws. It is particularly noticeable at weddings, when a long line forms at the faucets before the meal—while the uninitiated wonder what on earth is going on.

Another traditional *netilat yadayim* involves washing the hands six times on waking.

— ✥ —

Nevuá (Ashkenazi: **Nevúe**)   Prophecy

"What a dream . . . It was almost like a *nevua*."

Since the end of biblical times, *nevua* is said to have ceased. Instead of being in direct communication with God, humankind has had to make do with sages with the lesser gift of *ruach ha-kodesh* (the Holy Spirit; see entry).

The one exception is said to be *Eliyahu ha-Navi* (Elijah the Prophet), who occasionally returns to earth on special business. Otherwise, it's a matter of who is *not* a *navi*—with pride of place going to Israeli economists.

From the day the Temple was destroyed, *nevua* was taken away from the *nevi'im* and given to simpletons and children.

The Talmud, Bava Batra

— ✥ —

Nibúl peh (Ashkenazi: **Níbul peh**)   Bad language (literally "fouling the mouth")

"Did I hear you call him a *mamzer*! Come on, no *nibul peh* on *Yom Kippur*!"

Why, people often ask, do Israelis seem to curse in Yiddish, Arabic, Russian, English—but not in Hebrew?

Actually they do curse in Hebrew a bit. But the fact is that *nibul peh* doesn't come that effortlessly in Hebrew. It doesn't flow. The great philosopher Maimonides would have been pleased: He opined that Hebrew was called *Leshon ha-Kodesh* (the Holy Tongue) because it was devoid of all the *nibul peh* of other languages.

We trust that he would have no objections to this book.

— 🙠🙡 —

Nichúm avél (Ashkenazi: **Níchum óvel**)   Consoling the mourner

"The whole community came to the house to do *nichum avel*."

See *Avel*, "Mourner."

Nichum avel is a duty of great import and is still widely practiced in traditional form: lining up to offer the ancient words of consolation to the mourners after the funeral, and visiting their home during the week of *shiva* that follows in order to keep them company and speak in praise of the deceased.

— 🙠🙡 —

Niftár, fem. **niftéret** (Ashkenazi: **Nífter**, fem. **niftéres**)   To die; the deceased

"The family was around him when he was *niftar*."

"Four generations are present here today to pay respect to the *nifteret*."

Niftar is used by the Orthodox in the phrase "to be *niftar*," "was *niftar*" as a way of referring to dying, and also as a noun denoting the deceased themselves. *Niftar* originally meant "to be released."

— 🙠🙡 —

Nigún, pl. **niguním** (Ashkenazi: **Nígn**, pl. **nigúnim**)   Tune

"Let's have a schnapps and I'll teach you a *nigun* I heard from my uncle."

A *nigun* is a way of serving the Almighty. It's a tune, any tune, that Chasidim sing to make *simcha* (joy).

There are *nigunim* that come from heaven only knows where. There are *nigunim* that were lifted right out of the mouths of the Gentiles— like Napoleon's March, which Lubavitcher Chasidim sing at the end of *Yom Kippur*, and the waltzes that the Chasidim up the street sing every Friday night. What counts is not where they come from, but where they're going.

When I hear a Jew singing a *nigun*, I can tell how far he's got in *yiras shomayim* [fear of Heaven].

Rabbi Yisroel Toyb of Modzitz

There is nothing in the world that does not have its own *nigun*. Even *apikorsus* [freethinking] has its own *nigun*.

Rabbi Nachman of Bratzlav

— ❧ —

Nisán (Ashkenazi: **Nísen**)   The month of Nisan

Nisan is the first month of the Jewish year, the month of new beginnings: of Passover and the Exodus, of spring cleaning all the *chametz* out of the house, of spring.

— ❧ —

Nu?   "Well?" (in expectation or impatience)

"So your daughter's still doing her Ph.D.? So *nu*? When does she go into practice?"

"*Nu*? The light's turned green!"

Here's a word that seems to have no right to be in a book about Hebrew. Russians will say it's Russian. To Poles *nu*? (or, to be more exact, *no*?) is pure Polish. To Litvaks it's Yiddish.

They're right. But to four million Israelis (five million if you include the inhabitants of Gaza, Nablus, and so on), *nu*? is Hebrew. Babes at the breast say *nu*?, boyfriends say *nu*?, and the entire membership of the Moroccan Immigrants Association say *nu*?

— ❧ —

Od chazón la-moéd (Ashkenazi: **Ohd chózon la-móed**)   "Be patient and it will happen" (literally a "vision of that time is still to come")

"It's frightening how long it's taking to stop nuclear proliferation."
   "Don't worry. *Od chazon la-moed . . .*"

This famous phrase comes from the biblical prophecies of Habakkuk. The event that he was referring to was the longed-for demise of Babylon (located in modern-day Iraq). A definite prediction of this might be delayed, but it would surely come. But which Babylon was he talking about?

— ❧ —

Olám ha-bá (Ashkenazi: **Óhlom há-bo**) The Next World
Olám ha-zé (Ashkenazi: **Óhlom há-ze**) This World

"Let the *mamzer* [swine] have his fun in *Olam ha-ze;* he won't have any in *Olam ha-ba."*

The Jewish goal of existence is to make the most of *Olam ha-ze,* so as to be able to make the most of the spiritual *Olam ha-ba.*

The very word *olam* is intriguing; it seems to come from the same root as *alum,* "concealed," as if the world as we know it is concealing reality from us. And *le-olam* means "forever."

Olam ha-ze is like a corridor to *Olam ha-ba.*

The Talmud, Avot

Everyone says there's an *olam ha-ze* and an *olam ha-ba.*

And we do believe that there is an *olam ha-ba,* and it's also quite possible that there is an *olam ha-ze,* somewhere—because down here it seems we're in *Gehinom* [Hell].

Rabbi Nachman of Bratzlav

Motke, a notorious scoundrel and lecher, came to visit the rabbi of his town. Now the rabbi was very ill; no one was allowed in to see him. But when he heard it was Motke outside, the rabbi ordered him to be let in forthwith.

"Why this honor?" asked Motke. "All your followers are kept away and I am allowed in?"

The rabbi shook his head. "All my followers I'll be able to meet, please God, in *Olam ha-ba.* But as for you—I think I may well be seeing you now for the last time."

Oléh, pl. **olím** Immigrant to Israel

"American *olim* are advised that it is difficult to obtain cranberry sauce in Israel."

Literally "someone who ascends," the *oleh* is the lifeblood of Israel, a "visionary society" (as political scientists put it) founded on the hope that all or most Jews will make *aliyah* (see entry). Some types of *olim* arouse little attention. Others create excitement and romance—the black *olim* from Ethiopia, the tiny Jewish community of Albania . . .

Ómer. See **Sefirat ha-Omer.**

Óneg shabbát (Ashkenazi: **Óhneg shábes**)   Sabbath party

"We're having an *oneg shabbat* this evening at eight, at our place. Can you come?"

Oneg, "pleasure" is one of the chief ingredients of the Sabbath. It's at one and the same time a spiritual and a physical ingredient, and so people often arrange an *oneg shabbat* at their home—with refreshments and perhaps one or two *divrey torah* (short Torah thoughts) and some songs. It's particularly customary in Israel.

If you cease to tread Shabbat underfoot
and keep my holy day free from your own affairs,
If you call Shabbat an oneg
and the Lord's holy day a day to be honored . . .

Isaiah 58

– 🙖 –

Oy!   "Oh!"

"*Oy,* I'm almost out of detergent!"

Let no person discredit *oy!*—prince of interjections.

To those whose thoughts immediately return to the *oy vey!* and *oy gevalt!* of their grandmothers' homes, I say: Open Isaiah, nay, open Numbers, and you shall find it. At the crescendo of his prophecy, the heathen prophet Balaam declared (and I hesitate to translate his cryptic Hebrew words): "*Oy,* who shall survive God's devastation?"

The same, but a trifle stronger—and also a pedigree biblical word: *Oy va-avoy!*

For the precise tone of voice: Listen to any Israeli for less than five minutes.

– 🙖 –

Oy le-rashá oy lishchenó (Ashkenazi: **Oy le-rósho oy lishchéynoh**)
"Woe to a villain, woe to his neighbor"

This celebrated maxim from the Talmud restates the opening motif of the biblical Book of Psalms: If individuals hang around with a bad crowd, they will be held responsible for the bad effect it is bound to have on them.

Jewish folklore abounds in tales of people who got caught up in the schemes of their neighbors—such as the tribe of Reuven whose men joined the rebellion of their neighbor Korach and were all swallowed up by the ground.

– ✿ –

Oy li mi-yotsrí, ve-oy li mi-yitsrí (Ashkenazi: **Oy li mi-yóhtsri, ve-oy li mi-yítsri**) "I'm damned if I do and damned if I don't"

See *Yetser ha-ra,* "Evil impulse."

Literally, "woe to me from my Creator, and woe to me from my evil impulse," this Talmudic exclamation means that if you act foolishly God will make you regret it, but if you act with restraint your *yetser ha-ra* will plague you too. A very Jewish version of Scylla and Charybdis.

– ✿ –

Ozéret pl. **ozrot** Cleaning woman

". . . and on Tuesdays the *ozeret* hangs all the rugs over the balcony to beat them out. Then on Thursdays she mops all the floors . . ."

If they ever get round to doing an Israeli version of *Upstairs Downstairs,* it will surely be called *Ozeret.* Happy to take the bus at 5:30 A.M. from one of the inner neighborhoods of Jerusalem or Tel Aviv so as to be at your door at 6 A.M. sharp, she knows her rightful station. She will work her fingers to the bone, keeping dust off rugs, mold off clothes, *jukim* (roaches) off food; she holds the *sponja* (mop) with statuesque finesse. She is perhaps the last monument to the Dignity of Labor.

She *is* a great topic of conversation, the *ozeret*: her honesty or lack of it, the quality of her work, the frequency of her absences, her moods, her caprices, and "What do you pay yours?"

Having been in on such discussions, I've often been struck by the number of women who are daunted by their *ozrot,* and not just for fear of losing them to the competition. They go all out to stay in the *ozeret's* good graces, flatter her, pander to her whims, bribe her with food and presents.

Miriam Arad

– ✿ –

Parashá, pl. **parshiyót** (Ashkenazi: **Párshe,** pl. **párshes**) Weekly section read from the Torah

"Which *parasha* will Daniel be reading for his *Bar Mitzvah*?"

See *Sidra.*

The Torah is divided into fifty-four sections called *parshiyot* (or *sidrot*), traditionally read in the synagogue on successive Sabbaths, starting in the autumn. (As you can imagine, certain *parshiyot* have to be combined to fit in to the year.)

The names of the *parshiyot* are engraved in many schoolchildren's minds—and in mine. So is the name of every boy's *Bar Mitzvah parasha*.

— ഴ —

Párev, commonly spelled **párve**   Neither meat nor dairy

"Barbara, are you sure this is a *parve* cake?"

Tradition forbids the mixing of meat and dairy food, so Jews have always found it useful to have foods that are neither meat nor dairy, and to have a word for them, *parve*—fish, cakes using margarine rather than butter, veggie burgers, and always, always *parve* bread.

Where precisely the word *parve* comes from no one seems to know, but today it's part and parcel of Israeli Hebrew, which is why it's here.

— ഴ —

Parnasá (Ashkenazi: **Parnóse**)   Livelihood

"If he can build an extension for his mother-in-law, *parnasa* can't be that bad . . ."

How can I say anything about *parnasa*? It's the same problem the world over.

One Friday afternoon, just before the Sabbath, a beggar arrived in town. Quickly, he made his way to the rabbi, so that he could leave his pack and his earnings in his care over the Sabbath—and then hurried to prayers. But as the rabbi made to pick up the pack, out poured hundreds of coins!

That Sunday morning, the rabbi and the town council summoned the beggar.

"You're no beggar," they announced. "But we're offering you the choice: Either you move to the next town and open a business, so you have no further need to beg—or you return all the money forthwith."

The beggar gave it some thought.

"You know what?" he decided. "Keep all the money. After all, a *parnose* is a *parnose*."

— ഴ —

Paróchet (Ashkenazi: **Peróhches**)   Curtain drawn across the Holy Ark

Synagogue architecture is full of memories. Just like the *Aron Kodesh*, the Holy Ark containing the Torah scrolls, is a memory of Solomon's

Temple, so, too, the curtain drawn across it, the *parochet*, is a memory of the curtain that veiled the Holy of Holies from the eyes of the world. The *parochet* is sometimes also a stunning demonstration of Jewish weaving, embroidery, and design.

— ❧ —

Pársha. See Parashá.

— ❧ —

Pasúk, pl. psukím (Ashkenazi: **Pósek, pl. psúkim**)   Biblical verse

"Rivka, can you please read out the next *pasuk* for us?"

The small Jewish child was brought to school for the first time, and probably the first word that he or she heard was *pasuk*. Reading *psukim*, translating *psukim*, explaining *psukim* . . . for the next few years their life would revolve around *psukim*.

People traditionally have their "own" *pasuk*, that is, one that starts with the first letter of their name, and they recite it if they ever fall ill.

The emperor signed the genocide documents and gave them to Haman, who left the palace in an exuberant mood, with all his cronies and hangers-on. Suddenly, Mordechai the Jew crossed their path. But seeing three children coming out of school, Mordechai chased after them—and Haman and his cronies, seeing Mordechai chase after them, also chased after them, to see what he wanted to ask them.

"What *pasuk* did you just learn?" Mordechai asked one of the children.

"I learned the *pasuk* 'Fear not sudden terror or the destruction of the wicked when it comes,'" he replied.

Mordechai's face broke into a smile of joy.

Haman said to him, "What did those children say to make you smile?"

He replied, "Good tidings—that I should have no fear of your wicked schemes."

Haman was livid. "These children will be the first to suffer," he muttered.

The *Midrash* on the Book of Esther

— ❧ —

Pasúl (Ashkenazi: **Pósl**)   Unfit (for religious use)

"Hey, you can't wear those *tefilin*—they're *pasul!*"

"Surely a teacher who can't control his temper is *pasul* for the job."

Apart from sin and anti-Semitism, I can't think of anything that can cause so much anxiety to observant Jews as the thought that something may be *pasul*.

If a *sefer torah* (scroll of the Law) is found to be *pasul*, because, say, a letter has faded away, it will have to be sent for correction; if an *etrog* (citron fruit for Sukkot) is *pasul*, because, say, the tip has fallen off, you'll need a new one.

Recent reports in the Jewish press warned that most *mezuzot* (doorpost scrolls) were *pasul*—many were not even scribally written but photocopied! How many came from Taiwan, who knows . . .

— ✥ —

Peót (Ashkenazi: **Péyes**)   Sidecurls

"Some of the boys have *peot* but some don't."

Long *peot* are found among many traditional Jewish communities. But they are best known among Chasidim, who in fact have a custom of waiting until a boy is three before cutting his hair, and then cutting it very short while leaving the long *peot*.

The Torah actually proscribes the shaving of the "corners" (*peot*) of the head, commonly taken to include the sideburns.

— ✥ —

Pérek, pl. **prakím** (Ashkenazi: **Pérek**, pl. **prókim**)   Chapter

"Last week we stopped near the end of the first *perek* of Samuel."

Each book of the Bible is divided into *prakim*. In the *Chumash* (Five Books of Moses), there are usually several *prakim* to each *sidra*. In fact, a *sidra* can end in mid-*perek*. The *Mishna* and *Gemara* are also divided into *prakim*.

— ✥ —

Pérek. See **Pirkéy Avót.**

— ✥ —

Perúsh, pl. **perushím** (Ashkenazi: **Péyresh**, pl. **peyrúshim**)   Commentary

"Today we're studying the Book of Isaiah with the *perush* of Radak."

It has been said that the page of the average *sefer* (religious book) is like a dialogue of the dead. Clustered around or beneath the central text, be it Bible or Talmud, are one or even many *perushim* elucidating the text, adding to it, even using it as a springboard. And the eyes of any learned person will automatically be wandering up and down, back and forth across the page, from text to *perush*, from *perush* to *perush*—Rashi in dialogue with Ibn Ezra, Ibn Ezra with Onkelos . . .

The highest form of literary achievement is the *peyresh* [on the Talmud]. The authority of the book commented upon is taken for granted, but so is the right of the commenter to elaborate, to point to deficiencies, and to propose emendations. There are quite a number of commentaries on commentaries as well. Every latter-day scholar navigates freely in the "sea of the Talmud."

Max Weinreich

— ❧ —

Pésach   Passover

"So Blanche, when are you starting to clean the house for *Pesach*?"

Pesach literally means "passing over" or "sparing." And as the Bible makes clear, the festival commemorating the Exodus from Egypt was named *Pesach* precisely because God "passed over (*pasach*) the houses of the Israelites in Egypt."

   Pesach is celebrated in the spring, for seven or eight days—although the preparations for it in Orthodox circles can take weeks: Every particle of *chametz* (leaven) is removed, "*kosher*-for-*Pesach*" food brought in, and everything readied for the *Seder* night.

"Mama, school's out," I said, as I came running home from school a few days before *Pesach*.
   "Big deal! May you live to bring home better news," Mama said, completely in a dither prior to the holiday. She tied kerchiefs around both maids' heads, gave them brushes, brooms, and feather dusters. She herself had a kerchief on her head, and all three women cleaned and rubbed, washed and scrubbed, making everything *kosher*-for-*Pesach*. I didn't know what to do with myself. No matter where I sat or stood or went—it was the wrong place.

Sholom Aleichem

— ❧ —

Peshará (Ashkenazi: **Peshóre**)   Compromise

"Look, you'll have to face him in the street again. Settle for a *peshara*."

Peshara is an important value not only in everyday life but also in law. A *Bet Din* (Jewish court of law) will often recommend a *peshara*. The classic Talmudic scenario is of two ships heading along a river: If one tries to pass the other, they'll both founder—so let each take its turn.

The power of *peshara* is greater than the power of *din* (strict justice).

The Talmud, Sanhedrin

— ⚜ —

Peshat (Ashkenazi: **Pshat**)   Literal sense of a biblical (or any) text

"Before we start arguing about the report, let's make sure we agree what the *peshat* is."

See *Drash*, "Applied meaning."

Peshat is the obvious, literal meaning of a biblical text—and by extension, of any piece of Mishna, Gemara, or anything else. To get at the *peshat* of something has been given high priority in traditional Jewish learning. "What's *peshat*?" is a question constantly heard in *yeshivas*.

At the same time, there is a whole alternative tradition of nonobvious biblical interpretation called *drash* or *midrash*.

The modern state of mind demands a greater faithfulness to the simple, literal meaning (to the *peshat*), and a greater obligation to preserve it. Only in the face of virtually insurmountable problems is this approach abandoned. The presence of an extra word, letter, or even an entire phrase can be easily seen as a stylistic peculiarity. *Peshat*, from this point of view, is synonymous with exegetical truth, and one does not abandon truth lightly. But to the rabbis of the Talmud, deviation from *peshat* was not repugnant.

David Weiss Halivni

— ⚜ —

Petichá (Ashkenazi: **Psíche**)   Opening the Holy Ark in the synagogue

"When I was asked to do *peticha*, I couldn't get the curtain open . . ."

Whenever the Torah scrolls are brought out of the Holy Ark to be read, a worshipper is given the honor of *peticha*—drawing open the *parochet* (curtain) and then opening the ark and bringing out the Torah.

— ⚜ —

Pidyón ha-bén (Ashkenazi: **Pídyen ha-bén**)   Redemption of the first-born

"Oh, the baby will look so sweet in that blue suit for his *pidyon ha-ben*!"

Redemption of the firstborn has a grand biblical ring to it, and that's exactly what the *pidyon ha-ben* ceremony is like. Since biblical times, firstborn baby boys have to be "bought out" of priestly service—for which the Torah had originally intended them. This is done by inviting a *kohen* (a real "priest") on the baby's thirty-first day of life, and paying him five silver shekels (or five silver dollars) as a "redemption" fee. The baby is traditionally brought in on a silver tray dressed up in finery, there's lots of food and drink, and everyone rejoices.

Doubtless, the parents of some bawling infants must have thought about leaving them with the *kohen* and keeping the money. That, fortunately, is against regulations.

– ❧ –

Pikúach néfesh   Saving of life

"Get this man to the hospital right away—it's *pikuach nefesh!*"

Pikuach nefesh is a supreme value. For the sake of *pikuach nefesh*, the *halacha* (Jewish Law) warrants and demands the suspension of all other laws (except, of course, things like killing one person to use the organs in another person)—most notably, the laws of the Sabbath and of *Yom Kippur*. During the 1991 Gulf War, for example, religious Israelis kept their radios tuned in on the Sabbath because of *pikuach nefesh*. One early problem for the State of Israel in upholding official Sabbath observance was whether the running of major 24-hour industries counted as *pikuach nefesh*.

Pikuach nefesh overrides the Sabbath.

The Talmud, Shabbat

– ❧ –

Pilpúl (Ashkenazi: Pílpul)   Academic Torah discourse; hairsplitting

"Come on, Shimon, I want a simple answer—don't give me all that *pilpul* . . ."

Pilpul can be a good thing or a bad thing. It can denote the kind of intricate, academic analysis of a Talmudic problem—delivered aloud to a critical audience—which created the Jewish penchant for law and academe.

But uttered with a suitably scathing tone of voice, *pilpul* is also a putdown for farfetched, overintricate, overacademic analysis ("purely academic," as nonacademics say). For centuries, rabbinic leaders have been trying to stamp it out, but they probably never will, because young men at *yeshiva* who don't gamble, don't drink, and don't womanize must have some way of blowing their aggression—and there's no finer way than attacking a Talmudic problem. *Pilpul* forever.

In truth, *pilpul* has been unfairly maligned, for this is the way the intellect "plays," the way the mind indulges in its delightful games and exercises.

Norman Lamm

The Yahrzeit [anniversary of death] of Rabbi Zalman Spitzer was marked by a well-attended gathering on the second night of *Chanukah*. Rabbi Zev Feldman gave a *pilpul* and two *talmidim* of the Talmud Torah presented *divrey torah*.

From an Ultraorthodox newspaper report

— ⚜ —

Pirkéy Avót (Ashkenazi: **Pírkey Óves**)   *Ethics of the Fathers* (a collection of maxims)

"Every *Shabbat* afternoon, Grandpa taught us something from *Pirkey Avot*."

Pirkey Avot, or *Perek* as it is popularly known, is probably the most popular book of Jewish sayings—the sayings of the sages of the *Mishna*, such as Hillel and Rabbi Akiva. For centuries it has been synonymous with long summer *Shabbat* afternoons, and a favorite with itinerant preachers and girls' schools.

— ⚜ —

Pítta   Pitta bread

"How many *falafels* do you want in your *pitta*?"

Pitta is flat, round, chewy, just slightly leavened, with a pocket that just begs for falafel, salad, and (I've tried it) hot dogs. The bad news is that you can't really spread anything on it. The good news is that to dip it is a delight.

The word *pitta* isn't as Arabic as it sounds. It's also Aramaic (a language many Jews once spoke)—and if you think the Hebrew for bread has always been *lechem*, you'll be surprised to know that Judah the Maccabee or Rabbi Akiva would have said *pat*.

— ⚜ —

Piyút, pl. piyutím (Ashkenazi: **Píyut, pl. piyútim**)   Liturgical poem

"I can't understand half of these *piyutim* . . ."

Once upon a time, in the Byzantine and Moslem world, when the greatest celebrities (after the warlords) were the poets, Jews, too, hoped that their sons might grow up to write poetry. One result was the *piyutim*—hundreds upon hundreds of long, delicately crafted, wondrously allusive, and to us nowadays well-nigh incomprehensible poems for the synagogue. Some of them are still recited on festivals.

The *piyutim* and the refrains were created by masters of language and eloquence. Since then, however, they have been soaked in Jewish tears—to become *selichot* [prayers of forgiveness].

Rabbi Levi Yitschok of Berditchev

— ❧ —

Protéktsiya   Influential connections

"I'm not saying you won't be able to get a phone for the apartment within the year, but you'll need *protektsiya*."

Protektsiya (don't slur it; pronounce every consonant reverently) is one of the great legacies of the former Soviet Union. It is Russian for having the right connections—family, friends, neighbors—to get things done. Millions of *olim* (immigrants) will attest to the fact that it is now Hebrew too. Don't ever confuse the Hebrew word *protektsiya* with the Hebrew word *protekshn*. The latter denotes "protection money" and, unlike our dear *protektsiya*, it is a bad, bad thing.

— ❧ —

Purím (Ashkenazi: **Púrim**)   The festival of Purim

"This Purim, I'm getting dressed up as Queen Esther."

See *Megila, Matanot la-evyonim,* and *Mishloach manot.*

The biblical festival of *Purim* is usually some time in March, and it's wild. It marks the defeat by Jewish prayer and force of arms of the first recorded attempt at a Final Solution 2,500 years ago, by Haman the Persian premier. In synagogues, the *Megila* (the Scroll of Esther) is read, with the noise level reaching 127 decibels at each mention of Haman's name. Children dress up. The streets of Tel Aviv swarm with cowboys and princesses. At the best *yeshivot*, earnest students suddenly stand up and do spoofs of their venerable rabbis. During the day, gifts of food (*mishloach manot*) and charity (*matanot la-evyonim*) are traditionally distributed. The climax is the *Purim* feast in the late afternoon. The pious drink themselves drunk. Someone once suggested that *Purim* is a complement to the fast of *Yom Kippur(im)*—and that ultimately both serve some similar spiritual goal. They had a point.

People must get intoxicated on *Purim* until they cannot distinguish between "cursed be Haman" and "blessed be Mordechai."

The Talmud, Megila

Give a shoulder, close your eyes,
We have Purim, *forget everything.*
You got a pain? Crunch it underfoot.
Open your mouth and sing:
Let's all joke, let's drink, let's live, despite all our troubles.
Let's all joke, let's live and see wonders and miracles.

Translation of an Israeli children's *Purim* song

A *galach* (Christian priest) asked a rabbi:

"Why is *Purim* different from all other feasts? All your other feast days seem to begin on the evening before—but your *Purim* banquet only begins on the evening *after.*"

"Let me answer with a question," said the rabbi. "You Gentiles always say your days begin at midnight. Then why do your Christmas celebrations begin the evening before? . . . I'll tell you why: We Jews have a Gentile named Haman to thank for the festival of *Purim*—so we celebrate it Gentile-style. And you Christians have a Jew to thank for your Christmas—so you start the day the Jewish way!"

— ✣ —

Rábbi [rhymes with "hubby"]   (Historical title of) rabbi

"Toledo is the reputed birthplace of *Rabbi Avraham ibn Ezra.*"

See also *Rebbe* and *Rav.*

Where contemporary rabbis are referred to by a Hebrew title, it is *rav.* But rabbis of earlier times were given the title *rabbi*, and they still are referred to in this way: *Rabbi Akiva* and *Rabbi Tarfon* of the Mishna, *Rabbi Yosef Karo* of sixteenth-century Tsefat, and so on. *Rabbi* is literally "my master" (the *-i* suffix denoting "my").

— ✣ —

Rabotáy! (Ashkenazi: **Rabóhsay!**)   "Gentlemen!"

"*Rabotay*, time is getting on and we have to come to a decision."

This ancient form of address is still in common use throughout the Jewish world. The word *rabot* here is the plural of *rav*, but meaning gentleman, not rabbi.

— ✣ —

Rachmána litslán (Ashkenazi: **Rachmóne litslón**)   "God forbid"

"These urns can tip over and you can be seriously scalded, *rachmana litslan.*"

Like *lo alenu*, this expression is commonly used—mostly by the Ultra-orthodox—as a pious rapid response (by the hearer or speaker) to any mention of a tragedy that happened or might happen.

    Rachmana litslan is actually not Hebrew but Aramaic in form (Aramaic, the old international language of the Middle East, was once *the* Jewish vernacular), but it has long formed part of the Hebrew repertoire, like *bon appétit* in English.

— ❦ —

Rachmanút (Ashkenazi: **Rachmónes**)   Compassion

"Come on, Harvey, have some *rachmanut* for the kid—let him watch."

Rachmanut was the quality that Jews in antiquity felt set them apart from the Greeks and Romans and their Rambo culture. Jews saw themselves as *rachmanim bney rachmanim*, "compassion running in the family," which is precisely what the modern philosopher Nietzsche said dismissively about them in proposing his master society.

    Rachmanut has a warm motherly feel to it, helped by the fact that *rechem* is the Hebrew for womb.

— ❦ —

Ragláyim la-davár (Ashkenazi: **Ragláyim la-dóvor**)   "There is some factual basis for it"

Literally "the matter has legs," this Talmudic expression is an elegant way of saying that something may indeed be the truth.

— ❦ —

Rashá, pl. reshaím (Ashkenazi: **Róshe, pl. reshóim**)   Wicked man

"I can just sense deep down that he's a *rasha* . . ."

Rasha isn't exactly an expletive (when one talks about Hebrew four-letter words, one is referring to Divine names . . .), but it's fairly strong stuff. Commonly used of biblical Haman (*Haman ha-Rasha*) and the Roman general Titus, responsible for torching the Temple (*Titus ha-Rasha*).

    For referring to more recent nasties, see *yimach shemo*.

Four types of person are called *rasha*: he who raises his hand against his fellow, he who borrows and will not pay, the arrogant, and the quarrelsome.

The Midrash

From *reshaim* comes forth *resha* [wickedness].

First Book of Samuel 24:13

Not only is he who hates others a *rasha*—so too is he who hates himself.

Rabbi Menachem Mendel of Kotzk

— ❧ —

Rav, pl. rabaním (Ashkenazi: **Rav** or **Rov**, pl. **rabónim**)   Rabbi (of a synagogue)

"I hear his brother's been appointed *rav* of that new synagogue in Newton."

Every Jew in America or Israel can probably open an old family photo album and point to at least one "rabbi." This is largely because everyone whose great-grandfather had a *yarmulka* and a beard assumes that he was one.

However, the traditional significance of rabbi is that you have received ordination (see *smicha*). In the Old Country, this generally meant that you then became the rabbi of a community, that is, you became a *rav*. And the Orthodox still call their communal rabbis *rav* (or *rov*).

When non-Orthodox Judaism evolved its own ordination, it too began creating "rabbis"—and much conflict with the Orthodox.

Incidentally, "rabbi" is based on the old Hebrew title *rabbi* or *rebbi*, meaning "my rabbi"; see *rabbi* and *rebbe*.

A big *rav* in Vilna was approached by a servant girl with a *shayle* (question): "Please, sir, what shall I make for supper?"

The *rav* thought for a moment. "My dear, go and make *lokshn* [noodles]."

Everyone present was flummoxed at the *shayle* and at the *rav*'s answer—but not the *rav*'s wife:

"It was obvious," she said. "The servant girl must have asked her mistress what to cook for supper, and her mistress must have lost her temper, and shouted, 'Why are you asking me! Go ask the *rav*!'—and she of course didn't know any better and did just that."

— ❧ —

Reayá (Ashkenazi: **Ráaye**)   Proof

"They say the crossing's safe because no one's been killed there yet? That's no *raaye*!"

Reaya is a word out of the world of Talmud study, where everything's a matter of proof and counterproof.

— ✿ —

Rébbe, pl. **rebbéyim**   (Chasidic) rabbi-leader

"I say we go to the *rebbe* for advice. Perhaps he'll give us a *bracha* (blessing)."

The *rebbe* is no ordinary rabbi. Nowhere is there a seminary that trains or ordains *rebbeyim*. You have to receive a call based on your pedigree and/or your saintly qualities. A *rebbe* is a charismatic rabbi-leader of one of the many Chasidic groups found formerly in eastern Europe, virtually wiped out by Hitler and Stalin, but now reviving in Israel and the United States. (See *Chasid*.) A *rebbe* is credited with extraordinary powers of counsel. His blessings are sought after. One of the most revered *rebbeyim* is Rabbi Menachem Mendel Schneerson, the Lubavitcher Rebbe based in Brooklyn, New York.

The navi [prophet] *sees the future.*
The rebbe sees the present.
Sometimes it is harder to see the present than the future.

Rabbi Naftoli of Roptchitz

. . . my husband asked him: "How may a man come to this experience of the Divine?" The tutor whispered to him, "Let your honor make a journey to my *rebbe*, and he will know this and much more."

S. Y. Agnon

I would listen to them as night fell—between the prayers of Minha and Maariv—in the House of Study filled with the flickering shadows of yellow candles. The Elders spoke of the Great Masters as though they had known them personally. Each had his favorite *Rebbe* and a legend he liked above all others. I came to feel that I was forever listening to the same story about the same *Rebbe*. Only the names of people and places changed.

Elie Wiesel

— ✿ —

Rechilút (Ashkenazi: **Rechílus**)   Tattling

"Tell me again what she said about me—no, don't, it's just *rechilut*."

Like *leshon ha-ra* (see entry), *rechilut* is deemed a very serious offense in Judaism. Technically, *rechilut* means reporting back to someone what others have said about him or her, "mixing it" in common parlance.

— ✿ —

Refuá shlemá! (Ashkenazi: **Refúe shléyme!**)   A speedy recovery; "Get well soon!"

"Don't forget to wish your sister a *refua shlema* from all of us."

"Look after yourself, Alec, and *refua shlema*!"

Jews have been saying *refua shlema* since as far back as Second Temple times. Literally "a complete recovery," it is used for both major and minor illnesses. In synagogue, the reader may also "make a *refua shlema* for someone," that is, say a prayer for a sick person, mentioning their Hebrew name and the Hebrew name of their mother.

May it be Your will, Lord our God and God of our fathers, to send speedily a *refua shlema* from heaven, a healing of the spirit and a healing of the body, to the sick person _____ son/daughter of _____ among the sick of Your people, Israel.

Translation of a traditional prayer for the sick

Réga!   "One moment!"

"Oh no, the bus is going! Driver, *rega rega!*"

If Mexico is a *mañana* society, Israel is a *rega* society. The bureaucrat simply flicks slowly through your file and soothingly says *rega . . .*

But there is another *rega*, the *rega* that puts *you* in control: It stops taxis, halts trains in their tracks, and keeps the doors of buses open that extra moment for you to effect a miraculous exit. It is generally said recursively: *rega rega rega . . .*

Ribít (Ashkenazi: **Ríbis**)   Interest payments

"Don't worry, the community won't charge you any *ribit* on a loan they make you."

Ribit is the dirtiest word in Hebrew. Charging *ribit* on personal loans is deemed one of the basest of practices—even demanding or accepting favors after making a personal loan is considered *ribit*. (Jewish Law does, however, make special provisions for commercial interest.)

Why are the laws of *ribit* set down in the *Yoreh Deah* code, which deals among other things with *kosher* and non-*kosher* food? Surely to make the point that non-*kosher* money is just as prohibited as non-*kosher* food.

Attributed to Rabbi Sholom Shwadron, the *Maggid* of Jerusalem

Ribonó shel olám (Ashkenazi: **Ribóhno shel óhlom**)   Lord of the Universe

"Don't let it depress you. The *Ribono shel olam* has His own ways . . ."

"*Ribono shel olam!* How can they have *Chanukah* lights *and* a tree!"

Compare *olam* in *Olam ha-ba*, "The World to Come."

This is one of many intimate names for the Almighty that have been passed down the ages. It is common also among old-timers as an invocation or exclamation.

Rikudím   (Jewish/Israeli) dancing

"I hope there'll be *rikudim* at your *Bar Mitzvah* after the dinner."

Rikudim is just the regular Hebrew word for dancing, but to most Jews outside Israel *rikudim* is synonymous with horas, debkas, *Ushavtem Mayim, Od Nashuva,* and all the other folk dances that have become so-called Israeli dancing. *Rikudim* is a favorite at Y's, summer camps, and fitness centers. They say it's also coming back into fashion in Israel.

Rishón, pl. **Rishoním** (Ashkenazi: **Ríshen**, pl. **Rishóhnim**)   Medieval Torah authorities

"What was the attitude of other *Rishonim* to Maimonides and his philosophy?"

See also *Acharonim*, "Latter-day scholars."

What the Mishna took for granted, the Talmud had to spell out. And what the Talmud transcribes in a kind of live debate, the *Rishonim*, the medieval scholars, tried to codify and justify. The *Rishonim* were the giants of medieval Judaism: Rashi, Yehuda Halevi, Maimonides, Ramban, the Tosaphists . . . Then came the *Acharonim*, the "latter-day scholars."

In some ways, Jews have liked to see their history as downhill all the way—until the Messiah comes to fish them out of the stew they've gotten themselves into. The same goes for their intellectual history: downhill or uphill, depending on how you look at it.

Rosh Chódesh (Ashkenazi: **Rosh Chóhdesh**)   New Moon

"Wow, it's *Rosh Chodesh Adar* on Tuesday—only two weeks now till *Purim!*"

Literally "beginning of the month," that is, the new moon, *Rosh Chodesh* certainly feels like it should be a special day—there are much longer morning prayers, with a festive feel about them. Yet people go about their normal business, and that's that. No one seems to dress up, there are no special ceremonies, and there seem to be no special foods, although if men were to do all the housework, as was the custom in some places, there might certainly be something different about the food.

But *Rosh Chodesh* certainly helps you keep your bearings in the Jewish year. Come *Rosh Chodesh Nisan* (the beginning of the month of *Nisan*) and you know that Passover is just two weeks away; come *Rosh Chodesh Kislev* and it'll soon be *Chanukah*.

— ❧ —

Rosh ha-Shaná, commonly spelled **Rosh Hashanah** (Ashkenazi: **Rosh ha-Shóne**)   The New Year

"Frank always takes off for *Rosh Hashanah* and *Yom Kippur*."

The autumn festival of *Rosh Hashanah* is a New Year festival, but a serious one, with none of the revelry of December 31, and with a high moral tone instead. It is above all the Day of Judgment, spent largely (and still by a large proportion of Jews) at the synagogue in prayers of reverence and awe punctuated by the wail of the *shofar* (ram's horn). At home, there is a buoyant mood, scores of New Year cards from people you only hear from at *Rosh Hashanah*, and apple dipped in honey for a sweet new year. On Wall Street, trading is quieter than usual.

Rosh Hashanah among our Chasidic Jews is always a joyful festival. We are not frightened of the Day of Judgment. We know that we stand not in the presence of an alien overlord, but of our Father. Our Father in Heaven judges us! So we take a drink! And we dance at our prayers.

Yitzchak Leib Peretz

— ❧ —

Rúach   Spiritual atmosphere

"Didn't that singing group make a great *ruach* at the *simcha* [celebration]!"

See *Ruchniut*, "Spirituality."

Ruach is one of those words which, if you know their meaning already, seem to say it in their very sound.

In the Bible, *ruach* is "wind" and also the "spirit" that God breathed into the first human. Nowadays, by a nice extension, *ruach* is that spiritedness people love to create at parties and celebrations by singing Israeli songs or Chasidic *nigunim*, dancing the hora, and playing a guitar or a keyboard.

– ୨୧ୠ –

Rúach ha-kódesh (Ashkenazi: Rúach ha-kóhdesh)   The Holy Spirit

"They say that their *rebbe* had *ruach ha-kodesh* . . ."

Ruach ha-kodesh is the highest degree of godliness thought to be possible in this day and age—or since the end of prophecy in ancient times. Those rare individuals credited with *ruach ha-kodesh* could foresee, forewarn, inspire, and have generally left behind remarkable works of Torah. Folk talk in hushed tones about who has or who had *ruach ha-kodesh*. I name no names.

Rabbi Shneur Zalman used to say:
"Never mind *nisim* [miracles]! Never mind *nevues* [prophecies]! If you had visited my teacher, the holy *maggid* of Mezeritch, you could have imbibed *ruach ha-kodesh* by the bucketful, and *nisim* were lying around there under your bench, but we were just so engrossed in Torah that we never had the time to pick them up!"

– ୨୧ୠ –

Ruchniút (Ashkenazi: Rúchnies)   Spirituality

"We have to put some *ruchniut* back into our lives in suburbia."

In *ruchniut* and *gashmiut*—"spirituality" and "materiality"—Judaism might appear to have two opposites: the one good and the other rather bad. But Judaism has always stressed the need in this world for the two of them, in a consecrated and healthy tension. One expression of *ruchniut* is *Yom Kippur*, on which there is no eating, drinking, or marital relationships; but another is *Shabbat*, with its bread, wine, meat, and general good cheer—a perfect backdrop to prayer, study, and all manner of "spiritual" activities.

In *gashmiut* (materiality), where there is fear there is no joy and where there is joy there is no fear.

In *ruchniut*, fear, love, and joy dwell together.

Rabbi Israel Baal Shem Tov

– ୨୧ୠ –

Rut [rhymes with "foot"] (Ashkenazi: **Rus**)   The Book of Ruth

Rut, or *Megilat Rut* ("the Scroll of Ruth"), as it is often known, is one of
five short biblical books that are traditionally recited once a year in the
synagogue, each on a different festival or fast: *Shir ha-Shirim* on *Pesach,*
Rut on *Shavuot, Echa* on *Tisha be-Av, Kohelet* on *Sukkot,* and *Esther* on
Purim.

   A charming tale of simple country life, tragedy, and romance, *Megi-
lat Rut* is read on the festival of *Shavuot,* which commemorates the
Revelation of the Torah—and fittingly: The heroine, Ruth, becomes an
Israelite and ultimately an ancestress of King David himself.

– ✣ –

Sabra. See Tsabár.

– ✣ –

Sandák (Ashkenazi: **Sándek**)   Person who holds the baby during the
circumcision

"I thought for a moment that the *sandek* was going to pass out, but he
was just closing his eyes and saying something."

The greatest honor at a *brit mila* (circumcision) is to be given the baby
to hold on one's lap while the *brit mila* is performed. The person who
has the honor is called the *sandek* and will normally be a learned or
otherwise important person.

– ✣ –

Satán (Ashkenazi: **Sóten**)   Satan

"We had such difficulties raising money for that clinic—as if the *Satan*
were trying to screw things up."

The Hebrew *satan* and the English Satan may share the same spelling,
but that's where all similarity ends. *Satan* is no Devil, no figure of
dread and evil. He's just one of God's faithful angels with a job to do:
to test a person's sincerity, to sow obstacles in one's path, and to play
the prosecutor on high. A projection, if you like, of our *yetser ha-ra.*

   The word *satan* in the Bible is a common noun meaning simply
"adversary."

The *Satan* only accuses in times of danger.

The Jerusalem Talmud, Shabbat

God's reproach upon you, *Satan*!

Oriental Jewish reproach to those who lose their temper

– ᆋᇔ –

Savlanút   Patience

"*Savlanut*, ladies and gentlemen! We are assured that our speaker will be here very shortly."

The welfare of the State of Israel is predicated on two ideals. One has absorbed the energies of its greatest politicians, thinkers, and educators. The other hasn't. One is called Zionism; the other is called *savlanut*.

– ᆋᇔ –

Sechách   Greenery for covering the *sukkah*

"Don't try using sycamore for *sechach* for the *sukkah*—it'll shrivel within a couple of days."

See *Sukkah*, "Booth."

Sechach is one of the hardest Hebrew words to pronounce, so it's fortunate people only talk about it once a year, at the festival of *Sukkot*. *Sechach* is the vegetation, or even ex-vegetation, that you use for roofing your *sukkah* (see entry)—in fact, it's what makes a *sukkah* a *sukkah*. The best *sechach* is evergreen foliage, such as pine and especially laurel. I myself use reusable bamboo, but anything will do as long as it gives you proper cover and it's not at the expense of a tropical rain forest.

– ᆋᇔ –

Séchel   Common sense

"The car won't start? Well, don't keep on pumping it. Use a bit of *sechel*."

There's no need to say anything lofty or spiritual about *sechel*. It denotes plain old common sense.

For *sechel* a person should be praised.

Book of Proverbs

A person's *sechel* does not depend on their wisdom but on their actions.

Rabbi Moshe of Kobryn

– ᆋᇔ –

Séder, pl. **sedarím** (Ashkenazi: **Séyder**, pl. **sdórim**)   Commemorative ceremonies on Passover evening

"We have twelve people coming to our *Seder!* Who are you having for *Seder* night?"

See also *Be-seder*, "OK" and *Haggadah*, "Passover Story."

Every year, on the first evening of the Passover festival, Jews gather at home for the *Seder* night: to retell the story of slavery and exodus that was the birth of the Jewish people—and to drink four glasses of wine, to eat *matzo*, bitter herbs, *charoset*, and to join in all manner of other customs that go to make a remarkable evening. Although *Seder* means "order (of ceremonies)" and there is a customary text, the whole thing is also gloriously informal. Much of it is aimed at the kids, who respond either by keeping it going till two in the morning or by sleeping through the whole thing.

Why is the *Seder* the most widely observed event in the traditional Jewish year (together with *Yom Kippur*)? Perhaps because it's about the birth of a nation, perhaps also because it has always brought together the whole *mishpacha* (extended family).

Sefardí, pl. **Sefardím**, commonly spelled **Sephardi** (Ashkenazi: **Sfárdi**, pl. **Sfárdim**)   a. Jew of Mediterranean or Mideastern background; b. Pertaining to Jews of Mediterranean or Mideastern background

"If she's marrying a *Sefardi*, then she'll have to take on all the *Sefardi* customs."

In its narrowest sense, *Sefardi* refers to Spanish and Portuguese Jews, claiming descent from the medieval Jews of Iberia banished and scattered some 500 years ago—still maintaining their ancient Spanish language in Turkey and the Balkans up until modern times and exceedingly proud of being *Sefardim tehorim*, "pure Sefardim." But in a broader sense, all Mediterranean and Eastern Jews—be they Moroccan, Baghdadi, Yemenite, or whatever—like to call themselves *Sefardim*, by virtue of sharing the same basic heritage of religious customs as laid down by Maimonides nearly 800 years ago.

Séfer, pl. **sfarím** (Ashkenazi: **Séyfer**, pl. **sfórim**)   Religious book

"So what should we give him for his *Bar Mitzvah*, money or a *sefer*?"

A *sefer* is not just like any other book in Jewish Law and folklore: If it falls, you rush to pick it up and kiss it. You don't sit on it or lean on it. There are even customs about keeping it in the marital bedroom. And when a *sefer* reaches the end of its life, you don't just rip it up or toss it in the garbage—you take it to a synagogue to be buried.

This use of the word *sefer* is a Diaspora use. (To Israelis, *sefer* simply means book.) And it speaks for the spiritual charge with which Yiddish endowed the Hebrew language—using the Germanic word *bukh* for secular books, and keeping the Hebrew word for religious books, as indeed it did for most things Jewish.

Séfer toráh, pl. **sifréy toráh** (Ashkenazi: **Séyfer tóre**, pl. **sífrey tóre**) Torah scroll

"Two of the oldest *sifrey torah* in the ark were brought over from Slovakia."

A *sefer torah* is the most sacred object in modern-day Jewish life. It contains the *Torah* (Five Books of Moses), written by a scribe on a scroll of parchment, mounted on wooden rollers, or housed in a casing, and robed and adorned in splendor. When it is brought out of the Holy Ark, people stand, bow, and kiss it. It is read aloud every few days, and to read it with the correct chant and pronunciation is a great art.

A new *sefer torah* was being dedicated in the synagogue. Reb Dovid Moshe of Tchortkov held it joyously in his arms and exulted. But it was a very large *sefer torah* and extremely heavy. His Chasidim clamored to offer to take it from him.

"No, no," said Reb Dovid, "once you have it in your arms, it just doesn't weigh you down."

Sefirát ha-Ómer (Ashkenazi: **Sfíres ho-Óhmer**)   The Counting of the Omer; the Omer period

"Have you done *Sefirat ha-Omer* today, Alan? It's the twenty-third day."

"You can't have the wedding then, because it's during the *Sefirat ha-Omer*."

For forty-nine days in the spring, Jews traditionally count down the days leading from Passover to the festival of *Shavuot*—that being the long-awaited date on which the Torah was revealed to the Israelites.

The countdown, and the period itself, is called the *Sefira*, literally "counting," or more fully the *Sefirat ha-Omer*, "the counting of the measure" (the measure being the measure of barley offered on Passover in the Temple). Every evening, one declares in Hebrew: "Today is the —th day of the Omer."

At the same time, the *Omer* period has sad historical associations; and so festivities are prohibited, at least until the day of *Lag ba-Omer* (see entry).

Today is twenty-four days, which make three weeks and three days of the *Omer*.

An example of the daily Hebrew *Sefirat ha-Omer* count

— 🙦🙦 —

Segulá, pl. segulót (Ashkenazi: **Sgúle, pl. sgúles**)   Charm

"Did she really ask you for a *segula* for an easy labor?"

The old books are full of *segulot* for all manner of crises, troubles, and misfortunes. They can involve saying *pesukim* (biblical verses) or special actions or both. Don't think they're history: In Ultraorthodox and other traditional circles, *segulot* are alive and well. In fact, a friend of mine claimed to have recovered from hepatitis with a *segula* that involved placing doves on his navel.

A *segula* for women to have easy childbirth:
    They should eat something on every Saturday night for the *mitzvah* of the *Melaveh Malka* meal, and also say aloud "toward the *mitzvah* of the *Melaveh Malka* meal," and thus they will give birth easily with God's help.

Rabbi Avrohom Yitzchok Sperling

— 🙦🙦 —

Selichót (Ashkenazi: **Slíches**)   Prayers for forgiveness

"The first *Selichot* service will be on Saturday night at 12 P.M. in the synagogue."

A few days before *Rosh Hashanah* (the Jewish New Year), synagogues all around the world are opened at the crack of dawn for the faithful to say *Selichot*, prayers for forgiveness. For this is the season of repentance, continuing through to *Yom Kippur*.

The opening *Selichot* service is actually on Saturday night at midnight, and in some places it has become something of a choral spectacular, attracting both the faithful and the less-than-faithful.

— 🙦🙦 —

Sephardi. See **Sefardi.**

— ✤ —

Se'udá (Ashkenazi: **Súde**)   Festive meal

"Who are you inviting for the *Purim se'uda*?"

See *Se'uda shlishit*, "Third Sabbath Meal."

The idea of a *se'uda* is as ancient as the Israelites. It was with a *se'uda* that they marked their liberation from Egypt. And there isn't a Sabbath or festival or any kind of religious celebration—*Brit Mila*, *Bar Mitzvah*, *Weddings*, and so on—that isn't celebrated with a *se'uda*. (See the entry *ruchniut*, "spirituality.") Even the fast of Yom Kippur has a *se'uda*, two in fact: one before the fast and one after the fast.

— ✤ —

Se'udá Shlishít (Ashkenazi: **Sháleshúdes**)   The Third Sabbath Meal

"It's beginning to get dark, so we'd better begin *Se'uda Shlishit*. Where's the herring?"

The *Se'uda Shlishit* has powerful associations for anyone who has experienced this traditional Sabbath custom. It's not just "a third meal," which is what the words literally mean—it's the intimate meal or snack taken in the twilight, at home or in the synagogue, as the Sabbath begins to slip away. Wistful Hebrew spirituals, the Twenty-third Psalm, *chulluh* and herring, bits of this and bits of that, Chasidic tales and a *devar Torah*. Jewish blues.

I come to do the *mitzvah* of the *Se'uda Shlishit* of *Shabbat* in commemoration of Jacob, father of a throng of seventy souls. By his virtue may we be spared the wars of Gog and Magog and merit the fulfillment of the verse "And I shall feed you the heritage of Jacob your father, a heritage that has no bounds . . ."
Introductory Hebrew words to the *Se'uda Shlishit* meal

— ✤ —

Sha'atnéz (Ashkenazi: **Shátnes**)   Forbidden mix of wool and linen

"You'll need to have this coat tested for *sha'atnez*."

The Bible prohibits the wearing of garments containing *sha'atnez*, any admixture of wool and linen, and Orthodox Jews still keep it up.

Like observing *kosher*, observing *sha'atnez* has gone high tech, and unavoidably so. Not so long ago, you simply went to your local tailor and said, "Make me a kosher wool suit, Morrie," and he would ensure that there was no linen in the collars or the buttonholes or whatever. Nowadays, the Orthodox will probably buy their jackets or coats off the rack—and that means either going to a special *sha'atnez*-free store or else spending a few dollars on sending your new garment to a *sha'atnez*-testing laboratory for seams to be opened and fibers tested under the microscope.

You shall not wear *sha'atnez*, wool and linen together.

Deuteronomy

Non-Shatnes.
Shatnes-Laboratory.
203 Lee Ave, Brooklyn, NY.

Legend on a *shatnes*-tested jacket

– ৩৫৯৯ –

Shabbát (Ashkenazi: **Shábes**)   Sabbath

"What time does *Shabbat* come in this Friday?"

Shabbat is one Hebrew word for which no English translation exists. The word Sabbath itself is no more than a pale transliteration.

   Shabbat calls a halt to a Jew's *melacha* (creative work) and makes twenty-five hours' time for study, prayer, and sanctified eating, drinking, and relaxing.

   The word itself is intriguing. It seems to be based on a verb meaning "to rest," but at the same time it echoes the word for seven, *sheva* . . .

What is *Shabbat*? A reminder of every man's royalty; an abolition of the distinction of master and slave, rich and poor, success and failure.

Abraham Joshua Heschel

If the Jewish people were properly to keep *Shabbat* twice in succession, Redemption would swiftly follow.

The Talmud, Shabbat

Seen on a car bumper sticker:
   This car runs on gas, not on Shabes

– ৩৫৯৯ –

Shabbát Shalóm!   Literally "Sabbath of Peace." A greeting used instead of "hi" or "bye" when Jews meet on the Sabbath

There is something soothing and restful in the words *Shabbat Shalom*. In the alliterative *sh* . . . and in the meaning of these two words and their associations: *Shabbat*, "Sabbath" echoes the Hebrew verb meaning "to stop work," and *shalom* means "peace." For traditional Jews, the *Shabbat* means banishing any workaday worries and concentrating the mind on prayer, study, and the enjoyments of food and love. The Sabbath is, in fact, perceived as a mystical foretaste of the messianic days to come, of a time when the whole world will be at peace.

Shabbat, Shabbat, *whence comest thou?*
Shalom *to you, maiden, how fair thy face!*
Thy face is comely, thou art a rich garden,
All who are sick shall gaze on thee and live.
Shabbat shalom, Shabbat shalom!

> From a Hebrew poem by Moshe Hayyim Luzzato

— ❧ —

Shacharít (Ashkenazi: **Sháchris**)   Morning prayers

"You'll have to get up at 6:45 if you want to say *Shacharit* before you go to work."

Traditionally, group prayer is held three times a day: mornings (*Shacharit*), afternoons (*Mincha*), and evenings (*Ma'ariv*). Early each morning, in every Israeli neighborhood—and more than a few American ones—you can see men heading for synagogue, clutching bags containing their *tallit* and *tefilin*. Forty minutes later, they'll be on their way to work. But *Shacharit* comes first.

Rabbi Yisroel of Rizhyn was visiting the Rabbi of Apt. As was his custom, he let a large part of the morning go by before reciting *Shacharit*. "*Nu? Well?*" his disciples asked him impatiently—but all he could do was to shrug his shoulders and tell this story:
  A king had arranged a fixed time for his subjects to come for a free hearing. Once a beggar turned up at a different time and asked to see the king. The guards growled. Did he not know the ruling? The beggar nodded dismissively: "That's only for those asking for their own needs; but I want to speak to the king about the country's needs." They promptly let him in.
  "And so," Rabbi Yisroel concluded, "how can I tell when I should say *Shacharit?*"

— ❧ —

Shadchán (Ashkenazi: **Shádchen**)   Matchmaker. See **Shiduch**.

— ❧ —

Sháleshúdes   The Third Sabbath Meal. See **Se'uda Shlishit**.

— ❧ —

Shalíach, pl. shlichím   Israeli emissary

"That new *shaliach* from Israel came to give a talk on Bible history to our youth group."

See *Sheliach tsibur*, "Prayer leader."

Literally "messengers," *shlichim* are sent in scores from Israel to every land of the Diaspora. In the best of all possible worlds, they would simply be spending a couple of years teaching about life and culture in Israel in order to encourage Diaspora support and immigration. In practice, however, the *shaliach* and his wife will be the workhorses of local Jewish education—sometimes, sadly, they are the only Jewish educators in town.

— ❧❧ —

Shalóm!   "Hello!," "Good-bye" (literally "Peace!")

See also *Shalom alechem*, "Greetings!", *Shelom bayit*, "Peace in the home."

Words get eroded through constant use. May *shalom* be spared.

Shalom is an ancient Talmudic greeting. In the Bible, it meant "all is well." The rabbis taught that it is also a name of God. Throughout the centuries, Jews have greeted each other with *shalom alechem*, "peace be upon you." With the revival of spoken Hebrew at the beginning of this century, the standard "How are you?" became—and still is—*ma shlomcha* and *ma shlomech* (to men and women, respectively).

It is a cheering thought that Jew and Arab use almost identical greetings, testifying to a linguistic kinship. The Arabic is *salemmoo aleekum*.

When meeting someone, be the first to say *shalom*.

The Talmud, Avot

The Hebrew word for peace, *shalom*, is derived from a root denoting wholeness or completeness, and its frame of reference throughout Jewish literature is bound up with the notion of *shelemut*, perfection. Its significance is thus not limited to the political domain—to the absence of war and enmity—or to the social—to the absence of quarrel and strife. It ranges over several spheres and can refer in different contexts to bounteous physical conditions, to a moral value, and, ultimately, to a cosmic principle and divine attribute.

Aviezer Ravitzky

May the Lord raise His face unto you and give you *shalom*.

The finale of the biblical priestly blessing

— ❧❧ —

Shalóm alechém! (Ashkenazi: **Shólem aléychem!**) "Greetings!"

"Rabbi Lefkowitz, *sholem aleychem!*
  Aleychem sholem, Rachel!"

Shalom alechem has been in use for at least 2,000 years, and is still in active service in traditionalist-minded circles. Literally "peace upon you," it is said when meeting someone—generally for the first time in a while. You respond by repeating *alechem shalom!* ("upon you peace").

  Shalom alechem is less common than it used to be, though. As for Israel, the usual greeting there is simply *shalom!*

  Sholem (or *Sholom*) *Aleichem* is familiar also as the name of the great Yiddish-Hebrew author of the original story of *Fiddler on the Roof.* In fact, it was his nom de plume—a kind of Mr. How Ya Doin'?

— 🙦🙤 —

Shalóm zachár (Ashkenazi: **Shólem zócher**) Friday night drinks on the birth of a boy

"Mr. and Mrs. Dan Levy invite the congregation to a *sholem zocher* at 8:30 P.M."

It is a custom among the Orthodox to mark the first Friday night after the birth of a boy by throwing a small party, called a *sholem zocher*. This curious name seems to translate literally "peace of the male" (nothing, nothing at all to do with the *brit mila*), and seems to express the hope that one more Jewish male child in the world means more peace and not more war.

  What makes a *sholem zocher* curiously different from any other party are the bowls of boiled chick-peas on the tables—a food of mourning, symbol (it is said) of the fact that the soul has been born willy-nilly into this hard world and has had to forget all the Torah it once knew.

— 🙦🙤 —

Shamásh (Ashkenazi: **Shámes**) a. Synagogue usher; b. Extra light from which the Chanukah lights are lit

"You don't have a prayer book, Nancy? So ask the *shames* for one."

"Light the *shames* first, Judah."

Rejoice! The American Heritage Dictionary actually lists the word *shammes*, and defines it as a "beadle" or a "sexton." I must confess that

I'm not quite sure what a beadle or a sexton does, but I'm pretty sure *they* don't hand out prayer books, prayer shawls or yarmulkes, let alone ask people their Hebrew name when they are about to be called up, or shush people when the rabbi's going to make a speech.

But king of the *shameses* was the *shames* who served the Chasidic rabbis of the Old Country. A combination of receptionist and bouncer, his self-selected role in life was to protect the *rebbe* from the contact with the great masses that he craved.

The *menorah* (candelabra) lit on the festival of *Chanukah* has eight branches or holders, for the eight lights, plus an extra one for the *shames*—the "servant" light, lit as an extra light lest one make profane use of the "real" lights.

When you come to a town and wish to size up the townsfolk, size up the *shamashim*. If they are good and wise, so too are the townsfolk. If they are not, neither are the townsfolk.

Rabbi Pinchas of Koretz

Shaná tová! (Ashkenazi: **Shóne tóhve!**)   "A Happy New Year!"

"*Shana tova*, Cheryl, and wish all your family *Shana tova* too."

As *Rosh Hashanah* (the Jewish New Year) approaches in the early autumn, people begin to wish each other *Shana tova!* (literally "a good year"), and go on doing so through the festival. Some may also send *Shana tova* cards.

Among the Orthodox, a series of other greetings is preferred. See *ketiva ve-chatima tova!* and *gmar chatima tova!*

Shas   The Mishna and Talmud

"What? His father-in-law didn't buy him a *Shas* for his wedding present?"

"The first-year students learn *Shas* and *Chumash-Rashi*."

Shas denotes the two ancient anthologies of Jewish Law and ideas, the *Mishna* and the *Gemara* (see entries). When you've reached the age of *Bar Mitzvah*, you're a man—but when you start studying *Shas*, you're a MAN.

A set of *Shas* can typically take up some twenty bulky volumes, stretching right across many a living room. A wonderful wedding present for a son-in-law. You can also buy a mini-*Shas* to take with you on vacation, but then half of the things on the page—which are already printed in small enough type in the big edition—become positively microscopic. They say that the *Shas* will soon be available on CD-Rom, but I myself am waiting for the interactive video version that allows you to talk back to it.

— ✄ —

Shátnes. See **Sha'atnez.**

— ✄ —

Shavúa tov! "Have a good week!"

"Is *Shabbat* out? *Shavua tov*, everyone!"

On Saturday evening, once *Shabbat* (the Sabbath) is over, Israelis say to one another *Shavua tov!* "a good week!"—the new Jewish week has now begun, buses are a-running, cars a-honking, and millions of dishes are sitting in the sink about to be washed up.

Shavua tov! is also becoming widespread around the Jewish world. When Sephardim say it, a traditional response is *Eliyahu ha-Navi zachur la-tov!* "Elijah the Prophet, may his memory be a boon" (see the entry *Eliyahu ha-Navi*).

— ✄ —

Shavuót (Ashkenazi: **Shvúes**)   The festival of Shavuot

"I can still remember the cheesecake last *Shavuot* . . ."

See *Tikun Leyl Shavuot.*

Shavuot is a biblical festival in the late spring, marking the giving of the *Torah* and—more so in Israel—the first fruits of summer. *Shavuot* is cheesecake and other milky foods (*Torah* is like mother's milk), scent-laden flowers decorating the synagogue, marathon through-the-night study sessions (called *Tikun Leyl Shavuot*), and loads and loads of sleep to cope with it all. It all lasts just a day or two, and most nonreligious Jews don't see it and don't know it.

— ✄ —

Sháyle   Ritual question to a rabbi. See **She'elá.**

— ✄ —

Shechiná (Ashkenazi: **Shechíne**)   The Divine Presence

"When you visited his grandmother on *Shabbat* and saw the candles burning, you felt like the *Shechina* was there in the room."

The *Shechina* is an ancient name for God's presence, felt at certain times, or by certain people, or in certain places, and above all in His "dwelling place," the *Bet ha-Mikdash* that stood in Jerusalem. For as long as the Jews have been in exile, the *Shechina* has generally been thought of as exiled too, only dimly operative to keep the Jewish people and the world in existence.

The *Shechina* does not move from the *Kotel Ma'aravi* [the Western Wall].

The Midrash on Exodus

The *Shechina* does not dwell amid sadness but only amid *simcha shel mitsva* [joy at performing commandments].

The Talmud, Shabbat

. . . suddenly, in the midst of the day, as I was studying tractate Yevamot [of the Talmud] in the name of the eternal God, in order to adorn the *Shechina* with all my might, a great light fell upon me. The whole house became filled with light, a marvelous light, the *Shechina* resting there. This was the first time in my life that I had some little taste of His light, may He be blessed . . .

The Secret Diary of Rabbi Isaac Eizik of Komarno

— ❧ —

Shechitá (Ashkenazi: **Shechíte**)   *Kosher* slaughter. See **Shochet**.

— ❧ —

She'elá, pl. **she'elót** (Ashkenazi: **Sháyle**, pl. **sháyles**)   A ritual question to a rabbi

"What, you're calling the rabbi at 11 P.M. with a *she'ela* about a turkey!"

Once upon a time, *she'elot* were every rabbi's bread and butter. At any time of day or night, men, women or children might knock at his door with a *she'ela*: *she'elot* about kosher food, about Passover cleaning, about *Bar Mitzvahs*, about marriage, about anything.

"I found a reddish spot in this egg. Is it kosher?" "We found an old Hebrew book. Shall we bury it?" "So-and-so died and his in-laws have to come from Minsk. Can we delay the funeral?" "Mrs. X is in labor. Can we say charms for her?"

When he didn't know, he would ask a "bigger" rabbi than he. And there were known to be rabbis who were strict in their interpretation of the law, and others who were more lenient . . .

An English rabbi in Middlesborough was asked by the synagogue management to explain why he could always be seen at his desk studying all through the night.

"I have to study the Torah," he pointed out. "I might be asked a *shayle.*"
The management were astonished. "But when we appointed you, we thought you'd studied the Torah already!"

— ❧ —

She-hecheyánu (Ashkenazi: **Shecheyónu**)   Blessing for a happy event

"What a beautiful coat! It's really something to say *she-hecheyanu* over."

On happy events—when becoming a parent, when tasting a new fruit in season, when putting on an expensive new garment for the first time or buying a new car, when first performing some *mitzvah* in season, such as lighting the festival candles or hearing the *shofar*—a Jew traditionally says the beautiful blessing known as *She-hecheyanu* (literally "who has kept us alive").

Blessed are You, Lord, our God, Ruler of the Universe, Who has kept us alive, preserved us, and brought us to this season.

Translation of the She-hecheyanu blessing

— ❧ —

Shéket!   "Quiet!"

"OK, guys, *sheket!* I want you all back at the bus in forty-five minutes, got it?"

Its bright new Israeli sound came as a welcome substitute for the old Yiddish silencer *sha!* Three generations of American Jewish children have been schooled on the word *sheket!*—for many, the one word of spoken Hebrew that they remember from their Jewish school or their summer camp.

— ❧ —

Shelíach tsibúr (Ashkenazi: **Shlíech tsíbur**)   Prayer leader

"We're lucky that quite a few of our members can act as *sheliach tsibur.*"

Wherever Jews pray as a congregation, they choose a *sheliach tsibur*, literally "a representative of the community," to stand in front and lead the prayers, or part of the prayers.

It's no easy job being the *sheliach tsibur*: Not only must you keep the worshippers in sync (no mean feat among Ashkenazim, who have an ancient tendency toward religious individualism), you must also be prepared for half of them to say you were too quick and the others that you were too slow. But you can console yourself with the thought that if you were a professional cantor they'd be asking why they're paying you to pray like this.

... the model, and possibly the actual source, for the "representative of the community" in prayer is the prophet who prayed for his people. The exemplary individual prays for his community because of his superior gifts, but his prayer is also uniquely potent because the claims of the community as a whole, as a *tsibur*, crystallize in him as its representative.

Gerald Blidstein

Shelom báyit (Ashkenazi: **Shólem báyis**)   Peace in the home

"Come on, let's make up. *Shelom bayit!*"

In the list of *mitzvot* commanded in the Torah, you won't find *shelom bayit*, but it is a value that underwrites the whole of Jewish life: whether it's making the home bright on *Shabbat* or keeping the peace between husband and wife. Even God told a white lie to Abraham about Sarah to prevent a row between the childless couple and maintain *shelom bayit*.

A woman used to attend Rabbi Meir's Friday evening *drasha* [sermon]. Once he spoke longer than usual. She returned to find the house in darkness and an irate husband. "You won't enter this house until you go and spit at that preacher," he yelled. Three weeks later, her neighbors persuaded her to return to Rabbi Meir—who knew all . . . "I have a sore eye," he said. "I need someone who knows charms to spit on it."
    The woman's neighbors propelled her to Rabbi Meir. "Go on, now's your chance! Spit on him!" they said. "Spit seven times," he said to her, "and now go tell your husband." And she did.
    "Rabbi!" his students asked. "How could you demean yourself?"
    "For the sake of *shelom bayit*," he said.

Abridged from the Midrash on Leviticus

Sheloshím (Ashkenazi: **Shlóhshim**)   Period of thirty days of mourning

"He can't come to the wedding, because he's still in the *sheloshim*."

Sheloshim literally means "thirty." For thirty days following the funeral, custom forbids a close relative to go out to entertainment, to wear new clothes, and to have a haircut. (Mourning for a parent extends for one whole year.) The concept of thirty days of mourning goes right back to the month of mourning for the death of Moses.

— ✂ —

Sheluchéy mitzváh enám nizokím (Ashkenazi: **Shlúchey mítzvo éynom nizóhkim**)   "Someone sent on a *mitzvah* (good deed) comes to no harm"

There is a widespread Jewish folk custom to give a coin to someone setting out on a long journey, for it to be given on arrival to *tsedaka* (charity). By making that person a token *sheluach mitzvah* (agent for a *mitzvah*), folk hope to merit the maxim *sheluchey mitzvah enam nizokim*—God looks after those engaged on a righteous mission. This Talmudic proverb is still said when someone sets out on one.

— ✂ —

Shemá   The Shema declaration

"No more bedtime stories now. So hands over your eyes, say *Shema*, and go to sleep . . ."

The *Shema* is the first Hebrew sentence that many Jews learn to say—and for some, their dying words. It's not so much a prayer, in the narrow sense of the word, as a biblical declaration of belief: in one God, in *mitzvot*, in Divine reward and punishment, and so on.

Even a Jew who doesn't say the *Shema* in synagogue may well say the first few words of it before going to sleep, as he or she was taught to do in childhood, and join the rest of the community at the finale of *Yom Kippur* in a cathartic *Shema* that comes from deep in the Jewish psyche, fed perhaps by the collective memory of martyrs going to their death with the words *Shema yisrael*.

A translation of the first few words of the *Shema*, taken from the Book of Devarim (Deuteronomy) and other ancient sources:

Hear O Israel [Shema Yisrael], *the Lord is our God, the Lord is One.*
Blessed be the name of His glorious kingdom for ever and ever.
And you shall love the Lord your God with all your heart and with all your soul and with all your might.

— ✂ —

Sheminí Atséret (Ashkenazi: **Shmíni Atséres**)   The festival of Shemini Atseret

See also *Simchat Torah.*

Shemini Atseret is a festival that comes on the day after *Sukkot* in the autumn. The name means "eighth day of assembly," which isn't exactly a very distinctive name—but then *Shemini Atseret* was originally the only festival where nothing distinctive happened, which is no bad thing after a whole month of general festivities and emotions ranging from fear to cheer.

But perhaps the idea of a festival where you just sit down and relax was just too much for people, for in Israel today—and among Chasidim just about everywhere—*Shemini Atseret* is total merriment and abandon: the day chosen for concluding the annual reading of the Torah and for starting it all over again, and for celebrating this all with singing and dancing and lots and lots of drink. (Most Jews outside Israel hold these celebrations on the day after this, a day they name *Simchat Torah.*)

— 🙌 —

Shemitá (Ashkenazi: **Shmite**)   Sabbatical year

"The rabbi won't buy any Israeli produce during the *shemita* year."

Every seventh year in Israel is a *shemita* year—a sabbatical year, not in the contemporary sense of people having a year off but in the biblical sense of the land being left fallow and no business being conducted with its produce. Many Orthodox growers adhere strictly to the ancient laws of *shemita,* and many Orthodox consumers (both in Israel and in the Diaspora) endeavor not to buy Israeli produce grown on Jewish-owned land at that time. Many stalls in Jerusalem and elsewhere sprout signs reassuring the public that their produce is "free of suspicion of *shemita.*"

— 🙌 —

Shemonéh-esréh (Ashkenazi: **Shmóne-ésreh** or **Shímen-ésre**)   Silent standing prayer. See **Amida.**

— 🙌 —

Shemót (Ashkenazi: **Shemohs**)   The Book of Exodus

Shemot is the second book of the Torah. Despite its rather prosaic-sounding name (meaning "names," and taken from the opening words *Ve-ele*

shemot, "And these are the names of . . ."), *Shemot* is action-packed: the slavery in Egypt, the Exodus, the Ten Commandments, and a multitude of other laws. While the first book of the Torah, *Bereshit*, is largely narrative, *Shemot* and the three remaining books amply entitle us to call the Torah "the Law."

Shemot is read in synagogues through the winter.

— ❧ —

Shemura matzo   Matzo protected from time of harvest. See **Shmúre mátze**.

— ❧ —

Sherút   Shared interurban taxi

"You'll find there's a *sherut* direct from downtown Haifa to Jerusalem."

The unsuspecting visitor to Israel may marvel at how half the cars on the road seem to be large Mercedes, all packed solid with perspiring people reading newspapers or elbowing one another in the ribs.

These are the *sherut*, the Middle East's one and only contribution to fossil fuel conservation. Instead of waiting on line for a bus between cities, many Israelis prefer to share a seven-seater *sherut* Mercedes for about the same price. The only disadvantage, apart from the crampedness, is that the passenger next to the driver is forbidden to fall asleep (a pure safeguard for the driver), though dozing off is very hard to do while you're wondering how the driver quite manages to decelerate from 90 to 0 in less than five seconds.

You can learn good ways from everything. From a *sherut* you learn humility: There's no way you can get in without bending down.

Rabbi Aharon Rokeach of Belz

— ❧ —

Shev ve-al taaséh (Ashkenazi: **Shev ve-al táaseh**)   Wait and see

"Look, the likelihood is that nothing serious will develop, so my advice to you for the moment is *shev ve-al taaseh*."

Literally "sit and don't act," *shev ve-al taaseh* is used whenever it's best to sit tight and do nothing for the moment. It's actually a Talmudic legal concept. For physicians who are sick of prescribing antibiotics because their patients want them to do something, *shev ve-al taaseh* is the ideal thing to frame and hang on the office wall—assuming their patients read Hebrew.

At times a person has to keep to *shev ve-al taaseh* in thoughts too. For thought is a kind of action.

Rabbi Nachman of Bratzlav

Shéva brachót (Ashkenazi: **Shéve bróches**)   Party for the bride and groom during the week following the wedding

"Miriam, we're making *Sheva brachot* at our house tomorrow evening for Eli and Shoshana. Can you come?"

For those who have not espoused the Western idea of a honeymoon on a tropical lagoon, the old tradition of *Sheva brachot* is a delightful way of celebrating the first week of marriage.

Sheva brachot literally means "seven blessings." For seven consecutive evenings following the wedding, relatives and friends of the couple throw a party for them—and recite seven marriage blessings.

. . . soon, O Lord our God, may the cities of Judea and the streets of Jerusalem hear the sound of glee and joy, the voice of groom and bride . . .

From the Seventh of the Seven Blessings

Shéva mitzvót livnéy nóach (Ashkenazi: **Shéva mítzves lívney nóach**)   The Seven Noahide Laws

Seven *mitzvot* (commandments) were divinely given to Noah and all humankind, according to tradition—the *Sheva mitzvot livney noach*, "the seven commandments to the descendants of Noah." They prohibit polytheism, sexual immorality, murder, blasphemy, anarchy, theft, and eating a live creature's limb.

The general view among Jews today is that these are all taken care of in Western law—though some Jewish circles feel that a bit of campaigning for the *Sheva mitzvot livney noach* is overdue.

Shevarím (Ashkenazi: **Shevórim**)   The ram's horn note *Shevarim*

See also *Tekia* and *Terua*.

The blowing of the *shofar* (ram's horn) on the New Year involves permutations of three notes. One is *shevarim* (literally "fragments"), three broken blasts, something like a moaning.

I was sounding *shevorim*. I tell you it was a real broken *shevorim*, a *shevorim* with all the fear of heaven in it. Suddenly there was a lot of loud whistling in the street, shouting, bells ringing! The pogromists had arrived in the market place! God in heaven, what a panic there was! The people tried to rush out, to escape. . . . The old rabbi, blessings on his memory, was still alive. He jumped up on a chair, and cried, "Stay where you are!" And they all stayed where they were.

Yitzchak Leib Peretz

– 🙚🙘 –

Shevat (Ashkenazi: **Shvat**)   The month of Shevat

Shevat, the eleventh month of the Jewish year (January-February), is the time when trees in Israel start their growth and the time for celebrating *Tu bi-Shvat*, "the New Year for Trees."

– 🙚🙘 –

Shéymes   Tattered religious books consigned to be buried

"Don't throw those books away. They're probably *sheymes*."

"Here, Esther, you'd better put this *siddur* into *sheymes*."

Jewish tradition prohibits the burning or destruction of writings or printed books containing the Divine names. So when they are tattered or unwanted, they are stored and often buried respectfully in a cemetery. The Hebrew word for "names" is *shemot*, or in its Ashkenazi form *sheymes*. Hence the Ashkenazi term *sheymes* for writings or books consigned to burial (Sephardim and Israelis have no word for this), or for the place where one keeps such things—in my synagogue it's a wooden chest, and at a summer camp I attended it was a pit in the ground. (For this, Sephardim and Israelis say *geniza*.)

In some pious circles, any and every scrap of Hebrew is regarded as *sheymes*. Where they put it all, I can't imagine. Meanwhile, modern technology has created the problem of whether the Torah intended the Divine name on photocopies to be kept away from the shredder. And in my local Jewish newspaper, the "Ask the Rabbi" column recently pondered whether the digitalized Divine name on cassettes and even diskettes might be considered *sheymes*.

– 🙚🙘 –

Shidúch (Ashkenazi: **Shídech**)   A match; an arranged marriage

"Your friend's brother's still unattached? Maybe we can find a *shiduch* for him . . ."

"Estelle says they met on vacation, but I think it was a *shiduch*."

Not too long ago, when Jewish girls lived sheltered lives, most marriages were *shiduchim*—and the role of *shadchan* (matchmaker) was an important one in any town or village. Even today, in Orthodox circles, formal or informal *shiduchim* are the way in which young people date (and sometimes they end up under the *chupa* without even having had much of a "date" . . .).

Your workaday affairs are forbidden
And even calculating accounts;
Just thinking is permitted,
And making shiduchim *for maidens . . .*

From a Sabbath zemira (mealtime melody)

"Do I have a good-looking *shidech* for you!" said a *shadchan* to a modern young Jewish fellow.
      "Forget it."
      "You don't care about looks? Then I have another *shidech*—she's worth 5,000!"
      "Forget it. Money isn't everything by me."
      "Ah, you're after *yiches* [good ancestry]? Then I have a girl from a line of 15 rabbis."
      "Look—I don't want a *shidech*. I want to marry for love."
      "Ah, you're after love? No problem either—I have just the girl for you . . ."

What Chasidim call a doubles match: A tennis *shidech*.

— ৡৢৢ —

Shikór (Ashkenazi: **Shíker**)   Drunk

"Every *Purim* Bernie gets *shiker* and I end up having to drive him home."

Drunk you musn't get, but *shiker* you may. If you want to know the difference, don't bother looking in a dictionary—dictionaries tell you the meanings of words, but not their feelings. And *shiker* simply feels safer, homier than "drunk."
      Perhaps that's why Jews have gone on using the Hebrew word for it over so many centuries. There's even a special day to get *shiker*: the feast of *Purim*, on which the rabbis recommend getting *shiker* enough for you not to be able to distinguish between "Cursed be Haman" and "Blessed be Mordechai." The original Jewish breathalyzer.
      Trivia: *Shiker* went into Greek and thence into Latin and finally into French *cidre*. The result: Cider!

Before he drinks wine, a man is a lamb;
When he drinks properly, a man is a lion;
When he drinks too much, a man is a pig;
When he gets shikor, *a man is an ape . . .*

The Midrash

– ৯৽৽ৎ –

Shin Bet   Israeli internal secret service

"He was under suspicion for a while, but we understand that the *Shin Bet* have eliminated him from their inquiries."

Shin Bet are the Hebrew initials for *Sherutey Biyun,* "intelligence services." They have the task of keeping undercover tabs on any threat to internal security. The *Shin Bet* is not as well known as the *Mosad,* Israel's equivalent of MI6 and the CIA (*lehavdil*), but it is, we might say, fairly well known.

– ৯৽৽ৎ –

Shir ha-Shirím (Ashkenazi: **Shir ha-Shírim**)   The Song of Songs

"It was my grandfather's custom to read *Shir ha-Shirim* every week before *Shabbat.*"

The biblical book *Shir ha-Shirim* is a sequence of love songs that have inspired a whole mystical tradition exploring the love between the Creator and Israel—and countless poets and musicians, religious and secular. *Shir ha-Shirim* is particularly familiar to Sephardim and Chasidim, who recite it every Friday to usher in *Shabbat.*

Said Rabbi Akiva: Never was the world so deserving as on the day that Shir ha-Shirim was given to Israel. And why? Because while all the Scriptures are holy, Shir ha-Shirim is holy of holies.

The Midrash

Shir ha-Shirim *of Solomon:*
Let him kiss me with the kisses of his mouth—
For your love excels wine.

Translation of the opening lines of *Shir ha-Shirim*

From the town strange noises arise—a roaring, a boiling, a seething. It is the day before Passover, a rare and wonderful day. In one instant the world is transformed. Our yard is a king's court. Our house is a palace. I am a prince and Buzie is a princess. The logs of wood piled about our door are the cedars and cypresses that are mentioned in *Shir ha-Shirim.* The cat that lies near the door warming herself in the sun is a roe or a young hart that is mentioned in *Shir ha-Shirim*. The women and the girls who are working outdoors, washing and cleaning and getting ready for *Pesach*, are the daughters of Jerusalem mentioned in *Shir ha-Shirim*. Everything, everything is from *Shir ha-Shirim*.

Sholom Aleichem

Shiúr, pl. shiurím (Ashkenazi: **Shíer, pl. shiúrim**)   Religious class

"Were you at the rabbi's *shiur* last Tuesday?"
    "What was it on, Talmud?"

To appreciate what a *shiur* is, you have to know what it isn't.

It isn't a *drasha* (sermon), where an eloquent rabbi seeks to move a captive synagogue audience. Rather, it's typically an informal gathering of adults to study classic Jewish texts with a rabbi or some other learned person—maybe in the synagogue, maybe in someone's home. Someone passes round the Sanka and the cookies, maybe the rabbi goes off on an interesting tangent, and all return home feeling they've done a little bit to get Jewish life back to where it was before mass migration, TV, and all the other disruptions: a life of learning. You come home from work, you eat, and you go to a *shiur*.

— ❧ —

Shivá (Ashkenazi: **Shíve**)   Week of mourning

"Is your aunt sitting *shiva* at her own home or at your cousin's?"

The basic meaning of *shiva* is "seven."

The *shiva* is the week of mourning for a close relative following a funeral. During this time, the *avel* (mourner) traditionally remains indoors and, rather than repressing emotions and memories, is encouraged to mourn—by abstaining from working, bathing, shaving, and so on. Religious services are held at the house, and friends and family visit to console and to reminisce about the deceased. The term "sit *shiva*" refers to the custom of sitting on low chairs.

Quite a few of the injunctions governing the observance of *shiva*, such as the prohibitions against washing, the use of cosmetics, ointments, wearing shoes, and sex life, are reminiscent of *Yom Kippur*. Somehow, we arrive at a strange equation: the act of mourning equals the act of expiation. The *halacha* commands the mourner to expiate his guilt . . ."

Joseph B. Soloveitchik

— ❧ —

Shivá Asár be-Tamúz (Ashkenazi: **Shíve Óser be-Támuz**) Fast of the seventeenth of Tamuz

"Tomorrow the camp theme is Jerusalem, because it's *Shiva Asar be-Tamuz.*"

In midsummer, and usually in the middle of the camping season, comes the unpleasant day of *Shiva Asar be-Tamuz*—anniversary of the forcing of the walls of Jerusalem and the beginning of the end of ancient Jewish independence. The tradition is to fast. But nearly as grim are the three weeks that follow *Shiva Asar be-Tamuz*, when all festivities are curtailed—culminating in the somber fast of *Tisha be-Av.*

— ❦ —

Shivím paním la-torá (Ashkenazi: **Shívim pónim la-tóhro**) "The Torah has seventy faces"

See also *Elu va-elu divrey elokim chayim.*

The Torah is to be taken in so many different ways. There are so many levels—ranging from the multiple possibilities of *peshat* (literal meaning) to the mysteries of letter recombinations and numerical equivalents. Hence *shivim panim la-torah,* "the Torah has seventy faces."

— ❦ —

Shlitá (Ashkenazi: **Shlíte**) "Long may he live"

"The photo on the wall is of Rabbi Ovadya Yosef, *Shlita.*"

Shlita is an abbreviation of the phrase *she-yichye leorech yamim tovim amen,* "May he live a long and good life, Amen." It is customarily added by the Ultraorthodox when mentioning the name of a revered rabbi.

On the masthead of a Chasidic newsletter:
  In honor of the Lubavitcher Rebbe, shlita.

— ❦ —

Shmúre mátze, usually spelled **Shemura matzo** Matzo protected from time of harvest

"Did you buy enough *shmure matze* for both *Seder* nights, Phillip?"

Shmure matze is the real McCoy. For the ceremonial eating of *matzo* on the Passover *Seder* night, the zealous insist on eating *shmure matze,* literally "protected *matzo.*" Whereas most *matzo* is from flour set aside and carefully kept dry (to stop it rising) from the moment it has been ground, *shmure matze* is zealously kept dry from the moment the wheat has been harvested.

Shoáh   Nazi Holocaust

"He came to Canada as a survivor of the *Shoah.*"

Shoah, literally "destruction" and used by the prophet Isaiah in reference to the fate of the evil as well as the fate of the good, has come to refer in recent years specifically to the Nazi Holocaust.

Most people of our time have the face of Lot's wife turned toward the *Shoah* and yet they are always escaping.

Yehuda Amichai

Shochét (Ashkenazi: Shóychet)   *Kosher* slaughterer

"They eat so much meat in their house. I guess their father's a *shoychet.*"

Torah law requires all meat and fowl to be slaughtered in a particular manner, by highly qualified and pious personnel, to avoid any pain to the animal. Thus even when an animal is in itself *kosher* (i.e., a religiously permitted species, such as a cow), it has to be readied for consumption in a special *kosher* way.

A Jewish communal representative was summoned to testify in a Polish court.
  "*Shoychet* Levy!" called the judge.
  "With respect, your honor, my name isn't *Shoychet* Levy. I am Mr. Levy."
  The judge was adamant. "In my records it states that you are a slaughterer by profession. Thus it is perfectly proper to call you *Shoychet* Levy."
  "Your Honor," replied Levy with dignity, "when I stand before the Court I am Mr. Levy; when I stand before my congregation and lead the prayers, I am *Chazan* Levy—and when I stand before an ox, I'm *Shoychet* Levy."

Shofár (Ashkenazi: Shóhfer)   Ram's horn

"Jonathan blows the *shofar* every year for the people at the Old Age Home."

To hear the *shofar* is to walk right into a biblical time frame. The same instrument that sounded the war alarm or trumpeted triumph is sounded every *Rosh Hashanah* (Jewish New Year) in synagogues everywhere—to stir, to cajole, to warn. The *shofar* was also famously sounded at the capture of the Western Wall in 1967, and every once in a while you may see photographs of Yemenite-looking sages with long beards and *peot* blowing long twirly *shofarot* at some other festivity.

A Chasid was once appointed to blow the *shofar* or ram's horn on *Rosh Hashanah*. He began to make elaborate inner preparations in order to experience the intimate mystical contemplations prescribed for this moment by the *Kabala*. Whereupon Reb Bunam turned to him and said:

"The prayer book says 'S.B.' This abbreviation means 'Simpleton, blow!' You need not indulge in contemplations. Just think '*tekia*' [blow] to carry out God's will."

Abraham Joshua Heschel

The month of Elul came, and in the Chasidic synagogue in our courtyard they blew the *Shofar* every day to frighten off Satan, the accuser.

Isaac Bashevis Singer

— ❧ —

Shólom aléychem! See **Shalom alechém!**

— ❧ —

Shomér shabbát, pl. shomréy shabbát (Ashkenazi: **Shómer shábes, pl. shómrey shábes**)   Sabbath observant; a Sabbath observer

"I didn't know that Beth's father is *shomer shabbat*."

"Do you run any safaris for *shomrey shabbat*?"

See also the opposite of *Shomer shabbat*: *Mechalel shabbat*.

Someone who observes the Sabbath laws in the traditional way is called *shomer shabbat*. The phrase is often used to indicate whether someone is considered religiously observant altogether: The observance of the Sabbath is more tangible, as well as more indicative of Orthodoxy, than many other practices.

— ❧ —

Shomrón   Samaria

"David and Rachel live on a small *yishuv* [village] somewhere in the *Shomron*."

Shomron is the geographical name for the mountainous part of Erets-Yisrael from Jerusalem northward to the Valley of Yizreel, including towns such as Shechem (Nablus) and Jenin.

In biblical times *Shomron* also denoted the Northern Jewish Kingdom—and in modern times the land from Jerusalem northward captured by Israel from Jordan in 1967, now undergoing gradual Jewish settlement. To the great powers, the names *Shomron* and *Yehuda* are loaded, expansionist names; they prefer the name chosen by the Jordanians, "the West Bank."

— ❦ —

Shtachím   The Israeli-administered territories acquired in 1967

"Is this new town inside the Green Line or in the *Shtachim*?"

The *Shtachim* (literally "the territories") is the popular name often used by Israelis for the territories captured from Jordan, Egypt, and Syria in 1967 and currently administered by Israel: Judea, Samaria, Gaza, and Golan. The line delineating the *Shtachim* is popularly called *Ha-Kav ha-Yarok*, the Green Line, because that was the color of the temporary borders as shown on pre-1967 Israeli maps.

— ❦ —

Shuk   Market

"And for Joan I bought this headscarf real cheap in the *shuk* . . ."

Any street market in Israel is a *shuk*—a word conjuring up sacks upon sacks of nuts and beans, enticing spices, pirate videos, strung-up chickens, and beggars.

— ❦ —

Shulchán Arúch (Ashkenazi: **Shúlchen Órech**)   The *Shulchan Aruch* code

See *Kitsur Shulchan Aruch*

Since its composition four centuries ago by Yosef Caro, the *Shulchan Aruch* has become almost synonymous with Jewish Law.

The *Shulchan Aruch* is what the Torah and *Mishna* and *Gemara* are not: a comprehensive and systematic code of practical living—taking in not only everyday do's and don'ts but also a vast body of criminal and civil law.

But it's hard going, even in watered-down English, and is essentially the preserve of rabbis and *yeshiva* students.

The unpretentiousness of the *Shulkhan Arukh* is striking. Where Maimonides opens his code with answers to the most terrible questions of theology, Caro reverts to the old tone of the Talmud and starts by telling what the pious Jew does when he gets up in the morning.

Herman Wouk

My father used to say to me that besides the "Four Parts of the *Shulchan Aruch*" there is need for a fifth—laying down how to behave toward others. To my mind, we need a sixth part—about how to behave toward scoundrels.

Rabbi Moshe of Kobryn

After we have been privileged to attain the religious level of life of the "commandments of men," inculcated by the regimen delineated in the *Shulchan Aruch* that the proponents of purified religion so despise, we will strive to advance further toward a religious existence in full consonance with the proper intentionality and spiritual awareness.

Yeshayahu Leibowitz

— ৪৫৬ৡ৯ —

Shushán Purím (Ashkenazi: **Shúshan Púrim**)   The festival of *Shushan Purim*

"Let's drive up to Jerusalem to see the fun on *Shushan Purim*."

A day after *Purim* (see entry) comes the festival of *Shushan Purim*. Because the Jews in the ancient Persian capital, Shushan, took an extra day to rout their enemies, the Bible records that their annual celebrations took place on the day after *Purim*. Whether the Glorious Iranian Revolution has left any Jews in Shushan today is doubtful (if indeed such a place still exists), but *Shushan Purim* is still a reality—because, not to be outshone by Shushan, the Jews in all the ancient biblical cities adopted the custom of celebrating *Shushan Purim*.

So to this day, whereas Tel Aviv celebrates *Purim*, Jerusalem celebrates *Shushan Purim* on the day after. In some Israeli cities they don't know which one they're celebrating, because the rabbis can't decide. And by the time *Purim* is over and the rabbis have all knocked back a few, they probably don't know which one they were celebrating either.

— ৪৫৬ৡ৯ —

Siddúr (Ashkenazi: **Sídder**)   Prayer book

"Dear Grandma,
    Thank you for the *siddur* that you gave me for my *Bar Mitzvah*. It will always sit on my shelf."

Of all the books that Jews have cherished, none has had greater use than the *siddur*. Even where women's literacy was at its most basic, they might at least expect to learn to read the regular prayers from the *siddur*.

An ignoramus had a *siddur* with a rare and beautiful commentary in the margins. Hearing of it, a scholar came and offered him 10 rubles.
  "10 rubles?!" said the ignoramus. "I'm not selling such a special *siddur* at any price."
  "But what use is such a *siddur* to someone like you?" asked the other in amazement.
  "It's tremendous!" replied the ignoramus. "With so many moths in my room, all nibbling away at the edges of my books, I've never had a *siddur* I could pray from. But in this one, all they'll ever manage to eat is the commentary in the margins!"

— ❀ —

Sidrá, pl. **sidrót** (Ashkenazi: **Sédre**, pl. **sédres**)   Weekly section read from the Torah

"Why are you back so early from *shul* [synagogue]? Was it a short *sidra*?"

Like the word *parasha*, the term *sidra* refers to the weekly portion (there are fifty-four of them) read from the Torah. The two words are used interchangeably.
  "What's this week's *sidra*?" schoolteachers ask their pupils the world over, every Monday morning. And the study of that particular week's *sidra* will be at the center of the traditional religious curriculum. In fact, if you invite yourself in to an Orthodox household on a Friday afternoon (decidedly *not* the best time to invite yourself in), you may find Father reading and then rereading the *sidra*, to fulfill the rule of "twice through the text and once in translation."
  Then comes *Shabbat*, and the *sidra* is chanted aloud in the synagogue.

— ❀ —

Simán, pl. **simaním** (Ashkenazi: **Símen**, pl. **simónim**)   Sign, portent

"Funny how they offered me an interview out of the clear blue. I think it's a good *siman* . . ."

Simanim can be taken seriously or spuriously, depending on whom you ask. Judaism seems to be in two minds about them. See *mazal* (luck). But everyone, including the rabbi, sings a hearty *Siman tov!* as the bride and groom enter the hall.

Siman tov u-mazal tov yihye lanu! [May we have a good sign and a good star!]
                                            Traditional wedding song

— ❀ —

Simchá (Ashkenazi: **Símche**)   Joy; a celebration

"Just look at her face—did you ever see such *simcha*?"

"Thank you for your kind gift on the occasion of our *simcha* . . ."

For all the sufferings, for all the fast days and commemorations of catastrophe, Judaism is a religion of *simcha*. The Bible warns of calamity if the Jew fails to serve the Creator with *simcha*. Despite repeated efforts by Western assimilationists to impose a staid decorum on Jewish life, the tradition of singing, dancing, whooping it up, and letting your hair down is alive and well, among both Ashkenazim and Sephardim.

There is no *simcha* without wine.

The Talmud, Pesachim

Greet every person with *simcha*.

The Talmud, Avot

Jewish experience is a testimony to *simcha shel mitzvah*, to the joy of doing a *mitzvah* [divine commandment].

Abraham Joshua Heschel

— ❧ —

Simchát Toráh (Ashkenazi: **Símches Tóre**)   Festival of Simchat Torah

"I danced so long on *Simchat Torah* that the heel came off my shoe."

See *Hakafot*, "Circle dancing," *Chatan Torah*, "Bridegroom of the Torah," and *Chatan Bereshit*, "Bridegroom of Genesis."

The very last day of the autumn season of festivals is called *Simchat Torah*, literally "the rejoicing of the Torah," and the name says it all: On this day the final section of the Torah is read out—and then it's promptly back to the beginning again with the story of Creation. And all of this amid exceedingly great rejoicing: singing, circle dancing (*hakafot*) with the Torah scrolls, horas, and congas that last hours, cookies and candies galore, even the dentists managing a smile. Everyone is given an *aliyah* to the Torah, with pride of place going to the two "bridegrooms" for the day, the *Chatan Torah* and *Chatan Bereshit*, who end and begin the reading, respectively. Everyone throws candies at them, and they throw a party.

The angel Michael makes a crown from the shoes that fall from the feet of Jews that dance on *Simchat Torah*.

Rabbi Israel Baal Shem Tov

— ❧ —

Sinát chinám (Ashkenazi: **Sínas chínom**)   Pointless hatred

"There's no reason he shouldn't lend it to you—it's pure *sinat chinam*."

There hasn't been a Jewish moralist who hasn't identified *sinat chinam* as the greatest enemy of the Jewish people. The First Temple fell through idolatry—and the ensuing exile lasted some seventy years; the Second Temple fell through sheer *sinat chinam*—and after nearly 2,000 years the ensuing exile is still not quite over.

Rav Kook, the popular and venerated Chief Rabbi of Mandate Palestine, felt a tolerance, even a respect, for the irreligious pioneers on the kibbutzim.
"How can you? They're heathens," he was asked.
"Better that I should err on the side of *ahavat chinam* [pointless love] than *sinat chinam*," he retorted.

Siván (Ashkenazi: **Síven**)   The month of Sivan

Coming in May-June, *Sivan*, the third month of the Jewish year, evokes flowers and first fruits and short summer nights—it's the time of the festival of *Shavuot*.

Siyáta dishmáya (Ashkenazi: **Siyóse dishmáye**)   Help from Heaven

"You've done all you can—now you'll have to ask for *siyata dishmaya*."

See *Be-siyata di-shmaya*, "With the help of Heaven."

Siyúm (Ashkenazi: **Síyem**)   Party celebrating the end of a program of study

"If Tanya's bringing cookies for the *siyum*, you can take soda, can't you?"

Eskimos are reputed to have scores of words for different kinds of snow. The British make fine distinctions between types of rain. Hebrew abounds in words for religious meals and parties: the *kiddush*, the *se'uda*, the *simcha* (see these entries), and—my personal favorite—the *siyum*.
When you have finished studying some book or even some chapter of a book, feel free to celebrate by making a *siyum*. Invite your friends,

and the rabbi of course—but don't let them drive home themselves. As a child, I got a *siyum* on every *parasha* (section) of the Torah; as a teenager, on every *masechta* of the *Mishna*; now I feel I should wait till I've got through a whole *masechta* of *Gemara* (which isn't too often).

— ❦ —

Smichá (Ashkenazi: **Smíche**)   Traditional rabbinic ordination

"Their new rabbi has *smicha* from one of the top *yeshivot* on the East Coast."

To be a rabbi in the Orthodox world you need to have *smicha*. You should also be pious and generally immersed in Torah, but being a rabbi—or *rav* as he is always called—has traditionally meant fulfilling a very communal role: being able to give advice and rulings on everyday matters of Jewish Law, especially *kashrut* (dietary laws) and familiar rituals. And this means many long, grueling years of study, culminating in an oral examination, and the award of *smicha*.

— ❦ —

(The) **Sochnút**   The Jewish Agency

"What size are the apartments that the *Sochnut* provides Russian families?"

The *Sochnut* facilitates immigration and other practical ties between Israel and the Diaspora. Many are the Jewish organizations whose name evokes stifled yawns or blank ignorance. The *Sochnut* is not one of them.

Every *oleh* (immigrant) has his or her own *Sochnut* tale of Byzantine bureaucracy and interminable delays; but the *Sochnut* is so much a part of the Israeli landscape—some cite it in explanation for why the Israelites about to enter the Holy Land had to wander for forty years in the wilderness—that it is impossible to imagine *aliyah* (immigration) without it.

— ❦ —

Sofér, pl. sofrím (Ashkenazi: **Sóhfer, pl. sóhfrim**)   Scribe

"These *tefilin* look like they got damp. You'll have to take them to a *sofer* to be checked."

Sofer is from the same root as *sefer*, "book."

If the Torah and the rest of the Bible have been preserved for millenia with such incredible accuracy—as we can now prove that they have been—it's due to the professionalism of the *sofer*.

Copyist, proofreader, and calligrapher all in one, the *sofer* works with a goose quill on parchment to write *tefilin, mezuzot,* and sometimes a *sefer torah*. To write a *sefer torah* can take a year, but the *sofer* has plenty of challenge just writing a *mezuzah*: One mistake in the shape of a letter, and you have to start all over again. But modern technology has been able to help where it matters most: Computerized scanners now pick up faults in a Torah scroll in a whoosh, and save the *sofer*'s time—and his eyes.

— ✺ —

Stam   Without any thought to it, for no particular reason

"I'm fed up with him, he does everything so *stam* . . ."

The classic guides to Jewish living are full of exhortations to do everything "in the service of the Creator"—which means not to do things *stam*. But people will be people, and so most things seem *stam*. When Kafka's Joseph K. walked out of his room, he discovered for himself— and for a lot of other people—precisely how *stam* the world appears to be; and if Kafka had been able to go on acquiring Hebrew and planning *aliyah* as intently as he had been doing before his untimely death, I fancy the word *stam* would have loomed large in his opus.

— ✺ —

Sukkáh, pl. **sukkót** (Ashkenazi: **Súkke**, pl. **súkkes**)   Booth for the *Sukkot* festival

"I brought five soups out into the *sukkah*, but some leaves fell into one of them so we'll need one more."

Just before the festival of *Sukkot*, the whole Israeli landscape seems to sprout *sukkot*. On roofs, on balconies, on every spare patch of ground, even along sidewalks, people are putting up little booths—ranging from the flimsy to the very flimsy—and preparing to spend the next seven days "under vegetation." In the religious neighborhoods, the very apartment buildings have staggered balconies to accommodate the *sukkot*. Living in the *sukkah* is not only a *mitzvah* (religious duty), it's also great fun, not least for kids who go on long candy-foraging "*sukkah* crawls," although one night I slept in such a wind that I dreamed that the sky was caving in.

Jews elsewhere build *sukkot*, but more discreetly—and with roofs designed to be lowered the moment it rains, as it always does.

Seven days you shall dwell in *sukkot*, every Israelite shall dwell in *sukkot*. In order that your generations may know that I had the Children of Israel dwell in *sukkot* when I brought them forth from the Land of Egypt . . .

Leviticus 23

To me it is the finest time of the year. Each day is a gift from heaven. The sun no longer bakes like an oven but caresses with a heavenly softness. The woods are still green, the pines give out a pungent smell. In my yard stands the *sukke*—the *sukke* I have built for the holiday, covered with branches, and around me the forest looks like a huge *sukke* designed for God Himself. Here, I think, God celebrates His holiday, here and not in town, in the noise and tumult . . .

Sholom Aleichem

— ✤ —

Sukkót (Ashkenazi: **Súkkes**)   The festival of *Sukkot*

"Have you got enough greenery and decorations for *Sukkot*?"

See *Sukkah*, "Booth."

Five days after *Yom Kippur*, in mid-autumn, comes the festival of *Sukkot*, which has to be seen to be believed. The word literally means "booths." For the week-long festival, Jews traditionally eat, drink, and sleep "under the sky"—in a little *sukkah* (see entry) roofed over with temporary vegetation, commemorating the wandering in the wilderness. This is also the harvest season and a time of judgment for rain, and there are a plethora of other customs and ceremonies to match. Provided it doesn't pour with rain, *Sukkot* fully lives up to its nickname of *zman simchatenu*, "our season of joy."

— ✤ —

Syag la-chochmá shtiká (Ashkenazi: **Syog la-chóchme shtíke**)
"Silence is a safeguard to wisdom"

See *Leshon ha-ra*, "evil language."

This maxim of Rabbi Akiva, one of the greatest rabbis of antiquity, reflects a philosophy of not speaking unless one has something significant to say. The tongue is a loaded weapon. Handle with care.

— ✤ —

Tá'am   Taste

"I don't really like the way they've done up the house. It has no *ta'am*."

In Israel, *ta'am* means the taste of the food, the taste of furnishings . . . any kind of taste. To Diaspora Jews, it means tastefulness—taste in the abstract, if you like.

– ❦ –

Ta'anít, pl. **ta'aniyót** (Ashkenazi: **Táanis**, pl. **taanéysim**)   Sad fast

"We can't go out next Wednesday because it's a *ta'anit*."

Not that long ago, the *ta'anit* seems to have been a regular part of Jewish life. There was the *ta'anit yachid*, a personal fast: You had a bad dream and you undertook to fast (a *ta'anit chalom*). Someone in the family was ill and you fasted. On the anniversary of a parent's death, you fasted.

And there was the *ta'anit tsibur*, the public fast—in drought, in war, in poverty. Nowadays, few rabbis will readily call for a *ta'anit tsibur* or recommend a *ta'anit yachid*. We're all too weak, it is said. (A few more *ta'aniyot* might actually be physically good for many of us—but that's another matter.)

And so, apart from fasting for a deceased parent, the only common *ta'aniyot* are the five statutory sad fasts that come round every year (*Asara be-Tevet, Ta'anit Ester, Shiva Asar be-Tamuz, Tisha be-Av, Tsom Gedalya*), commemorating great catastrophes that are still with us.

A *ta'anit* acts on a dream as fire acts on sawdust.

The Talmud, Shabbat

Answer us, O Lord, answer us on the day of our *ta'anit*, for we are in great trouble. Turn not to our wickedness and do not hide Your face from us or ignore our pleas. Be close, we beg, to our cries, and let Your kindness comfort us. Even before we call on You, answer us . . .

Translation of the beginning of a prayer said on every *ta'anit*

A Chasid came to his *rebbe* with a desperate look on his face. He wanted to elevate his soul, and had been observing a personal *ta'anit* once a week—but to no avail.

The *rebbe* shook his head—and told him this story: the saintly *Baal Shem Tov* once had his horses harnessed and set off on an urgent mission. The horses passed all their familiar inns and drinking troughs, but time was of the essence and on they galloped.

"Maybe we're no longer horses but humans," the horses thought. "So we'll eat when we get to the next city." But the next city came and went.

"Maybe we're angels . . ." said the horses. "Angels never eat."

Finally, however, they reached their destination—and there the horses were led to the stable, where they ate and ate—like horses.

"So, my good friend," said the *rebbe*, "it's not just the *ta'anit*—it's also how you conduct yourself after the *ta'anit*."

— ୨ୡୡ —

Ta'anít Bechorím (Ashkenazi: **Táanis Bechóhrim**)   The Fast of the Firstborn

"Are you going to the *Ta'anit Bechorim* service in the synagogue tomorrow?"

On the morning before the *Pesach* festival, firstborn men and boys traditionally gather in the synagogue for *Ta'anit Bechorim*, the fast day commemorating the sparing of the lives of the Jewish firstborn (*bechorim*) in ancient Egypt. Except that they don't fast: Custom obligingly arranges for a *siyum* party (see entry) to be held that morning following prayers, which cancels out the fast, and everyone has a little drink and goes away very relieved. The Jewish people have enough fast days—with this everyone, even the most pious, would agree.

— ୨ୡୡ —

Ta'anít Estér (Ashkenazi: **Táanis Éster**)   The Fast of Esther

"Gila isn't fasting on *Ta'anit Ester* because she's pregnant."

Ta'anit Ester, the day before the mega-festival of *Purim*—when everyone is meant to have a riot of a time—is a time for fasting. Its purpose is to recall how close the Jews of the vast Persian Empire came to suffering genocide, and how Queen Esther herself (a Jewish girl out of her depth, if ever there was one) dared to fast and wear sackcloth in the harem of the Persian emperor.

— ୨ୡୡ —

Tachanún (Ashkenazi: **Táchanun**)   Daily prayer of pleading

The *Amida* prayer is said standing to attention. Following it comes a prayer in a quite different physical mode: *Tachanun* is said drooping over a table or the back of a chair, with one's head leaning on one's arm. *Tachanun* means "pleading." It's about suffering. But on any festive or vaguely festive occasion—indeed, whenever a bridegroom is present—*Tachanun* is omitted. A "no-*Tachanun* day" is almost synonymous with "a happy day."

— ❦ —

Táchles   Practical considerations; let's talk business

"Come on, George, the economy's in a mess, you've got to talk *tachles*."

"Wow, you know it's 10 o'clock and we haven't got to the main agenda! Now *tachles*, what jobs are going to go?"

There is a certain irony in the fact that the very word *tachles* is an out-and-out Ashkenazi-sounding word, still suggestive of smoke-filled rooms of humorless Russian-Zionist revolutionaries. For over forty years, Israel's Ashkenazi-dominated political parties have talked about talking *tachles*. Whether they have indeed succeeded, you must judge.

— ❦ —

Tafásta merubéh, lo tafásta (Ashkenazi: **Tofáste merúbe, lo tofáste**) "Don't bite off more than you can chew" (literally "If you grab a lot, you grab nothing")

Like so many graphic expressions, this one grew out of a Talmudic legal maxim (establishing certain legal minimums—I won't go into it here). If you think about it, the legal maxim itself sounds very much as if it grew out of a popular saying of the ancient Israelite-in-the-street.

— ❦ —

Tahará (Ashkenazi: **Táare**)   Cleansing of the dead prior to burial

"They've contacted the hospital about performing *tahara* there."

Tahara, literally "purification," involves (among other things) cleansing the dead with hot water, combing and trimming the hair, and dressing the body in white linen *tachrichin* (a shroud)—in preparation for the resurrection of the dead. A man is customarily wrapped in the *tallit* (prayer shawl) that he wore in his life.

— ❦ —

Taharát mishpachá (Ashkenazi: **Táares mishpóche**)   Marital purity

"Rabbi Feldman gave an impassioned plea for the promotion of *taharat mishpacha.*"

See *Mikveh,* "Pool for religious immersion."

Taharat mishpacha is a delicate way of referring to the practice of avoiding physical contact between wife and husband for twelve (occasionally more) days a month, culminating in the wife's immersion in a *mikveh* pool.

Since the mass migrations 100 years ago, *taharat mishpacha* became a rarity outside strictly Orthodox circles, but it is now enjoying a comeback—due undoubtedly to a search for spiritual and aesthetic values, a recognition of the therapeutic qualities of separation, and perhaps to an appreciation that *taharat mishpacha* gives a woman the right to say no.

Tallít, pl. tallitót (Ashkenazi: **Tállis, pl. talléysim**)   Prayer shawl

"His Uncle Itz bought him a real old-fashioned woolen *tallit* for his *Bar Mitzvah,* instead of that silk one."

Worn at morning prayers, the traditional *tallit* is a massive square woolen garment, bearing at each corner a *tsitsit* with its knots and eight strands. Enveloping as it does the whole of one's back—and in pious circles often the head too—it gives the worshipper a sense of envelopment and intimacy with God. Among Chasidim, the *tallit* is reserved for married men.

The *tallit* is larger than life. It accompanies a Jew through this world and envelops the body in its final journey. One may see all manner of innovative *tallit* patterns and hues, but those elemental thick stripes on a white field are engraved on the collective mind's eye.

One morning before prayers Rabbi Chayim of Zans lay down for a nap. Just then, a soldier came to collect taxes. Awaking and seeing him, Rabbi Chayim gave a shudder. When the soldier had gone, he said to his servant:

"Look, that soldier was a mere peasant, but when he appears in the king's uniform he inspires fear and dread. Let us put on the uniform of the True King of Kings, the *tallit* and *tefilin,* and all the nations will feel fear and dread."

Tallít katán (Ashkenazi: **Tállis kóten**)   Four-cornered garment

"Put your *tallit katan* on, sweetheart, before you start walking around the house."

The *tallit katan* is also known popularly as an *arba kanfes*. See also *tsitsit* and *tallit*.

The *tallit*, the prayer shawl, is a familar sight. Less familiar, if only because it's usually worn under the shirt, is the *tallit katan*, literally "mini-*tallit*." It doesn't usually have those bold stripes characteristic of the *tallit*, but it does have the same four corners, and at each corner a *tsitsit*, "tassel" consisting of eight wool strings—in observance of the biblical command to wear *tsitsit*.

Orthodox men and boys keep up the tradition of the *tallit katan*, and among the Ultraorthodox you may see the *tsitsit* themselves hanging out from the sides of the shirt.

Talmíd, pl. **talmidím** (Ashkenazi: **Tálmid**, pl. **talmídim**)   Disciple; pupil

"I'm going to give that guy a lift—he's a *talmid* of mine."

Talmid traditionally suggests a mentor-disciple relationship, something more spiritual than merely a teacher-pupil relationship—though here, as with so many other Hebrew words, modern Israeli Hebrew uses it precisely in the pupil-teacher sense.

A man is envious of all except his son and his *talmid*.

The Talmud, Sanhedrin

There are four types of *talmid:*
  Quick to grasp and quick to forget—their gain is wiped out in their loss.
  Slow to grasp and slow to forget—their loss is wiped out in their gain.
  Quick to grasp and slow to forget—a wise person.
  Slow to grasp and quick to forget—a villain.

The Talmud, Avot

Much have I learned from my teachers, and still more from my friends, and most of all from my *talmidim*.

The Talmud, Ta'anit

Talmíd chachám, pl. **talmidéy chachamím** (Ashkenazi: **Tálmid chóchem**, pl. **talmídey chachómim**)   Man of Jewish learning

"Now his uncle, he was a real *talmid chacham*—he knew *Gemara* backward."

Why all the Jewish Nobel laureates? Thanks, above all, to the *talmid chacham*.

Not so long ago, Torah study was the highest Jewish value, and society operated by a simple rule: If you can, learn; if you can't, earn. And those who were learning rather than earning didn't need to chase a girl with some money—the girl's father chased *them*.

Who is a *talmid chacham*? Someone who has learned "the whole of *Shas*" (*Shas* means the Talmud). He should be getting through it once in seven years. Ninety-nine percent of Jews today have never got through it once.

Talmidey chachamim increase the peace of the world.

The Talmud, Keritot

$$-\text{\clubsuit}-$$

Talmúd (Ashkenazi: **Tálmud**) Talmud

"Sorry, Joel's not in, he's either jogging or at the early morning *Talmud* class."

Orthodox Jews usually refer to *Talmud* as *Gemara*. The *Talmud* is built on a central core of legal rulings called *Mishna*. For another word from the same root, see *Melamed*.

(The) *Talmud* is a vast anthology of Jewish law and thought—and complex discussions—set down in the fifth and sixth centuries as the authoritative source book of Judaism. *Chumash* (the biblical Five Books of Moses) and *Talmud* are the heart and brains of the Jewish people. To study *Talmud* you don't have to be a lawyer, but it helps; if you're a bit of a poet and philosopher, it's also a good thing. In many "modern" Jewish circles, *Talmud* study is now "in."

The impact of the *Talmud* upon the Jewish people has been immeasurable. Throughout the generations, Jewish education demanded considerable knowledge of the *Talmud*, which functioned as the basic text of study for all. Indeed, much of posttalmudic Jewish literature consists of commentaries, reworkings, and new presentations of the *Talmud* . . .

Adin Steinsaltz

A Jewish peasant begged a rabbi to teach him some *Talmud*.

"OK," said the rabbi reluctantly, "but listen carefully. If two burglars break into a house down the chimney, one with a grimy face and one with a clean face, which of them will wash?"

The peasant reflected. "The one with the grimy face, of course!"

"See?" said the rabbi, "I knew that a peasant couldn't learn *Talmud*. The one with the clean face looked at the one with the grimy face and, thinking his own face was also grimy, he washed it of course, while the one with the grimy face, seeing the clean face of his colleague, was quite sure his own face was clean and thus it never occurred to him to wash it."

The peasant cocked his head, thought this over—and grasped the rabbi's hand: "Thank you, Rabbi, thank you. I've learned some *Talmud!*"

The rabbi shrugged his shoulders. "What did I tell you: A peasant can't learn *Talmud*. Who but a peasant would imagine that if you have two burglars climbing down a chimney, only one of them will have a grimy face?"

— ✣ —

Talmúd Toráh (Ashkenazi: **Tálmud Tóre**)   Study of Torah; traditional communal Jewish religious school

"After Moishe finishes *Talmud Tore*, he'll start *yeshive*."

The word *Talmud* basically denotes "*study*," and by extension, "the Talmud." See also *Torah*.

Talmud Torah is one of the core components of Jewish life, and it's not just an act of study, it's an act of communion.

The phrase also came to denote a place of study—and to most American Jews, studying in a *Talmud Tore* conjures up scenes of prewar inner-city New York or Chicago, but with a decidedly better image than the *cheder* (the privately run traditional school). Although generally confined to after school-hours, the Orthodox *Talmud Tore* was able to attract some good teachers and good kids, and kept Jewish education alive long enough for there to be something to rescue by the day schools in the 1950s and 1960s.

Nowadays you'll still find *Talmud Tores*, lots of them in fact. The Ultraorthodox sector in the United States and Israel is bursting out all over, and with it the idea of all-day religious education.

These things have no set quantity: leaving the corner of a field to the poor, first fruits, festival sacrifice, acts of kindness, and *Talmud Torah*.

These are things whose revenue is enjoyed in this world while they themselves remain for the World to Come: honoring parents, acts of kindness, and making peace between people—but equal to them all is *Talmud Torah*.

The Mishna, Peah

From a pragmatic standpoint, much *Talmud Torah* is futile or irrelevant, or both. Religiously regarded, however, it is eminently sensible. The bather is refreshed, regardless of where he dips into the ocean. Does he refrain from going to the water merely because he cannot reach the other shore?

Aharon Lichtenstein

— ✣ —

Tamúz (Ashkenazi: **Támuz**)   The month of Tamuz

The fourth month of the Jewish year, *Tamuz* falls in June-July, which should have been a carefree time—except that right in the middle of it comes the Fast of *Tamuz*, followed by the semimourning of the "Three Weeks," leading up to the dreaded Fast of *Av*.

– ✾ –

Tanách. See **Tenach.**

– ✾ –

Taryág mitzvót (Ashkenazi: **Táryag mítzves**)   The 613 commandments

"May you grow up to keep *taryag mitzvot* and be a credit to your people."

The number of *mitzvot* (commandments) in the Torah is traditionally put at 613. Hebrew loves to convert numbers into words and words into numbers. It does it by the ancient code of *gematria* (see entry)—and 613 comes out as *taryag*.

– ✾ –

Tashlích (Ashkenazi: **Táshlech**)   Tashlich ceremony

"So we'll all meet for *Tashlich* by the stream at 4:30, OK—and don't forget your *siddur*."

On the first afternoon of *Rosh Hashanah* (the New Year), there is a custom to gather by a river, shore, or reservoir and say *Tashlich*, prayers for forgiveness that implore God to "cast sin into the deep sea." *Tashlich* means "cast." Folk say there is indeed something humbling and cleansing in contemplating the mighty sea or a river that flows and flows.

Who is God like You—forgiving iniquity and overlooking sin for the remnant of His inheritance; He does not maintain His anger forever, for He desires loving-kindness. May he have renewed mercy on us, suppress our iniquities—and cast [*tashlich*] all their sin into the deep sea.

Verses from the Book of Micah read on Tashlich

– ✾ –

Techína   Sesame paste

"Don't pour too much *techina* into the *pitta* because it'll drip everywhere."

Like *pitta* and *chumus*, the word *techina* is now Hebrew through sheer usage. Made from sesame seeds and sold in jars, it is the great Middle Eastern appetizer—and now shows up regularly at United Jewish Appeal (UJA) fund-raising buffets and at the American synagogue *kiddush*, with celery sticks, carrot spears, and cauliflower clumps in attendance.

— ❧ —

Techiná, pl. techinót (Ashkenazi: **T'chíne, pl. t'chínes**)   Personal prayers

"The prayer book opens automatically to the *t'chines* that my grand-mother used to say on Friday night."

T'chines are the Cinderellas of the Jewish prayer book: personal prayers, composed down the ages, often in Yiddish and for women, often by women for women. When my grandmother passed away, I thought I might never hear a *T'chine* again—my mother does not read Yiddish. Nor does my wife.

But slowly, women are reawakening to the sensitivity of these *t'chines* and asking for them to be translated into Hebrew or English.

— ❧ —

Techiyát ha-metím (Ashkenazi: **Techíyes ha-méysim**)   Resurrection of the dead

"There were so many people there that we haven't seen for ages—it was like *techiyas ha-meysim*."

Judaism teaches that at the end of days the righteous will come back to life in this world.

Three keys are in God's hands, and were given to no other agent: the key to rain, the key to childbearing, and the key to *techiyat ha-metim*.

> The Talmud, Ta'anit

Queen Cleopatra once asked Rabbi Meir:
  "I understand that the dead will rise, but will they rise naked or clothed?"
  "Your Majesty," replied Rabbi Meir, "think of wheat and there is your answer: If an ear of wheat, which is buried naked in the soil, can emerge clothed in layer upon layer, so surely can the righteous, who are buried in their clothes . . ."

> The Talmud, Sanhedrin

Berel was a poor fellow who had never managed to find a bride. Let's face it, he had absolutely nothing to offer. But the *shadchen* (matchmaker) wouldn't give up.

"How about Yente?" he said.

"What! Yente the *Malach-hamoves* ["Angel of Death"]!? No way."

But she was rich, and he was persuaded to marry her. She proved, however, to be a shrew and a vixen . . .

"Oh Lord," prayed Berel, "whichever of us dies first, I will build my wife a golden tombstone."

And die she did. As they bore her to her grave, Berel feigned grief. But suddenly, as they were crossing a bridge, the pallbearers gave a jolt. Yente gave a start and awoke.

"Oy . . . *Techiyes ha-meysim! Techiyes ha-meysim!*" they all shrieked.

And indeed, she had come back to life, and returned to live with Berel—until, three years later, she died once again. And, to tell the truth, he did feel some grief this time, and as they bore her to her grave, Berel wept. But as they reached the bridge, he had second thoughts.

"Gently does it," he called to the pallbearers, "don't jolt her . . ."

– ✂ –

Tefilá, pl. tefilót (Ashkenazi: **Tfíle, pl. tfíles**) Prayer; a prayer

"Morning *tefilot* are at 7 A.M. during the week and at 9 A.M on *Shabbat*."

The word "prayer" is still foreign to many English-speaking Jews. The word *davning* (from the Yiddish verb *davn*) feels better—or increasingly the old-new Hebrew word *tefila*.

Theologians like to emphasize that many of the *tefilot* are not prayers, in the sense of praying for something, but rather praise, gratitude, and self-judgment. The very word *tefila* seems to be part of a family of words denoting judgment.

Tefila must spin out like a thread. The slightest interruption—and the thread snaps.

Rabbi Shneur Zalman of Ladi

Before *tefila*, I pray that during my *tefila* I shall be praying.

Rabbi Chayim of Zans

– ✂ –

Tefilát ha-Dérech (Ashkenazi: **Tfílas ha-Dérech**) Prayer for the journey

"Are we out of Chicago? Then it's time to say *Tefilat ha-Derech*."

On planes, trains, cars, or on foot, Jews traditionally say a short prayer on leaving a built-up area. In Israel, cabs seem to display *Tefilat ha-Derech* very prominently on the dashboard—and verily the mention of "daylight robbery and evil animals" in modern versions of the prayer might not seem entirely inappropriate to the circumstances. El Al also include *Tefilat ha-Derech* in their in-flight material, but a shade more discreetly.

Said Rav Chisda: "Anyone setting out on the road must say *Tefilat ha-Derech*."

Tefilat ha-Derech is as follows: "May it be Your will, O Lord, my God, that You lead me in peace, make me tread in peace, support me in peace, and save me from every enemy and ambush on the road, and give me favor, kindness, and mercy in Your eyes and in the eyes of all who see me. Blessed are You, O Lord, who listens to prayer." Said Abaye: "One should always mention the community when mentioning oneself."

The Talmud, Brachot

Tefilín (Ashkenazi: Tfílin)   Phylacteries

"Are you packed now, John? You have your passport, tickets, credit cards, *tefilin*?"

Tefilin are a pair of small black leather boxes containing biblical verses on parchment, tied by leather straps around the left arm and the head—traditionally worn by men at weekday morning prayers, in fulfillment of the verse "And you shall bind them as a sign on your arm and an emblem between your eyes."

The father of a *Bar Mitzvah* boy traditionally buys him *tefilin* to put on in synagogue—and in the weeks before the big day, the boy will spend many difficult hours getting used to winding them round, stowing them away, and feeling grown up about it.

Around them is a circle of Divine commands: *tefilin* on their hands, *tefilin* on their arms, *tsitsit* on their clothes, and *mezuzot* on their doorways.

The Midrash on Deuteronomy

My deepest revulsion is incited by the man who cheats the God he knows, the man who discusses his business prospects while wearing his *tefilin*.

Martin Buber

Franz-Josef, Emperor of Austria, was friendly to his Jewish subjects. Whenever he paid a visit to the city of Kraków, he visited a synagogue in which his portrait hung prominently, and was duly impressed.

The day dawned when the Emperor was due once again in Kraków, but—horror of horrors—the portrait was nowhere to be found. Franz-Josef swept in, noticed the empty space on the wall, and demanded an explanation.

"Your Majesty," said the rabbi, racking his brains, "You see us today all wearing *tefilin*, a symbol of our faith. But on the Sabbath, we do not wear them. The Sabbath is so holy a symbol that no other, lesser symbol such as *tefilin* is allowed to compete. The same goes for your portrait: While you are not with us, we have it to remind us of you. But when we are able to gaze upon your features in person, how can we allow a mere copy of them to hang upon the wall?"

— ❧ —

Tehilím (Ashkenazi: **Tehílim**)   Psalms

"All through the missile attacks we said *Tehilim*."

The Book of Psalms is called *Tehilim*. (There are 150 in total.) And reciting any or all of them is called "saying *Tehilim*."

No book in the Bible has been so intimately familiar to the Jew as *Tehilim*. Its pages are full of joy and depression, love and hatred, war and peace, piety and confusion. Every community had its *chevra Tehilim* (*Tehilim* society) that recited it once every week. And everywhere, the response to a personal crisis or public disaster was—and among traditional Jews still is—to say *Tehilim*. Nearly everyone knew a few; in the prayer book you find them everywhere, a verse here, a snatch there.

I was once waiting blankly at a Jerusalem bus stop for the bus that never comes; in a doorway, an elderly woman was crouching, waiting like me . . . but saying *Tehilim*.

When King David had finished composing the Book of *Tehilim*, he felt self-satisfied. Said David to God: "Lord, can there be a creature in Your world that sings Your praises more than I?"

At that moment, a frog hopped by. "David," said the frog, "do not be so self-satisfied—for I sing God's praises more than you."

Perek Shira (an ancient midrash)

— ❧ —

Tekiá, pl. **tekiót** (Ashkenazi: **Tekíe**, pl. **tekíes**)   Blast of the *shofar*

"I felt a sudden shiver down my spine during the *tekiot*."

See *Baal tekia*, "*Shofar* blower," *Shevarim*, and *Terua*.

I wonder what goes through people's minds during the *tekiot*, those 100 blasts of the *shofar* heard around the world on *Rosh Hashanah*. Awe? Remorse? Nostalgia? A warmth of peoplehood? Custom requires a complex permutation of three notes, *Tekia, Shevarim, Terua*—long notes, moaning notes, and sobbing notes. And the message of this ancient instrument of alarm that is known as the *shofar* is itself a very complex one.

— ❧ —

Tenách The Bible (alternative pronunciation: **Tanách**)

"I'm sure this place is mentioned in *Tenach*. If you have a *Tenach* handy, we'll look."

The word *Tenach* is formed from the initials of *Torah + Nevi'im + Ktuvim*: "Teaching + Prophets + Writings."

The *Tenach* is a traditional Jewish name for what Christians, for Christian reasons, have preferred to call The Old Testament. The whole *Tenach* is deemed the word of God, received either directly or through the prophets over a period of maybe 1,000 years—a period which came to an end in Second Temple times . . .

Since then the *Tenach* has been handed down by meticulous scribal transmission. (The discovery of the Dead Sea Scrolls, some 2,000 years old, confirmed this.) Meanwhile, the *Tenach* is usually read in book form, though Jerusalem synagogues sometimes have it on parchment scrolls.

There is only one way to salvation—where we have sinned, there must the atonement begin: forget the inherited opinions and misconceptions about Judaism: return to the sources, *Tanach, Midrash, Shas*; read them, study them, grasp them—for the sake of life . . .

Samson Raphael Hirsch

Tenaím (Ashkenazi: **Tnóim**)   Engagement contract; engagement party

"Guess what! The rabbi's daughter's getting married. They held *tnoim* last night."

When a young couple decide to marry, there is a widespread Chasidic custom of drawing up a binding engagement contract between the two families, called *tnoim*. They drink a *le-chayim* and both mothers-in-law-to-be break a plate, to symbolize that there's no going back. In fact, if either side wants out, they will rather marry and divorce than break the *tnoim*.

Teruá (Ashkenazi: **Terúe**)   The *terua* note on the ram's horn

See also *Tekia* and *Shevarim*.

Terua is one of the three traditional notes sounded on the *shofar* (ram's horn) on the New Year. It consists of nine or more short sharp bursts— a bit like sobbing.

Teshuvá (Ashkenazi: **Teshúve**)   Literally "return." Denotes repentance

"He comes into synagogue for half an hour and he's already dashing back to the office? He must have discovered a new quick way of doing *teshuva.*"

See also *Baal Teshuva,* "Penitent."

Teshuva is the foundation of Jewish morality. Prophets and rabbis have forever come back to the image of a "return" to God—a return from what is surely just a temporary estrangement.

"... and *teshuva, tefila* [prayer], and *tsedaka* [charity] cancel the stern decree."
From the High Holy Day prayers

Teshuva, return, is the name given to the act of decision in its ultimate intensification; it denotes the decisive turning point in a man's life, the renewing, total reversal in the midst of the normal course of his existence.
Martin Buber

Advertisement in a synagogue magazine: "Do *Teshuva* now and avoid the *Yom Kippur* rush."

— ❧ —

Tevét (Ashkenazi: **Téyves**)   The month of Tevet

In darkest winter, *Tevet,* the tenth month of the Jewish year, starts off with the last few days of *Chanukah*—but then comes the fast of *Asara be-Tevet.*

— ❧ —

Tikún Leyl Shavuót (Ashkenazi: **Tíken Leyl Shvúes**)   Shavuot night learn-in

"The *Tikun Leyl Shavuot* was just great up until three-thirty. Then I fell asleep ..."

Staying up through a summer night to hear the dawn chorus and greet the sun is always a joy—and all the more when it's combined with the custom of *Tikun Leyl Shavuot.* On the first night of the festival of *Shavuot* in early summer, the hardy, the pious, and the plain romantic get together to study Torah through the night, in commemoration of the Giving of the Law on this very day. More and more synagogues are organizing learn-ins of all sorts, accompanied (of course) by endless coffees and chocolate chip cookies. How things work in Australia, I don't quite know.

— ❧ —

Tinokót shel bet rabán (Ashkenazi: **Tinóhkes shel beys rábon**)
Children at Jewish school

"Funding priority must go to securing the future of *tinokot shel bet raban.*"

Warmth and nostalgia surround the term *tinokot shel bet raban,* literally "the children of our rabbi's house," children learning in the traditional ways of Ashkenazi and Sephardi Jewry—particularly since nowadays the word *tinokot* tends to be used in the sense of "babes."

The world survives only by the breath of *tinokot shel bet raban.*

The Talmud, Shabbat

Tinokot shel bet raban may not be taken away from their studies even to rebuild the *Bet ha-Mikdash* [the Temple].

The Talmud, Shabbat

Tishá be-Av (Ashkenazi: **Tíshe B'ov**)   Fast of the ninth day of Av

"Everyone's putting out such low vibes, it's almost like *Tisha be-Av . . .*"

See *Echa,* "Book of Lamentations" and *Kinot,* "Dirges."

The day of *Tisha be-Av* casts a shadow over the summer for many Jews. It's the anniversary of the destruction of the First and Second Temples, of the 1492 expulsion from Spain, of the outbreak of World War I—and marked by fasting, sleeping without a pillow, sitting on low seats, chanting laments, and feeling thoroughly miserable. The 1990 invasion of Kuwait began the day after *Tisha be-Av,* but who knows what that signifies?

One *Tisha be-Av,* Napoleon is said to have passed a synagogue and seen people chanting and wailing. On being told why, he exclaimed:
   "A people that mourns such an ancient national destruction is entitled to have hope for a national reconstruction."

Tishréy (Ashkenazi: **Tíshrey/Tíshri**)   The month of Tishrey

The seventh and most serious month of the Jewish year, *Tishrey* opens with the festival of *Rosh Hashanah,* continues with *Yom Kippur* and *Sukkot,* and comes to a hectic end with *Simchat Torah*—days of repentance and then days of relief and rejoicing and mellow fruitfulness. September-Octoberish.

Tóches   Posterior. See under **Túches**

Tochó ke-varó (Ashkenazi: **Tóhchoh ke-vóroh**)   He or she is a model of sincerity

This Talmudic expression means literally "His inside is like his outside."

Todá (rabá)!   "Thanks (a lot)!"

"And to all those people who helped make this dinner a success, *toda raba*."

This is the Israeli way of saying thanks. The traditional Ashkenazi way was to use another Hebrew expression, *yishar koach* (see entry)— but the Israelis didn't have to invent *toda*: It's one of those funny things about the new Hebrew that the word *toda* has always been obscurely familiar to virtually every Jew from the fourth line of the Chanukah song "*Maoz Tsur*." But there it means "thanksgiving offering." Plus ça change . . .?

Toráh (Ashkenazi: **Tóre**)   The Five Books of Moses; Judaism

"*Chanukah* isn't mentioned in the Torah, it's in the *Gemara*!"

"Instead of sitting in front of that video, why don't you learn *Torah*?"

"But how easy is it to find a psychiatrist with a *Torah* view on life?"

See *Sefer Torah*, "Torah scroll," *Torah she-be'al peh*, "Oral Torah."

Torah essentially means "teaching" (cf. *mora*, "teacher"). The fact that this word, better than any other, sums up traditional Jewish life shows the centrality of study—to men, women, and children alike.

As "*The Torah*," it denotes the Five Books of Moses (also called the *Chumash*), or more broadly the Five Books of Moses plus all the ancient commentaries and elaborations thereon (which are also called *Torah she-be'al peh*, "Oral *Torah*"). As simply *Torah*, it denotes the whole of Jewish religious lore—law, philosophy, history, and so on.

Torah without an occupation is bound to come to nothing.
                                             The Talmud, Avot

Whoever studies *Torah* and fails to review is like someone who sows and fails to harvest.
                                             The Talmud, Sanhedrin

If you have studied much *Torah,* do not congratulate yourself. You were created for this purpose.

The Talmud, Avot

– ❧ –

Toráh she-be'al peh (Ashkenazi: Tóre she-b'al peh)   The Oral Law

"The third grade gets three hours *Chumash* (Five Books of Moses) and one hour *Torah she-be'al peh.*"

"You shall not cook a young goat in its mother's milk," state the Five Books of Moses. And yet Jews have traditionally interpreted this as a ban on cooking, eating, or using any mix of meat and milk. The *Torah she-be'al peh* in action.

"People of the Book," the Koran called the Jews. A misleading name. As important as the written Five Books of Moses always were, they were always just one half of the Torah. The other half was the *Torah she-be'al peh,* the explanations and elaborations of the written Torah that were handed down by word of mouth—and *not* in book form—for many generations.

But following the Dispersion, the Rabbis ordered *Torah she-be'al peh* to be committed to writing, to become our modern-day *Mishna, Midrash,* and *Gemara.* Yet it went on being called *Torah she-be'al peh,* "Oral Torah"—and indeed it's the kind of thing that is very difficult to learn in any fashion except orally, from a teacher.

– ❧ –

Tovél ve-shérets be-yadó (Ashkenazi: Tóyvl ve-shérets be-yódoh) Pious hypocrisy!

Literally "immersed in water with a reptile in his hand," this is the Talmud's graphic metaphor for someone who has all manner of pious intentions but makes a nonsense of them in action. The image refers to the practice of doing immersions for self-purification from contact with impure objects, such as dead reptiles . . .

– ❧ –

Tóyvl   Immerse (cookware)

"There are six glasses over there that haven't been *toyvl'ed.* Would you *toyvl* them for me?"

Toyvl is the Ashkenazi term. Sephardim and Israelis use the noun *tevilat kelim,* "immersion of vessels."

To *toyvl* is to immerse newly purchased cookware, silverware, and dishes (of glass or metal) in "pure" water for a split second, to "purify" it before use. Tradition requires the *toyvling* to be done in a stream or lake or a specially constructed facility at the synagogue or *mikveh* (see entry). So the next time you see someone tramping along the seashore in midwinter with three pans and twelve sets of silverware, you'll know they're not having a picnic.

Treyf   Non-*kosher*, that is, not conforming to Jewish dietary law

"I think someone used that dairy knife on the meat, so assume it's *treyf*."

See *Kasher*.

For anything that isn't *kosher*—a non-*kosher* animal, an admixture of meat and dairy food, or any silverware, or dishes used for such—Ashkenazi Jews traditionally use the word *treyf*.

  Sephardim use *trefa* for meat that has not been traditionally slaughtered, and sometimes also as a no-holds-barred insult.

In our home, the "world" itself was *treyf*.

Isaac Bashevis Singer

Tsáar baaléy chayím (Ashkenazi: **Tsáar báaley cháyim**)   Animal suffering

"Don't kill that spider, just throw it out. It's *tsaar baaley chayim!*"

Avoiding *tsaar baaley chayim* is a big thing in the Torah: not muzzling an ox threshing grain, not standing by when a donkey collapses under its load, not taking eggs from the nest while the mother bird is there. They say that for fear of *tsaar baaley chayim* the great kabbalist, Rabbi Yitschak Luria, forbade his followers to kill even a louse. But if I were a household pet, what would most attract me to moving in with an Orthodox Jewish owner would be Passover—the thought that for one blissful week they'd be feeding me lox and raw meat instead of my regular *chametz*-ridden cat or dog food.

Tsáar gidúl baním (Ashkenazi: **Tsáar gídul bónim**)   The stress of raising children

"Have you seen how much camp costs this year? It's real *tsaar gidul baním*."

Although *gidul banim*, "raising children," is an essential *mitzvah*, the Torah never pretended that it's easy. It's a *tsaar*—though not of the same order as *tsaar baaley chayim* (see preceding).

Tsabár, pl. tsabarím   Native-born Israeli

"All three boys are *tsabarim*, so they'll automatically be called for army service."

Anyone who knows a little about Israel knows the word Sabra, denoting the native-born Israeli, named after the prickly pear that grows all over the country, which the Arabs call *sabr*.

But *sabra* (or, more accurately, *sabre*) is actually a Sephardi way of saying it. Most Israelis say *tsabar*.

Sabra humor hardly excels in the kind of biting, yet humane, self-irony that is the hallmark of traditional Jewish humor. It is cooler, a bit distant, or abstract, in the shaggy-dog style. In his humor, the *sabra* is critical not of himself, but of the high-sounding pathos of the older generation.

Amos Elon

Tsadík, pl. tsadikím (Ashkenazi: **Tsádik, pl. tsadíkim**)   Righteous man
Tsadéket, pl. tsadikót (Ashkenazi: **Tsadéykes, pl. tsadkóniyes**) Righteous woman

"I remember his grandmother. A real *tsadeykes* she was . . ."

"You want to send a New Year's Card to the IRS? What, are you some kind of *tsadik*?"

A word from the same root as *tsadik* is *tsedaka*, "charity." See also *Zecher tsadik livracha*.

Tsadik and *tsadeket* are powerful words. This is the ultimate compliment to someone or to someone's memory.

Not too long ago, Chasidic leaders in eastern Europe were referred to as *tsadikim*; nowadays, the usual term is *rebbe*.

Rabbi Israel Baal Shem Tov said: "I hope I can love a *tsadik* as much as God loves a wicked man."

Motl of Chernobyl used to call everyone *tsadik*. Once he was on a wagon with the driver. So he said to the driver, "Hey, *tsadik*"—that's how he called him—"when will we come to this place?"

The driver replied, "Hey, rabbi, I'm a *tsadik* and you're a *tsadik*. I have a daughter—you have a son. So let them get married."

Said Motl, "All right, you're a *tsadik* and I'm a *tsadik*. But my son is going to get married to a *tsadik* like I am, and your daughter is going to get married to a *tsadik* like you are."

Tsadikim are greater in their death than in their life.

The Talmud, Chullin

— ❧ —

Tsarát rabím chatsí nechamá (Ashkenazi: **Tsóras rábim chátsi nechóme**)   Literally "A public woe is half a comfort," that is, "When you suffer together, it makes it half bearable"

This piece of folklore is full of the Jewish experience. Everyone's personal sorrows seem to be diverted into the maelstrom of Jewish suffering. The prayers are overwhelmingly about *we* rather than *I;* even the mourner is comforted with talk of "the mourning for Zion and Jerusalem." And the Israelis under siege, with their own *tsarat rabim,* have found fresh truth and *nechama* in these words.

— ❧ —

Tsarot (Ashkenazi: **Tsóres**)   Troubles, crises

"Israel's having such *tsores* trying to find work for the new immigrants, and all he talks about are his own *tsores!*"

See *Daya le-tsara be-sha'ata,* "Don't try to find crises."

In the wilderness, the Israelites complained about their *tsarot.* Throughout the Middle Ages, Hebrew poets lamented their people's *tsarot.* Today Jewish life has changed beyond recognition, but people still talk about their *tsarot.*

— ❧ —

Tsava'á, pl. **tsava'ót** (Ashkenazi: **Tsavóe**, pl. **tsavóes**)   Last will and testament

"You should have heard Uncle Simon's *tsavoe!*"

Tsava'a is from the same root as *mitzvah,* "commandment, good deed."

It's hard to imagine anyone publishing an anthology of last wills and testaments, and even harder to imagine anyone wanting to read it, but that's precisely what people have often done with Jewish *tsava'ot.* The *tsava'a* was traditionally an occasion for a father to leave a compelling moral message to his offspring, and collections of *tsava'ot* make stirring reading today, if you like that sort of thing.

— ❧ —

Tsedá la-dérech (Ashkenazi: **Tséydo la-dérech**)   Food for a trip

"Here, take these grapes with you—*tseda la-derech.*"

This is a biblical expression, going back to the story of Joseph and his brothers' to-ing and fro-ing to Egypt.

Tsedaká (Ashkenazi: **Tsedóke**)   Charity

"Daddy, there's someone at the door asking for *tsedaka.*"

Tsedaka is the cornerstone of Jewish society. Not by chance is the word for "justice" *tsedek*. Some give 10 percent of their net income to *tsedaka*. And Jewish Law demands that no one asking for *tsedaka* for themselves be turned away empty-handed.

> Even a poor man who lives off *tsedaka* must give *tsedaka*.
>
> The Talmud, Gittin

"Do you give a lot of *tsedaka*?" a rabbi asked a wealthy congregant.
  "*Bli ayin ha-ra* [no evil eye], rabbi—I give enough. But I'm a modest man—I don't like to talk about it."
  "Talk more," said the rabbi, unimpressed—"and, while you're at it, give more!"

> *Tsedaka* counts as much as all the other *mitzvot* of the Torah.
>
> The Talmud, Bava Batra

Tsedaká tatsíl mi-mávet (Ashkenazi: **Tsedóko tátsil mi-móves**)
"Charity saves from death"

This verse from the biblical Book of Proverbs can be taken in two ways—and is. At funerals, the poor traditionally beg for *tsedaka* using this phrase.

> Instead of any formal visiting of the grave, I would prefer that the family try and observe a family day in the month of June at which reminiscence of happy incidents be the order of the day, and some worthy cause be remembered in fulfillment of the admonition *tsedaka tatsil mi-mavet.*
>
> Closing words of Jacob Weinstein's ethical will, 1971

Tseniút (Ashkenazi: **Tsníes**)   Physical modesty

"They don't want the guys or girls to wear shorts at prayers, because of *tseniut.*"

Tseniut has wide ramifications in Orthodox life, and even beyond. *Tseniut* demands that Orthodox womenfolk shun short skirts, and means that they are unlikely to wear jeans, or to sing in male company. Married women cover their hair with a headscarf or a wig. Men and women will not dance together, nor share the same beach, nor get into compromising situations. Separate seating at synagogues is another manifestation of *tseniut*.

— ❧ —

Tsevát bi-tsevát asuyá (Ashkenazi: **Tsvas bi-tsvas asúyo**)
The chicken or the egg

Literally "tongs made with tongs," *tsevat bi-tsevat asuya* belongs to the curious list drawn up by the ancient rabbis of things that must have been created separately from the rest of Creation, since they all partake of the supernatural. Why *Tsevat bi-tsevat asuya*? Because you would have needed tongs to hold the first tongs in the furnace.

Tsevat bi-tsevat asuya has come to be used of any "chicken or egg" situation.

— ❧ —

Tsibúr (Ashkenazi: **Tsíbur**)   The public

"Bob feels he should give of his time to the *tsibur*."

Over and over again, the word *tsibur* recurs in the classic sources—for social policy and politics are as important a part of Judaism as an individual's debt to the Creator. There are *tsorchei tsibur*, "public needs"—education, defense, welfare—and *tefila be-tsibur*, "public prayer," so much more powerful than individual prayer, and there is *tircha de-tsibura*, "public nuisance," such as synagogue services that overrun their time . . .

Said Hillel: "Do not withdraw from the *tsibur*."

> The Talmud, Avot

When the *tsibur* is in trouble, let no man say: "I shall go home and eat and drink, and peace be with me."

> The Talmud, Ta'anit

— ❧ —

Tsitsít (Ashkenazi: **Tsítsis**)   Tassels on the *tallit*

"Kiss the Torah with your *tsitsit* when they carry it past you."

Jewish men and boys traditionally wear a four-cornered garment (the *tallit katan*), under their shirt—with tassels consisting of eight wool strings on each corner. These tassels are the *tsitsit*. A larger four-cornered shawl (the *tallit*), also adorned with *tsitsit*, is worn at morning prayer. In ancient times, one of the eight strings was colored blue, but the tradition for producing the dye lapsed long ago.

Into the *tsitsit* of the corner they shall work a blue string, and whenever you see it you will remember all God's commands and obey them . . .

Numbers 15

When a simple wagon-driver kisses his *tsitsit*, it means more in Heaven than the praises of the archangel Michael.

Rabbi Israel Baal Shem Tov

One summer, on a sandlot in Gloucester, Moshe was playing baseball with a group of boys from town, none of them Jewish. As he ran around the field, his *tsitsit* strings began to fly from under his T-shirt. After the game, as the boys were finishing up and getting ready to leave, one of the townies asked Moshe, "What are those strings hanging out of your shirt?" Moshe, then fourteen, thought for a moment, grinned, and said, "Those are my soul threads."

Blu Greenberg

— ✿ —

Tsom Gedalyá (Ashkenazi: **Tsom Gedálye**)   The Fast of Gedaliah

"Does Chana fast on *Tsom Gedalya*?"

The day after the festival of *Rosh Hashanah*—and quite overshadowed by it—is the fast day of *Tsom Gedalya*. Few Jews have heard of Gedaliah, Governor of Judea, and few have read his sad story in the Book of Jeremiah. But the Orthodox continue the ancient fast on this day, because it commemorates the worst genre of calamity of them all: when Jew kills Jew—in this case, putting an end to the last chance of Jewish self-rule in biblical Judea.

— ✿ —

Tu bi-Shvat   Literally "The 15th day of the month of Shvat." Also known as New Year for Trees, a kind of Arbor Day

"Which fruits did you have for your *Tu bi-Shvat* party? We even had carobs from Israel!"

Tu bi-Shvat is a modest festival in early spring celebrating the trees of Israel. Since antiquity, *Tu bi-Shvat* has marked the start of the tree-planting season, following the winter rains. Diaspora Jews have kept the day alive by eating the fruits of Israel and praying for their growth. Israeli children mark *Tu bi-Shvat* by planting trees in vast numbers.

The almond-tree's in blossom
And a golden sun is shining.
Birds on top of every roof
Are heralding the festival.

Tu bi-Shvat *is here,*
The festival of trees!

> From a popular Israeli kindergarten song

Our God and God of our fathers, may it be Thy will that, by virtue of eating the fruits which we will now eat and say benedictions over, we may benefit from their heavenly roots by which they draw Divine favor and blessing, and may the regimen that controls them continue to make them grow and flourish from the start of the year to its finish . . .

> From a kabbalistically based Prayer for Trees

An unlettered Jew from the mountains came to stay one February with his son-in-law in the big city—and was surprised to find him preparing a festive meal.

"What's this? A festival?"

"Sure, tonight's *Tu bi-Shvat!*"

The father-in-law had never heard of *Tu bi-Shvat*, so his host explained to him that this was the New Year for Trees. But this was still puzzling. He knew all about *the* New Year, *Rosh Hashanah*, but how could trees have a New Year? He decided to go to the woods to see.

And in the snow-covered woods, he found all the trees clothed in white, just like at the New Year! And they were all swaying, just like people sway when they pray! And when the wind howled, it was just like the sound of the *shofar*! And in the middle stood one massive tree. That must be the cantor, he thought.

But suddenly a peasant woman came trudging through the woods—and got her dress entangled in one of the branches.

The old man hurried home to tell his son-in-law:

"You were right about *Tu bi-Shvat*—all the trees are standing and praying just like on *Rosh Hashanah*! But that cantor is such a joker. Fancy, I saw him flirting with one of the women!"

— ✿ —

Túches or **Tóches**   Posterior

"I can't spend another minute sitting on my *tuches* in front of that monitor."

Even if an Ashkenazi Jew knows a bare twenty words of Hebrew, *tuches* will probably be one of them—and perhaps the first Hebrew word he or she will ever have heard as children. Yes, it's Hebrew, although it's come down through Yiddish. A Jew needed a nice way of talking about posteriors, and *tuches* (or in its more classical form, *tachas* or *tachat*), simply meaning "underneath" in the Holy Tongue, was graciously willing to be raised to the task.

— ❧❦ —

Tumá (Ashkenazi: **Túme**)   Impurity

"Turn that video off already! Filth and *tuma* . . ."

Tuma is a strong word, much used by the Ultraorthodox. It simultaneously evokes and exorcises immodesty or depravity of any sort.

— ❧❦ —

Ulpán   Hebrew crash-course

"There's a morning *ulpan* at the community center this fall."

The word *ulpan* holds out promise that learning Hebrew can be fun, can be painless, can be natural. A kind of linguistic Lamaze, except that once you're six months pregnant there's no going back, while a lot of people who start an *ulpan* never push on to see the fruit of their labor.

   The whole *ulpan* idea was an Israeli response to mass immigration, using vogue ideas of teaching a language *in* the language and with as little grammar, paper, and pencil as possible. If it worked, it may be because an immigrant *had* to learn Hebrew to survive. Whether it works in London or Chicago, I don't know. There are a lot of people wandering around who know how to say the first half of a Hebrew sentence. But *ulpan* is one of the last great Zionist experiences. And *ulpan* is undeniably fun.

— ❧❦ —

Vayikrá (Ashkenazi: **Vayíkro**)   The Book of Leviticus

Vayikra is the third book of the Torah. Its present-day Hebrew name comes from the first word *vayikra*, "And He called (to Moses)." Even Jewish children well schooled in the Torah are unlikely to know most of *Vayikra* well, as it is largely occupied with the sacrificial and purificatory responsibilities of the ancient priesthood, hence its Latin name "Leviticus."

   And yet medieval German Jews had the custom of starting children's schooldays off with the first words of *Vayikra*. And there are teams of *kohanim* (priests) in modern times who have been studying these very regulations intensively, in expectation of the Third Temple.

– ❧ –

Vidúy (Ashkenazi: **Víduy**) Confession

See *Al Chet.*

To confess one's sins aloud to God is a vital feature of *teshuva* (repentance)—and a central part of the service on *Yom Kippur* (the *Al Chet* prayer) and on one's deathbed. It is traditionally accompanied by pounding the heart with the hand.

They summoned a rabbi to say the *viduy* with a wealthy old lady, who was seriously ill. After it was over, she leaned toward the rabbi and asked:
  "Rabbi, can I still have a glass of water, or must I die now?"

As the renowned sceptic, Yisroel Ostrin, lay dying, a pious friend came and pleaded:
  "Yisroel, Yisroel! Say a *viduy!*"
  But the sceptic was adamant. "I see you want me to make the Rabbis look like complete frauds," he said to his baffled friend. "Didn't the Rabbis say that the wicked don't repent even on the threshold of Hell? So then why are you trying to make me prove them wrong . . .?"

– ❧ –

Yam ha-Mélach The Dead Sea

Literally "the Salt Lake." Apart from being the lowest place on the world's surface, the site of Sodom and Gomorrah (you can't sink lower than that), utterly dead, and a delight to people who seek to smear themselves with mud or to float while reading newspapers, the *Yam ha-Melach* has provided Israel with a rich chemical industry.

  But *Yam ha-Melach* hasn't exactly entered the country's folklore or mythology, and as it's gradually drying up someone had better do something about that before it's too late.

– ❧ –

Yam Kinéret Lake Kineret = the Sea of Galilee

Whatever *Yam ha-Melach* lacks in romance, the *Yam Kineret* makes up for amply. It is truly a designer lake. Nestling between the mountains of the Galilee and the Golan, shaped like a heart or a lyre, and with a name to match (*Kinor* is "lyre"), *Yam Kineret* was immortalized in the lyrical songs of the poetess-pioneer Rachel.

Like most designer things, however, *Yam Kineret* faces utter exploitation—by tourism and, most tragic, by a water-wasting society that is pumping it dry.

And perhaps it never happened,
And perhaps I did not rise at dawn to till the garden with the sweat of my hands
And never—in those hot, searing days of harvest,
From atop a sheaf-laden cart—raised my voice in song,
Never was purified in the quiet blue and the perfection
Of Kineret *of mine,* Kineret *of mine—*
Did you exist? Or did I dream a dream?

A Hebrew poem by the poetess Rachel

Yamím Noraím (Ashkenazi: **Yómim Nohróim**)   High Holy Days

"Today I want to buy the children clothes for the *Yamim Noraim.*"

Yamim Noraim means "days of awe." This is the overall name for the autumn festivals of *Rosh Hashanah* and *Yom Kippur* and the days in between—ten days with a theme of awe and repentance, and a coloring to match: The normal *parochet* (curtain) over the Holy Ark and the coverings of the Torah scrolls are changed for white ones, and even colored *kipot* are changed for white ones. The *Yamim Noraim* mood builds gradually: for days, even weeks before, homes are being cleaned, children groomed, and clothes readied so as to look one's best before Heavenly King and people on the big days.

(The) **Yardén**   The River Jordan

As rivers go, the width or length of the *Yarden* is hardly impressive. But being the only serious river in Israel, and the scene of wonders and miracles, it means a lot. The name *yarden* means "descender," and in 150 miles or so it hurtles down from the foothills of Mt. Hermon, through verdure and wilderness, to reach the lowest place on earth, the Dead Sea.

"Onward, Yarden, *onward flow," murmur your waves.*
Wash onto your banks and roll away the sickness of your land.
Give out a thundering sound with your mass of waters,
Clear us a highway to Zion, and we shall follow you!

From an early twentieth-century Hebrew Zionist hymn

Yatsá secharó be-hefsedó (Ashkenazi: **Yótso s'chóroh be-hefséydoh**)
"They lose more than they gain"

"He wants to hire a car from the airport rather than call a limousine? But he'll lose his way . . . *Yatsa secharo be-hefsedo.*"

The classic case of *Yatsa secharo be-hefsedo*, in the Mishna, is someone who's hard to anger but hard to mollify (think about it . . .). The same Mishna gives better marks to someone who's easy to anger but easy to mollify: In their case, *yatsa hefsedo bi-secharo*, "They gain more than they lose."
 The expression is used of past, present, or future scenarios.

– ✿ –

Yehudá ve-Shomrón Judea and Samaria

"How do they feel about living in *Yehuda ve-Shomron*?"

See also *Shtachim* and *Shomron.*

Yehuda ve-Shomron is a common (and the official) Israeli name for the areas captured from Jordan in 1967 but never technically annexed.
 Yehuda is the area south of Jerusalem, roughly corresponding to the ancient province of *Yehuda* (Judea) in Maccabean times; the name goes back even further to the biblical kingdom of *Yehuda*, covering the whole southern half of Israel. It also gives us the word *Yehudi*, "Jew."
 While many Israelis refer to *Yehuda ve-Shomron* simply as *ha-Shtachim*, "the territories," nationalistic circles use the ancient name — as indeed did the British, until the Jordanians came up with the name West Bank.

– ✿ –

Yeridá Emigration from Israel

"No one's to blame for the *yerida*—it's just the economic reality."

Yerida is almost a taboo word. Although few Diaspora Jews would blame one another for not "making *aliyah*" or even for returning from living in Israel, there is a deep unease toward Israelis who leave permanently for the West. It is called *yerida*, "descent" (the opposite of *aliyah*, literally "ascent"), and someone who leaves is branded a *yored* (see entry).

– ✿ –

Yeridá le-tsórech aliyáh (Ashkenazi: **Yeríde le-tsórech alíye**)   Descent for the purpose of ascent

"Just don't treat it as a crisis. It's a *yerida le-tsorech aliyah.*"

Yerida le-tsorech aliyah is a Chasidic concept that the soul has to be brought down into this world in order to find the challenges that will raise it to a higher level than before—descent for the purpose of ascent.

The phrase can be used of any situation where you had to "go down" in order to "rise even higher." A good means of encouragement.

— ❧ —

Yeridát ha-dorót (Ashkenazi: **Yerídes ha-dóhres**)   The decline of the generations

"The kids nowadays don't want to do anything for themselves. It's a real *yeridat ha-dorot* . . ."

Deeply engrained in the Jewish psyche is the belief that, ever since the Revelation of the Torah, each successive generation has failed to reach the standards of the preceding one. Rabbi Akiva, in this light, didn't come up to Daniel, nor Maimonides to Rabbi Akiva, nor the Gaon of Vilna to Maimonides.

And *yeridat ha-dorot* is what makes today's rabbinic lawmakers so reluctant to challenge established precedent.

But equally engrained is the belief that when things are at their lowest ebb (now perhaps? or can things get even worse?), a Golden Age will dawn.

— ❧ —

Yerushá (Ashkenazi: **Yerúshe**)   Inheritance

"The only thing *we* were left in the *yerusha* was a matching pair of brass ducks."

Happy is the man or woman in this day and age who can leave children a *yerusha* worth squabbling over. The cost of college education in the United States or the need to provide marriageable daughters with an apartment in Israel, plus the attentions of the IRS, make a *yerusha* something you want to leave behind you well before you die.

Commit yourself to the study of Torah, for it cannot be treated as your *yerusha*.

The Talmud, Avot

— ❧ —

Yerushaláyim Jerusalem

Does any city on earth have so evocative and rhythmic a name as *yerushalayim*? The city chosen by David to be the eternal capital of the Jewish people contains within its name the letters *sh-l-m* spelling *shalem*, "whole" and *shalom*, "peace."

If I forget you, *Yerushalayim,* may my right hand lose its cunning.

Psalm 137

Said Rabbi Yochanan:
  Yerushalayim will one day be the capital of the world.

The Midrash

The mountain air is clear as wine, and the scent of pines
Is borne on the twilight breeze, with the sound of bells.
And in a slumber of tree and stone, captive to its dream,
Is the city that dwells alone—and in its heart, a wall.
Yerushalayim *of gold*
And of copper and light,
Let me be a lyre
To all your songs.

From Naomi Shemer's famous Hebrew hymn to Jerusalem

Yesh me-áyin Something out of nothing, ex nihilo

"You can imagine democracy in Czechoslovakia because they have a tradition of it, but in some eastern European countries it would have to be a case of *yesh me-ayin . . .*"

Yesh me-ayin, literally "existence out of nothingness," actually goes back to mysticism and Chasidic theology. *Yesh me-ayin* is how the universe was made. It has come to be used of anything apparently being made out of thin air.

Yeshivá, pl. **yeshivót** (Ashkenazi: **Yeshíve**, pl. **yeshíves**) Talmudic seminary

"After high school, Jonathan's spending a year in *yeshiva* in Israel."

See *Chavruta*, "Study twosome" and *Kolel*, "Married men's seminary."

Yeshiva is the powerhouse of traditional Jewish culture: a seminary where Jewish boys in their late teens or twenties receive intensive tuition in the Talmud and other classic Jewish sources—commonly for one year, sometimes for longer. Not so long ago, most American Jews considered *yeshiva* a thing of the past, an institution that belonged with *Fiddler on the Roof* or with the Ultraorthodox. Now the *yeshiva* is back. Most modern Orthodox Jews in the United States, Israel, and other countries send their sons to *yeshiva* after high school. (Increasingly, their daughters, too, go to women's *yeshivot*, called "sems.")

The atmosphere is one of piety; and the study system, based on a few *shiurim* (lectures) and ten to fifteen hours a day of learning in *chavruta* (twosomes), is arguably the best intellectual training that has ever been designed.

Yeshiva University in Manhattan was founded to combine an Orthodox *yeshiva* training with a college education.

It is the nation's schools—the *cheder*, the *yeshiva*, the *bet midrash*—that have been our safest strongholds throughout our long tough struggle to exist in the world as a distinct people among peoples. In times of storm and fury, we took cover behind their walls and there we sharpened the one weapon we had left—the Jewish mind.

Chaim Nachman Bialik

Yétser ha-rá (Ashkenazi: **Yéytser hóre**)   Evil inclination

"He was going to give up smoking—but his *yetser ha-ra* got the better of him."

Everywhere in traditional Jewish pyschology are the ideas of the *yetser ha-ra* and the *yetser ha-tov* ("the good inclination")—two ideas that are not necessarily what they seem: The *yetser ha-ra* is in fact the aggressive, impulsive inclination, also God given, also necessary to human survival, but to be treated with extreme watchfulness. The Talmud teaches that the word for the "creation" of Adam, *vayitser*, is spelled in the Bible with an extra letter *yod*, to emphasize that he was intended from the outset to have both a *yetser ha-tov* and a *yetser ha-ra*.

The *yetser ha-ra* only desires what is forbidden.

The Jerusalem Talmud, Yoma

Said Rav Assi: "In the beginning the *yetser ha-ra* is like a spider's thread, but in the end—like wagon ropes."

The Talmud, Sukkah

When the Bible says, "And God saw all that He had done, and behold it was very good," this refers to the *yetser ha-ra*. But is the *yetser ha-ra* very good? However, were it not for the *yetser ha-ra*, no person would build a house, or marry, or have children, or conduct business.

The Midrash on Genesis

Yetsiát Mitsráyim (Ashkenazi: **Yetsíes Mitsráyim**)   The Exodus from Egypt

"The children are going to dress up this *Pesach* as if they were taking part in *Yetsiat Mitsrayim*."

In virtually every prayer and in every festival, a Jew is enjoined to remember *Yetsiat Mitsrayim*. Even *Maoz Tsur*, the world's favorite *Chanukah* song, devotes an entire stanza to it. It doesn't seem to matter that no one alive today was in the Exodus (unless you believe in reincarnation). A kind of collective memory is involved. Only once in the year does it emerge, become tangible, for most people: at the Passover *Seder* night. But I suspect that deep down it's always there. *Yetsiat Mitsrayim* is the frame of reference for all that a Jew knows of God and of Jewish destiny.

. . . and You have given us in love, O Lord our God, this Day of Remembrance, a day for the blowing of the *shofar*, a holy festival in remembrance of *Yetsiat Mitsrayim* . . .

Translation of part of the Kiddush for Rosh Hashanah (The New Year)

— ✿ —

Yichúd (Ashkenazi: **Yíchud**)   Being alone with the opposite sex

"She always leaves the door ajar when he's here. She doesn't want to be in *yichud* with him."

Orthodox Jews try hard to avoid *yichud* with the opposite sex, being together in a place to which other people don't have easy access. Compromising situations, you might say. So an Orthodox young woman may wish to leave a door ajar if alone in the house with a male acquaintance. A married woman may feel the same way about being alone with another man if her husband is out of town. And there must be many men, too, who feel more secure thanks to the laws of *yichud* with women. Strongly recommended for all presidential hopefuls.

— ✿ —

Yichús (Ashkenazi: **Yíches**)   Family pedigree; status (in general)

"I've also got *yichus*—I go right back to Adam."

Yichus is still a valuable commodity, in certain circles, though whether a girl's dowry or her *yichus* count for more may be a debatable point. To be descended from rabbis is in itself no special distinction; after all, go back three generations and it seems like everyone in Poland or Morocco was a rabbi of some sort. What counts is which rabbis. Say "the Alter Rebbe" or "Baba Sali," and your *yichus* is real *yichus*.

Typists don't do too well; some receive a paltry three dollars a week. But typists have more *yiches* than shopgirls—it helps them find a husband, and they mix with a more refined class of person.

The Forward (New York Yiddish paper) 1905

— ❧ —

Yimách shemó   "May his name be blotted out"

"That portrait in the corner is of Tsar Nicholas, *yimach shemo*."

Hebrew never had the range of curses that Yiddish boasted. You can't wish in Hebrew for all of someone's teeth save one to fall out and for that one to hurt. Even Israelis don't wish someone to go to *gehinom*, "Hell." They say *lech la-azazel*, "go to Azazel" (see entry).

But if you want to redouble the curse on some notorious paragon of evil, *yimach shemo* is pretty effective. It expresses the hope that, far from being known, their memory should be wiped out—like the evil Haman in the Book of Esther, whose name is drowned out with stamping when the book is recited on the festival of Purim.

Yimach shemo is regularly appended (in writing or speech) to names like Hitler *yimach shemo*, Stalin *yimach shemo*, and Saddam Hussein *yimach shemo*.

— ❧ —

Yishár kóach! (Ashkenazi: **Yáshe kóyech**)   "Well done; thanks for your help"

"And to all those who have given of their time for this project, *yishar koach!*"

See *Koach*, "Strength."

Literally "may your strength be firm." A congratulations to people receiving an honor in the synagogue (their response is *baruch tihye*, "be blessed") or, in very traditional circles, a thanks for any help rendered.

— ❧ —

Yisraél (Ashkenazi: **Yisróel**)   A Jew who is neither *Kohen* nor Levite

"Excuse me, are you a *Kohen*?"
   "No, I'm a *Yisrael*."

A small percentage of Jews are categorized for religious purposes as *Kohanim*, "priests," claiming descent through their father and father's father from the first biblical high priest, Aaron. Another small percentage are *Leviyim*, "Levites," descended from the tribe of Levi. Anyone who is neither—the overwhelming majority—is simply termed "a *Yisrael*," literally "an Israelite."

For those people who always like to be a bit different, to be a *Yisrael* may sound a bit of a bore, but it makes little practical difference what you are (unless you particularly like to be called up first every time to the reading of the Torah). See *kohen* for details.

A very modern-looking, clean-shaven, hatless man once called on the old Rabbi of Slonim. The rabbi looked him up and down.

"Are you a *Kohen* or a *Levi*, my dear fellow?" the rabbi inquired.

"What makes you think I'm a *Kohen* or a *Levi*?" asked the other with some amusement.

"Well, you certainly don't look like a *Yisroel*," declared the rabbi.

— ✿ —

Yisurím (Ashkenazi: **Yisúrim**)   Trials and tribulations

"She's had so many *yisurim* from her children, she deserves some *nachat* [fulfillment]."

For *yisurim* look no further than the Book of Job. "Why do good people suffer" is high on the biblical and Talmudic agendas. Ultimately the rabbis of the Talmud have to admit that there is such a thing as *yisurim shel ahava*, "trials of love."

There is no one who has no *yisurim*.

The Midrash

. . . and cleanse what I have sinned in Your abundant mercies, but not by *yisurim* and grievous illnesses.

Prayers of *Yom Kippur*

"Rebbe," sobbed a young man racked by disease to Rabbi Yisroel of Rizhyn, "with *yisurim* like these, how can any normal person study or say prayers?"

Rabbi Yisroel put his arm around his shoulder: "It could be," he said, "that the Almighty values your personal *yisurim* more highly than all your studies and all your prayers . . ."

— ✿ —

Yiyéh tov   "It'll turn out OK"

"Danny's going into the army this week? Don't worry, *yiyeh tov* . . ."

Probably the most frequently used of all Israeli sayings. (If you get tired of it, try *yiyeh b'seder*, "It'll be all right," *bli panika*, "Don't panic," *al tidag*, "Don't worry," or *lo ason*, "It's not the end of the world.")

And hardly surprising: One hopes each war will be the last and that the economy couldn't possibly get any worse . . .

The other side of worry is the constant admonition not to worry, that everything will be all right. The sight of a broken-down car on the road, an unhappy expression on someone's face, the news of another border incident, all evoke a quick rejoinder of *al tidag* or *bli panika*.

Amos Elon

— ❧ —

Yizkór (Ashkenazi: **Yízker**)   Memorial prayer for close relatives

"He says he'll be in synagogue on Passover to say *Yizkor* for his parents."

The *Yizkor* prayer has some residual power to draw the masses back into the synagogue, for a few brief minutes, to pray for the souls of their dearly departed. *Yizkor* means "may He remember." Four times a year, on *Yom Kippur* and other festivals, the synagogue is in a brief hubbub as those who wish to say *Yizkor* pour in while—in keeping with folk custom—those who have not lost parents file out. The cantor will probably also say memorial prayers for the Six Million and for the Israeli war dead. And then, suddenly, everything returns to normal.

May God remember [*yizkor*] the souls of the pure martyrs who have been killed, butchered, burned, drowned, strangled for *kiddush ha-Shem* [sanctification of God]. We pledge charity in memory of their souls, so that their spirits be bound up in the bond of life with the souls of Abraham, Isaac, and Jacob, Sarah, Rebekah, Rachel, and Leah . . .

From a Hebrew *Yizkor* prayer for Jewish martyrs

— ❧ —

Yom ha-Atsmaút   Israel Independence Day

"The school is having a *Yom ha-Atsmaut* party. Do you have an Israeli flag to lend us?"

Jews find it easier to celebrate (or mourn) ancient happenings than modern ones. Take *Yom ha-Atsmaut*. It commemorates the declaration of Israeli independence in May 1948, and most Jewish communities hold festive services and perhaps a show or a party.

But *Yom ha-Atsmaut* has yet to take on a distinctive form and distinctive prayers or customs. You sense this clearly in Israel. Once there were big *Yom ha-Atsmaut* happenings and military parades, but now it's basically a day out in the car.

— ❧ —

Yom Kippúr (Ashkenazi: **Yom Kípper**)   The Day of Atonement

"If *Yom Kippur* comes in at 6:15, we'd better start the meal at 4:45."

The holiest day of the year. The day on which, to this day, a majority of Jews spend much of the day in the synagogue, praying for atonement (*kippur*) for the year's sins.

No eating. No drinking. No showering. For the traditional, no wearing of leather shoes. But this is no black fast. It is preceded by a festive meal and concluded with another festive meal to break the fast. Catharsis. The whole-iest day of the year.

If I were able, I would abolish every single ta'anit *[fast] save* Yom Kippur *and* Tisha be-Av—
On Yom Kippur, *who needs to eat?*
And on Tisha be-Av, *who's able to eat?*

Rabbi Avrohom Yehoshua Heschel of Apta

– ❧ –

Yómtov Shéyni   The extra festival day observed in the Diaspora

"Why don't you guys come for lunch on *Yomtov Sheyni*?"

Orthodox Jews in the Diaspora observe an extra day for each of the major biblical festivals (except *Yom Kippur*—phew!). It's called *Yomtov Sheyni,* literally "second festival." And so they have not one *Seder* night but two.

– ❧ –

Yom Yerushaláyim   Jerusalem Day

"The *Yom Yerushalayim* service in the synagogue will commence at 8 P.M."

Yom Yerushalayim marks the anniversary of the liberation of Old Jerusalem and the Temple site from Jordanian rule in June 1967. As on *Yom ha-Atsmaut*, there are special synagogue services and other happenings—ad lib.

– ❧ –

Yóntef, also spelled **Yom Tov**, pl. **Yómim tóhvim / Yontóyvem**   Festival

"Good *yontef*, Betty, how are you?"

". . . as for those loose hinges, I can't do anything till after *Yontef*."

N.B.: The singular, *yontef*, is also used (with a capital Y, as it were) as a proper name, in the same way as *Shabbat*: One prepares for *Shabbat*, one prepares for

Yontef. People also use the plural, "the *Yontoyvem,*" specifically for the major autumn season of High Holy Days.

The major biblical festivals—*Pesach, Shavuot, Rosh Hashanah, Yom Kippur, Sukkot*—are traditionally called, in Ashkenazi parlance, *yomim tohvim* or *yontoyvem. Yontef* actually comes from the Hebrew phrase *yom tov,* literally "good day," used since Talmudic times for "festival." The pronunciation *yontef* is due to Yiddish; but Yiddish continues to spell it and pluralize it the Hebrew way.

However, the word *yontef* has fallen on hard times. Israelis do not use it at all; they prefer the biblical word *chag* (see entry), as do many other people who wish to sound more modern.

Said Rabbi Eliezer: On *Yom Tov* a person should either eat and drink or sit and study. Said Rabbi Yehoshua: Divide it—half for food and drink and half for the House of Study.

The Talmud, Pesachim

Yoréd, pl. **yordím**   Israeli emigré

"Is her family just here temporarily from Tel Aviv, or are they *yordim*?"

Yored is virtually a taboo word, just like *yerida* (see entry). There is felt to be something reprehensible about leaving Israel permanently for the West. Most Israelis would like to think that those who have are actually only "on leave."

American-born Jews find it hard to relate to the *yored* in their midst, or in fact to Israelis in general. And Israeli *yordim* seem largely to live apart from other Jews, mixing among themselves. Nevertheless, Jewish education is largely dependent on them—they, for sure, have no need for this book.

(To be) **Yotsé** (Ashkenazi: **Yóytse**)   To have done what's required

"If I had to go out in the middle of the *shofar* blowing, am I still *yotse*?"

"OK, guys, you don't have to clear up anymore here—you're all *yotse.*"

To be *yotse* is to perform a *mitzvah* (religious duty) properly, being "quit" as it were (*yotse* literally means "go out, quit")—to be *yotse* with the way you read from the Torah, with the size of your *tallit,* with the shape of your *Chanukah menorah* . . . And, by extension, to be *yotse* with the number of times you called Aunt Sylvia last month and with the offerings you made to the synagogue.

— ৵৶ —

Zécher la-churbán (Ashkenazi: **Zéycher la-chúrben**)   Remembrance of the Destruction of the Temple

See *Churban*, "Destruction."

If you walk into an Orthodox Jewish home, you may sometimes see a small section of wall undecorated. This is a *zecher la-churban*, literally "a remembrance of the Destruction," a traditional mark of grief for the loss of the Temple and Jewish life 2,000 years ago. Another well-known *zecher la-churban* is the bridegroom's breaking of a glass underfoot at his wedding. Less well known is the custom in Jerusalem, to this day, of restricting the music at a wedding to one lone drum.

— ৵৶ —

Zécher tsadík livrachá (Ashkenazi: **Zéycher tsádik livrócho**) (Commonly abbreviated to **zatsál**)   "May the memory of the righteous be a blessing"

"Our tour of Poland took us to the tomb of Rabbi Moshe Isserles, *zecher tsadik livracho*."

See also *Zichrono livracha*, "May his memory be a blessing" and *Alav ha-shalom*, "Peace be upon him."

Rather like "may he rest in peace," this phrase is often appended (particularly by the Ultraorthodox) when one mentions the name of a great rabbi.

It is actually a direct quotation from the biblical Book of Proverbs: "The memory of the righteous is a blessing, and the name of the wicked will rot."

— ৵৶ —

Zechút, pl. zechiyót (Ashkenazi: **Zechús, pl. zechúsim**)   Merit; act of merit

"To raise a family and settle them is quite a *zechut* in these times."

"May the deceased's *zechut* be a source of blessing to you all in years to come."

See also *Melamed zechut*, "Give the benefit of the doubt."

By performing *mitzvot* (religious duties), people are said to amass *zechiyot* (merits), and to receive reward in this world or in the next.

Just as a person's *zechiyot* and sins are weighed at death, so too all mankind's sins are weighed against their *zechiyot* on the New Year festival.

Maimonides

— 🙞🙜 —

Zemirót (Ashkenazi: **Zmíres**)   Sabbath mealtime songs

"Let's sing some *zemirot* between courses. You start us off, Daniel."

Around the world, Jews have the custom of singing *zemirot* during the Sabbath meals. *Zemirot* are religious poems, medieval for the most part but sung to a variety of melodies. German Jewish *zemirot* remind one vaguely of carousing songs, many Chasidic numbers sound as if they've waltzed right out of a Viennese ballroom, while some of my more alternative friends favor a theme from *Appalachian Spring*, though I'm positive it has nothing to do with Aaron Copland being Jewish.

But it's the words that count.

— 🙞🙜 —

Zenut (Ashkenazi: **Znus**)   Sexual immorality; prostitution

If *zenut* has been left almost till the end of this book, it's thanks to the order of the English alphabet and not of the Hebrew. The word *zenut* is not a dirty word. In the Bible (and in the *Shema* recited twice a day), the idea of *zenut* is mentioned in the same breath as idolatry and godlessness.

— 🙞🙜 —

Zerizím makdimím le-mitzvót (Ashkenazi: **Zrízim makdímim le-mítzves**)   When duty calls, be the first

Literally "the quick get there first for religious duties," *zerizim makdimim le-mitzvot* is widely used for encouraging or congratulating anyone who jumps to it.

— 🙞🙜 —

Zichronó/zichroná livrachá (Ashkenazi: **Zichróhne livróche**)   "May his or her memory be a blessing"

"I got this book as a present from your grandmother, *zichrona livracha*."

See *Zecher tsadik livracha.*

When mentioning a departed relative or someone of stature, Israelis—and many Diaspora Jews, particularly the Orthodox—add this phrase of respect. The import of *zichrono livracha* is a profound one: that a person's memory can inspire the living to higher things, which in turn redound to the credit of the departed.

– ❧ –

(The) **Zóhar**   The classic book of the Kabbalah

Some swear by it; others studiously avoid it. But you can't ignore it.

Since its emergence into public view in thirteenth-century southern France, the *Zohar* has been the classic book of *Kabbalah* mysticism, and it is freely available to the public, if they wish to tangle with the obscure Aramaic. (English translations tend to be even more obscure.) The *Zohar* is studied intensively by many Sephardim. Chasidim, too, make abundant use of it. It has left its marks throughout Jewish laws and customs. It has even found its way into the standard American and British prayer books, though I'm not telling where . . .

The Words in
Their Hebrew Lettering

Acharón	אַחֲרוֹן
Acharón acharón chavív	אַחֲרוֹן אַחֲרוֹן חָבִיב
Adár	אֲדָר
Adón Olám	אֲדוֹן עוֹלָם
Afikomán	אֲפִיקוֹמָן
Aggadá	אַגָּדָה
Ahavát Yisraél	אַהֲבַת יִשְׂרָאֵל
(The) Akedá	עֲקֵדָה
Al Chet	עַל חֵטְא
Al ha-Nisím	עַל הַנִּסִּים
Al régel achát	עַל רֶגֶל אַחַת
Al tiftách peh la-satán	אַל תִּפְתַּח פֶּה לַשָּׂטָן
Aláv/aléha ha-shalóm	עָלָיו/עָלֶיהָ הַשָּׁלוֹם
Álef-Bet	אָלֶף-בֵּית
Aléynu	עָלֵינוּ
Aliyáh	עֲלִיָּה
Alyá ve-kóts ba	אֲלִיָּה וְקוֹץ בָּהּ
Am ha-Árets	עַם הָאָרֶץ
Amén!	אָמֵן
Amidá	עֲמִידָה
Aním Zemirót	אַנְעִים זְמִירוֹת
Apikóres	אֶפִּיקוֹרוֹס
(The) Aravá	עֲרָבָה
Aravót	עֲרָבוֹת
Árba kánfes	אַרְבַּע כַּנְפוֹת

Arbá kosót	אַרְבַּע כּוֹסוֹת
Arbá miním	אַרְבָּעָה מִינִים
Arón kódesh	אֲרוֹן קֹדֶשׁ
Asará be-Tevét	עֲשָׂרָה בְּטֵבֵת
Aséret yeméy teshuvá	עֲשֶׂרֶת יְמֵי תְּשׁוּבָה
Ashkenazí	אַשְׁכְּנַזִי
Asúr	אָסוּר
Av	אָב
Avatíach	אֲבַטִיחַ
Avél	אָבֵל
Averá	עֲבֵרָה
Avínu Malkénu	אָבִינוּ מַלְכֵּנוּ
Avrahám Avínu	אַבְרָהָם אָבִינוּ
Áyin ha-rá	עַיִן הָרָע
Báal ga'avá	בַּעַל גַּאֲוָה
Báal ha-báyit	בַּעַל הַבַּיִת
Báal koré	בַּעַל קוֹרֵא
Báal tekiá	בַּעַל תְּקִיעָה
Báal teshuvá	בַּעַל תְּשׁוּבָה
Bal tashchít	בַּל תַּשְׁחִית
Balagán	בַּלָגָן
Ba-Midbár	בַּמִדְבַּר
Bar Mitzváh	בַּר מִצְוָה
Barúch dayán ha-emét!	בָּרוּךְ דַיָן הָאֱמֶת
Barúch habá!	בָּרוּךְ הַבָּא
Barúch ha-Shém!	בָּרוּךְ הַשֵׁם
Barúch she-petaráni	בָּרוּךְ שֶׁפְּטָרַנִי
Batél be-shishím	בָּטֵל בְּשִׁשִׁים
Batlán	בַּטְלָן
Bat Mitzváh	בַּת מִצְוָה
Báu máyim ad néfesh	בָּאוּ מַיִם עַד נֶפֶשׁ
Bechirá	בְּחִירָה
Bechiyá le-dorót	בְּכִיָה לְדוֹרוֹת

Bedikát chamétz	בְּדִיקַת חָמֵץ
Be-ezrát ha-Shém	בְּעֶזְרַת הַשֵּׁם
Bereshít	בְּרֵאשִׁית
Besamím	בְּשָׂמִים
Be-séder	בְּסֵדֶר
Be-sha'á tová!	בְּשָׁעָה טוֹבָה
Be-shem omró	בְּשֵׁם אוֹמְרוֹ
Be-siyáta di-shmáya	בְּסִיַּעְתָּא דִשְׁמַיָּא
Bet Din	בֵּית דִּין
Be-teyavón	בְּתֵאָבוֹן
Bet ha-Mikdásh	בֵּית הַמִּקְדָּשׁ
Bet midrásh	בֵּית מִדְרָשׁ
Bevakashá	בְּבַקָּשָׁה
(The) Biká	בִּקְעָה
Bikúr cholím	בִּקּוּר חוֹלִים
Bimá	בִּימָה
Birkát ha-Mazón	בִּרְכַּת הַמָּזוֹן
Birkát Kohaním	בִּרְכַּת כֹּהֲנִים
Bitachón	בִּטָּחוֹן
Bitúl zman	בִּטּוּל זְמַן
Biúr chamétz	בִּעוּר חָמֵץ
Bli néder	בְּלִי נֶדֶר
Brachá	בְּרָכָה
Brit milá	בְּרִית מִילָה
Brógez	בְּרֹגֶז
Buréke	בּוּרֶקֶה
Bushá	בּוּשָׁה
Chad Gadyá	חַד גַּדְיָא
Chag	חַג
Chag saméach!	חַג שָׂמֵחַ
Chaláv yisraél	חָלָב יִשְׂרָאֵל
Chalitsá	חֲלִיצָה
Chaltúra	חַלְטוּרָה
Chalútz	חָלוּץ

Chamétz	חָמֵץ
Chanukáh	חֲנֻכָּה
Chanukiyá	חֲנֻכִּיָה
Charatá	חֲרָטָה
Charedí	חֲרֵדִי
Charóset	חֲרֹסֶת
Chas ve-shalóm!	חַס וְשָׁלוֹם
Chashásh	חֲשָׁשׁ
Chasíd	חָסִיד
Chasíd shotéh	חָסִיד שׁוֹטֶה
Chasidéy umót ha-olám	חֲסִידֵי אוּמוֹת הָעוֹלָם
Chasidút	חֲסִידוּת
Chatán	חָתָן
Chatán Bereshít	חֲתַן בְּרֵאשִׁית
Chatán Toráh	חֲתַן תּוֹרָה
Chatuná	חֲתוּנָה
Chavrúta	חַבְרוּתָא
Chay	חַי
Chazák u-barúch!	חֲזַק וּבָרוּךְ
Chazaká	חֲזָקָה
Chazál	חַיִּיל
Chazán	חַזָן
Chazanút	חַזָנוּת
Chazír	חֲזִיר
Chéder	חֶדֶר
Chérem	חֵרֶם
Cheshbón ha-néfesh	חֶשְׁבּוֹן הַנֶפֶשׁ
Chévra Kadísha	חֶבְרָה קַדִישָׁא
Chévre	חֶבְרֵייה
Chévreman	חֶבְרֶהייִמַן
Chidúsh	חִדוּשׁ
Chilúl ha-Shém	חִלוּל הַשֵּׁם
Chilúl shabbát	חִלוּל שַׁבָּת
Chinúch	חִנוּךְ
Chizúk	חִזוּק

Chóchem	חָכָם
Chochmá	חָכְמָה
Chol ha-Moéd	חוֹל הַמּוֹעֵד
Chumásh	חוּמָשׁ
Chumrá	חֻמְרָה
Chúmus	חוּמוּס
Chupá	חֻפָּה
Churbán	חֻרְבָּן
Chuts La-árets	חוּץ לָאָרֶץ
Chutzpáh	חֻצְפָּה
Daf Yomí	דַּף יוֹמִי
Dáled amót shel halachá	דָּלֶת אַמּוֹת שֶׁל הֲלָכָה
Datí	דָּתִי
Davíd ha-Mélech	דָּוִד הַמֶּלֶךְ
Dávka	דַּוְקָא
Dayá le-tsará be-sha'atá!	דַּיָּה לְצָרָה בְּשַׁעְתָּה
Dayán	דַּיָּן
Dérech	דֶּרֶךְ
Dérech érets	דֶּרֶךְ אֶרֶץ
Devár toráh	דְּבַר תּוֹרָה
Devarím	דְּבָרִים
Devarím begó	דְּבָרִים בְּגוֹ
Devekút	דְּבֵקוּת
Din	דִּין
Dína de-malchúta dína	דִּינָא דְּמַלְכוּתָא דִּינָא
Drash	דְּרַשׁ
Drashá	דְּרָשָׁה
Dúchen	דּוּכֶן
Echá	אֵיכָה
Echád ba-peh ve-echád ba-lev	אֶחָד בַּפֶּה וְאֶחָד בַּלֵּב
Égged	אֶגֶד
El Malé Rachamím	אֵל מָלֵא רַחֲמִים
Eliyáhu ha-Naví	אֵלִיָּהוּ הַנָּבִיא

Élu va-élu divréy elokím chayím	אֵלוּ וָאֵלוּ דִּבְרֵי אֱלֹקִים חַיִּים
Elúl	אֱלוּל
(The) Émek	עֶמֶק
Emét me-érets titsmách	אֱמֶת מֵאֶרֶץ תִּצְמָח
Emuná	אֱמוּנָה
En brerá	אֵין בְּרֵירָה
En chadásh táchat ha-shámesh	אֵין חָדָשׁ תַּחַת הַשֶּׁמֶשׁ
En me'arvín simchá be-simchá	אֵין מְעָרְבִין שִׂמְחָה בְּשִׂמְחָה
Érets Yisraél	אֶרֶץ יִשְׂרָאֵל
Érev	עֶרֶב
Érev Shabbát	עֶרֶב שַׁבָּת
Erúv	עֵרוּב
Éshet cháyil	אֵשֶׁת חַיִל
Et chata'áy ani mazkír hayóm	אֶת חֲטָאַי אֲנִי מַזְכִּיר הַיּוֹם
Et sefód ve-et rekúd	עֵת סְפוֹד וְעֵת רְקוֹד
Etróg	אֶתְרוֹג
Etsá	עֵצָה
Ézehu chachám? Ha-loméd mi-kol adám	אֵיזֶהוּ חָכָם? הַלּוֹמֵד מִכָּל אָדָם
Ezrát nashím	עֶזְרַת נָשִׁים
Faláfel	פָּלָפֶל
Fráyer	פְרַייֶר
Gabáy	גַּבַּאי
Galách	גַּלָּח
(The) Galíl	גָּלִיל
Galút	גָּלוּת
Gam zu le-tová	גַּם זוּ לְטוֹבָה
Gan Éden	גַּן עֵדֶן
Ganáv	גַּנָּב
Gaón	גָּאוֹן
Gariním	גַּרְעִינִים
Gashmiút	גַּשְׁמִיוּת
Gazlán	גַּזְלָן

Gehinóm	גֵּיהִנּוֹם
Gelilá	גְּלִילָה
Gemár chatimá tová!	גְּמַר חֲתִימָה טוֹבָה
Gemará	גְּמָרָא
Gemátria	גִּימַטְרִיָּא
Gemilút Chasadím	גְּמִילוּת חֲסָדִים
Genevá	גְּנֵבָה
Ger	גֵּר
Get	גֵּט
Ge'ulá	גְּאוּלָה
Gírsa de-yankúta	גִּירְסָא דְּיַנְקוּתָא
Golá	גּוֹלָה
Gólem	גֹּלֶם
Goy	גּוֹי
Hachnasát kalá	הַכְנָסַת כַּלָּה
Hachnasát orchím	הַכְנָסַת אוֹרְחִים
Hadasím	הֲדַסִּים
Haftará	הַפְטָרָה
Hagadá	הַגָּדָה
Hagbahá	הַגְבָּהָה
Ha-Kadósh Barúch Hu	הַקָּדוֹשׁ בָּרוּךְ הוּא
Hakafót	הַקָּפוֹת
Halachá	הֲלָכָה
Halél	הַלֵּל
Haleváy!	הַלְוַאי
Ha-motsí me-chaveró aláv ha-raayá	הַמּוֹצִיא מֵחֲבֵרוֹ עָלָיו הָרְאָיָה
Har ha-Báyit	הַר הַבַּיִת
Har Sináy	הַר סִינַי
Hararím hatluyím be-saará	הֶהָרִים הַתְּלוּיִים בְּשַׂעֲרָה
Hashavát avedá	הֲשָׁבַת אֲבֵדָה
Ha-Shém	הַשֵּׁם
Hashgachá	הַשְׁגָּחָה
Hashkafá	הַשְׁקָפָה
Ha-shomér achí anóchi?	הֲשׁוֹמֵר אָחִי אָנֹכִי

Haskalá	הַשְׂכָּלָה
Ha-Tíkvah	הַתִּקְוָה
Hatslócho Rábo!	הַצְלָחָה רַבָּה
Háva Nagíla	הָבָה נָגִילָה
Havdalá	הַבְדָּלָה
Hechshér	הֶכְשֵׁר
Hefkér	הֶפְקֵר
Hespéd	הֶסְפֵּד
Hetsíts ve-nifgá	הֵצִיץ וְנִפְגַּע
Hidúr mitzváh	הִדּוּר מִצְוָה
Híllel	הִלֵּל
Hirhuréy averá kashím me-averá	הִרְהוּרֵי עֲבֵרָה קָשִׁים מֵעֲבֵרָה
Hosháana Rabá	הוֹשַׁעְנָא רַבָּה
Hoshaanót	הוֹשַׁעְנוֹת
Ikár	עִקָּר
Ikvót meshícha	עִקְבוֹת מְשִׁיחָא
Ilúy	עִלּוּי
Im ba laharogchá, hashkém lehorgó	אִם בָּא לַהָרְגְךָ הַשְׁכֵּם לְהָרְגוֹ
Im eshkachéch yerushaláyim, tishkách yeminí	אִם אֶשְׁכָּחֵךְ יְרוּשָׁלַיִם תִּשְׁכַּח יְמִינִי
Im yirtséh hashém	אִם יִרְצֶה הַשֵּׁם
Inyán	עִנְיָן
Ípcha mistábra	אִפְּכָא מִסְתַּבְּרָא
Ísru Chag	אִסְרוּ חַג
Isúr	אִסּוּר
Ivrít	עִבְרִית
Iyár	אִיָּר
Iyóv	אִיּוֹב
Juk	גּוּק
Kabalá	קַבָּלָה
Kabalát Shabbát	קַבָּלַת שַׁבָּת
Kabdéhu ve-chashdéhu	כַּבְּדֵהוּ וְחָשְׁדֵהוּ

Kaddísh	קַדִּישׁ
Kalá	כַּלָה
Káshe	קוּשְׁיָה
Kashér	כָּשֵׁר
Kashrút	כַּשְׁרוּת
Kavaná	כַּוָּנָה
Kavód	כָּבוֹד
Kedushá	קְדֻשָּׁה
Kehilá	קְהִלָה
Ken yirbú!	כֵּן יִרְבּוּ
Keréach mi-kan u-mi-kan	קֵרֵחַ מִכָּאן וּמִכָּאן
Keriá	קְרִיעָה
Ketivá ve-chatimá tová!	כְּתִיבָה וַחֲתִימָה טוֹבָה
Ketubá	כְּתֻבָּה
Kéver avót	קֶבֶר אָבוֹת
Kíbúd av va-em	כִּבּוּד אָב וָאֵם
Kibbútz	קִבּוּץ
Kiddúsh	קִדּוּשׁ
Kiddúsh ha-Shém	קִדּוּשׁ הַשֵּׁם
Kiddúsh levaná	קִדּוּשׁ לְבָנָה
Kilachár yad	כִּלְאַחַר יָד
Kiná	קִינָה
Kipá	כִּפָּה
Kisé shel eliyáhu	כִּסֵּא שֶׁל אֵלִיָּהוּ
Kislév	כִּסְלֵו
Kitsúr Shulchán Arúch	קִצּוּר שֻׁלְחָן עָרוּךְ
Klal Yisraél	כְּלַל יִשְׂרָאֵל
Knésset	כְּנֶסֶת
Kóach	כֹּחַ
Kohélet	קֹהֶלֶת
Kohén	כֹּהֵן
Kol ishá	קוֹל אִשָּׁה
Kol ha-kavód!	כָּל הַכָּבוֹד
Kol ha-mosíf goréa	כָּל הַמּוֹסִיף גּוֹרֵעַ

Kol kevudá bat mélech peníma	כָּל כְּבוּדָה בַת מֶלֶךְ פְּנִימָה
Kol Nidréy	כָּל נִדְרֵי
Kol tuv!	כָּל טוּב
Kol yisraél arevím ze ba-ze	כָּל יִשְׂרָאֵל עֲרֵבִים זֶה בָּזֶה
Kol yisraél chaverím	כָּל יִשְׂרָאֵל חֲבֵרִים
Kolél	כּוֹלֵל
Kosher	כָּשֵׁר
(The) Kótel	כֹּתֶל
Kotsó shel yud	קוֹצוֹ שֶׁל יוּד
Kóva témbel	כּוֹבַע טֶמְבֶּל
Kriát ha-Toráh	קְרִיאַת הַתּוֹרָה
Kriát Shemá	קְרִיאַת שְׁמַע
Kriát Yam-Súf	קְרִיאַת יָם סוּף
Labriút!	לַבְּרִיאוּת
Lag ba-Ómer	לַייג בָּעֹמֶר
Lámed-vav tsadikím	לָמֶד וָו צַדִּיקִים
Lébn	לֶבֶּן
Le-cháyim	לְחַיִּים
Lech la-azazél	לֵךְ לַעֲזָאזֵל
Lechá Dodí	לְכָה דוֹדִי
Léchem mishnéh	לֶחֶם מִשְׁנֶה
Lehavdíl	לְהַבְדִּיל
Lehitraót	לְהִתְרָאוֹת
Le-shaná ha-baá birushaláyim!	לְשָׁנָה הַבָּאָה בִּירוּשָׁלַיִם
Leshém shamáyim	לְשֵׁם שָׁמַיִם
Leshón ha-Kódesh	לְשׁוֹן הַקֹּדֶשׁ
Leshón ha-rá	לְשׁוֹן הָרַע
Levayá	לְוָיָה
Leví	לֵוִי
Lo alécha ha-melachá ligmór	לֹא עָלֶיךָ הַמְּלָאכָה לִגְמוֹר
Lo alénu	לֹא עָלֵינוּ
Lo dubím ve-lo yáar!	לֹא דֻבִּים וְלֹא יַעַר
Lo hayá ve-lo nivrá!	לֹא הָיָה וְלֹא נִבְרָא

Lo mi-duvshách ve-lo mi-uktsách!   לֹא מִדֻּבְשָׁךְ וְלֹא מֵעֻקְצָךְ

Lúach   לוּחַ

Luláv   לוּלָב

Ma Nishtaná   מַה נִּשְׁתַּנָה

Ma pitóm!   מַה פִּתְאֹם

Ma'alín ba-kódesh ve-en moridín   מַעֲלִין בַּקֹּדֶשׁ וְאֵין מוֹרִידִין

Ma'arív   מַעֲרִיב

Ma'asér   מַעֲשֵׂר

Ma'aséy avót simán le-vaním   מַעֲשֵׂי אָבוֹת סִימָן לְבָנִים

Ma'ayán ha-mitgabér   מַעֲיָן הַמִּתְגַּבֵּר

Machlóket   מַחְלֹקֶת

Machmír   מַחְמִיר

Machzór   מַחְזוֹר

Madregá   מַדְרֵגָה

Madrích   מַדְרִיךְ

Maftír   מַפְטִיר

Magén Davíd   מָגֵן דָּוִד

Magén Davíd Adóm   מָגֵן דָּוִד אָדוֹם

Makólet   מַכֹּלֶת

Malách   מַלְאָךְ

Malách ha-mávet   מַלְאַךְ הַמָּוֶת

Mamásh   מַמָּשׁ

Mamzér   מַמְזֵר

Maóz Tsur   מָעוֹז צוּר

Marcheshván   מַרְחֶשְׁוָן

Marór   מָרוֹר

Mashál   מָשָׁל

Mashíach   מָשִׁיחַ

Mashkéh   מַשְׁקֶה

Matán Toráh   מַתַּן תּוֹרָה

Matanót la-evyoním   מַתָּנוֹת לָאֶבְיוֹנִים

Matzá   מַצָּה

Matzevá   מַצֵּבָה

Máyim acharoním   מַיִם אַחֲרוֹנִים

Máyim genuvím yimtáku	מַיִם גְּנוּבִים יִמְתָּקוּ
Mazál	מַזָּל
Mazál tov!	מַזָּל טוֹב
Mazík	מַזִּיק
Mechalél shabbát	מְחַלֵּל שַׁבָּת
Mecháye	מְחַיֶּה
Me-cháyil el cháyil	מֵחַיִל אֶל חַיִל
Mechirát chamétz	מְכִירַת חָמֵץ
Mechitsá	מְחִיצָה
Mechclass	מְחֻתָּן
Mechután	מְחֻתָּן
(The) Megilá	מְגִלָּה
Megíle	מְגִלָּה
Mekarév	מְקָרֵב
Mekél	מֵקֵל
Mekubál	מְקֻבָּל
Melachá	מְלָאכָה
Melámed	מְלַמֵּד
Melaméd zechút	מְלַמֵּד זְכוּת
Melavéh malká	מְלַוֶּה מַלְכָּה
Melíts yósher	מֵלִיץ יֹשֶׁר
Menoráh	מְנוֹרָה
Meshugá	מְשֻׁגָּע
Meshumád	מְשֻׁמָּד
Mesirút néfesh	מְסִירוּת נֶפֶשׁ
Met	מֵת
Metapélet	מְטַפֶּלֶת
Metsiá	מְצִיאָה
Méyven	מֵבִין
Mezonót	מְזוֹנוֹת
Mezúmen	מְזֻמָּן
Mezuzáh	מְזוּזָה
Mi she-béyrech	מִי שֶׁבֵּרַךְ
Midá	מִדָּה
Midá kenéged midá	מִדָּה כְּנֶגֶד מִדָּה
Midrásh	מִדְרָשׁ

Mi-kol melamdáy hiskálti	מִכָּל מְלַמְדַי הִשְׂכַּלְתִּי
Miktsát shivchó shel adám omrím befanáv	מִקְצָת שִׁבְחוֹ שֶׁל אָדָם אוֹמְרִים בְּפָנָיו
Mikvéh	מִקְוֶה
Miluím	מִלוּאִים
Min ha-katséh el ha-katséh	מִן הַקָּצֶה אֶל הַקָּצֶה
Min ha-shamáyim	מִן הַשָּׁמַיִם
Minchá	מִנְחָה
Minhág	מִנְהָג
Minyán	מִנְיָן
Mi-she-nichnás Adár, marbím be-simchá	מִשֶּׁנִּכְנַס אֲדָר מַרְבִּים בְּשִׂמְחָה
Mishebeyrach	מִי שֶׁבֵּרַךְ
Mishléy	מִשְׁלֵי
Mishlóach manót	מִשְׁלוֹחַ מָנוֹת
Mishná	מִשְׁנָה
(The) Mishná Brurá	מִשְׁנָה בְּרוּרָה
Mishpachá	מִשְׁפָּחָה
Mitóch she-ló lishmá, ba lishmá	מִתּוֹךְ שֶׁלֹּא לִשְׁמָה בָּא לִשְׁמָה
Mitzváh	מִצְוָה
Mitzvát anashím melumadá	מִצְוַת אֲנָשִׁים מְלֻמָּדָה
Mizrách	מִזְרָח
Modéh Aní	מוֹדֶה אֲנִי
Mohél	מוֹהֵל
Mosád	מוֹסָד
Mosháv	מוֹשָׁב
Moshé Rabbénu	מֹשֶׁה רַבֵּנוּ
Motsaéy Shabbát	מוֹצָאֵי שַׁבָּת
Motsí	מוֹצִיא
Mótek	מֹתֶק
Muát ha-machzík et hamrubéh	מוּעָט הַמַּחֲזִיק אֶת הַמְרֻבֶּה
Muktséh	מֻקְצֶה
Mumchéh	מֻמְחֶה
Musáf	מוּסָף
Musár	מוּסָר

Náchat	נַחַת
Naé dorésh ve-naé mekayém	נָאֶה דוֹרֵשׁ וְנָאֶה מְקַיֵּם
Nána	נַעְנַע
Naví	נָבִיא
Nechbá el ha-kelím	נֶחְבָּא אֶל הַכֵּלִים
Nedavá	נְדָבָה
(The) Négev	נֶגֶב
Ne'ilá	נְעִילָה
Ner tamíd	נֵר תָּמִיד
Nes	נֵס
Neshamá	נְשָׁמָה
Neshamá yeterá	נְשָׁמָה יְתֵרָה
Nesiá tová!	נְסִיעָה טוֹבָה
Netilát yadáyim	נְטִילַת יָדַיִם
Nevuá	נְבוּאָה
Nibúl peh	נִבּוּל פֶּה
Nichúm avél	נִחוּם אָבֵל
Niftár	נִפְטָר
Nigún	נִגּוּן
Nisán	נִיסָן
Nu?	נוּ
Od chazón la-moéd	עוֹד חָזוֹן לַמּוֹעֵד
Olám ha-bá	עוֹלָם הַבָּא
Oléh	עוֹלֶה
Ómer	עֹמֶר
Óneg shabbát	עֹנֶג שַׁבָּת
Oy!	אוֹי
Oy le-rashá oy lishchenó	אוֹי לְרָשָׁע אוֹי לִשְׁכֵנוֹ
Oy li mi-yotsrí, ve-oy li mi-yitsrí	אוֹי לִי מִיּוֹצְרִי וְאוֹי לִי מִיִּצְרִי
Ozéret	עוֹזֶרֶת
Parashá	פָּרָשָׁה
Párev	פַּרְוֶה
Parnasá	פַּרְנָסָה

Paróchet	פָּרֹכֶת
Pársha	פָּרָשָׁה
Pasúk	פָּסוּק
Pasúl	פָּסוּל
Peót	פֵּאוֹת
Pérek	פֶּרֶק
Perúsh	פֵּרוּשׁ
Pésach	פֶּסַח
Peshará	פְּשָׁרָה
Peshat	פְּשָׁט
Petichá	פְּתִיחָה
Pidyón ha-bén	פִּדְיוֹן הַבֵּן
Pikúach néfesh	פִּקוּחַ נֶפֶשׁ
Pilpúl	פִּלְפּוּל
Pirkéy Avót	פִּרְקֵי אָבוֹת
Pítta	פִּתָּה
Piyút	פִּיּוּט
Protéktsiya	פְּרוֹטֶקְצִיָה
Purím	פּוּרִים
Rábbi	רַבִּי
Rabotáy!	רַבּוֹתַי
Rachmána litslán	רַחְמָנָא לִצְלַן
Rachmanút	רַחְמָנוּת
Ragláyim la-davár	רַגְלַיִם לַדָבָר
Rashá	רָשָׁע
Rav	רַב
Reayá	רְאָיָה
Rébbe	רִבִּי
Rechilút	רְכִילוּת
Refuá shlemá!	רְפוּאָה שְׁלֵמָה
Réga!	רֶגַע
Ribít	רִבִּית
Ribonó shel olám	רִבּוֹנוֹ שֶׁל עוֹלָם
Rikudím	רִקּוּדִים

Rishón	רִאשׁוֹן
Rosh Chódesh	רֹאשׁ חֹדֶשׁ
Rosh ha-Shaná	רֹאשׁ הַשָּׁנָה
Rúach	רוּחַ
Rúach ha-kódesh	רוּחַ הַקֹּדֶשׁ
Ruchniút	רוּחָנִיּוּת
Rut	רוּת
Sabra	צַבָּר
Sandák	סַנְדָּק
Satán	שָׂטָן
Savlanút	סַבְלָנוּת
Sechách	סְכָךְ
Séchel	שֵׂכֶל
Séder	סֵדֶר
Sefardí	סְפָרַדִי
Séfer	סֵפֶר
Séfer toráh	סֵפֶר תּוֹרָה
Sefirát ha-Ómer	סְפִירַת הָעֹמֶר
Segulá	סְגֻלָּה
Selichót	סְלִיחוֹת
Sephardi	סְפָרַדִי
Se'udá	סְעוּדָה
Se'udá Shlishít	סְעוּדָה שְׁלִישִׁית
Sha'atnéz	שַׁעַטְנֵז
Shabbát	שַׁבָּת
Shabbát Shalóm!	שַׁבַּת שָׁלוֹם
Shacharít	שַׁחֲרִית
Shadchán	שַׁדְכָן
Sháleshúdes	שָׁלוֹשׁ סְעוּדוֹת
Shalíach	שָׁלִיחַ
Shalóm!	שָׁלוֹם
Shalóm alechém!	שָׁלוֹם עֲלֵיכֶם
Shalóm zachár	שָׁלוֹם זָכָר
Shamásh	שַׁמָּשׁ

Shaná tová!	שָׁנָה טוֹבָה
Shas	שַׁ״ס
Shátnes	שַׁעַטְנֵז
Shavúa tov!	שָׁבוּעַ טוֹב
Shavuót	שָׁבוּעוֹת
Sháyle	שְׁאֵלָה
Shechiná	שְׁכִינָה
Shechitá	שְׁחִיטָה
She'elá	שְׁאֵלָה
She-hecheyánu	שֶׁהֶחֱיָנוּ
Shéket!	שֶׁקֶט
Shelíach tsibúr	שְׁלִיחַ צִבּוּר
Shelom báyit	שְׁלוֹם בַּיִת
Sheloshím	שְׁלֹשִׁים
Sheluchéy mitzváh enám nizokím	שְׁלוּחֵי מִצְוָה אֵינָם נִזּוֹקִים
Shemá	שְׁמַע
Sheminí Atséret	שְׁמִינִי עֲצֶרֶת
Shemitá	שְׁמִיטָה
Shemonéh-esréh	שְׁמוֹנֶה-עֶשְׂרֵה
Shemót	שְׁמוֹת
Shemura matzo	מַצָּה שְׁמוּרָה
Sherút	שֵׁרוּת
Shev ve-al taaséh	שֵׁב וְאַל תַּעֲשֶׂה
Shéva brachót	שֶׁבַע בְּרָכוֹת
Shéva mitsvót livnéy nóach	שֶׁבַע מִצְווֹת לִבְנֵי נֹחַ
Shevarím	שְׁבָרִים
Shevat	שְׁבָט
Shéymes	שֵׁמוֹת
Shidúch	שִׁדּוּךְ
Shikór	שִׁכּוֹר
Shin Bet	שִׁין בֵּית
Shir ha-Shirím	שִׁיר הַשִּׁירִים
Shiúr	שִׁעוּר
Shivá	שִׁבְעָה
Shivá Asár be-Tamúz	שִׁבְעָה עָשָׂר בְּתַמּוּז

Shivím paním la-torá	שִׁבְעִים פָּנִים לַתּוֹרָה
Shlitá	שְׁלִיטָיָיא
Shmúre mátze	מַצָּה שְׁמוּרָה
Shoáh	שׁוֹאָה
Shochét	שׁוֹחֵט
Shofár	שׁוֹפָר
Shólom aléychem!	שָׁלוֹם עֲלֵיכֶם
Shomér shabbát	שׁוֹמֵר שַׁבָּת
Shomrón	שׁוֹמְרוֹן
Shtachím	שְׁטָחִים
Shuk	שׁוּק
Shulchán Arúch	שֻׁלְחָן עָרוּךְ
Shushán Purím	שׁוּשָׁן פּוּרִים
Siddúr	סִדּוּר
Sidrá	סִדְרָה
Simán	סִימָן
Simchá	שִׂמְחָה
Simchát Toráh	שִׂמְחַת תּוֹרָה
Sinát chinám	שִׂנְאַת חִנָם
Siván	סִיוָן
Siyáta dishmáya	סִיַעְתָּא דִשְׁמַיָא
Siyúm	סִיּוּם
Smichá	סְמִיכָה
(The) Sochnút	סוֹכְנוּת
Sofér	סוֹפֵר
Stam	סְתָם
Sukkáh	סֻכָּה
Sukkót	סֻכּוֹת
Syag la-chochmá shtiká	סְיָג לַחָכְמָה שְׁתִיקָה
Tá'am	טַעַם
Ta'anít	תַּעֲנִית
Ta'anít Bechorím	תַּעֲנִית בְּכוֹרִים
Ta'anít Estér	תַּעֲנִית אֶסְתֵּר
Tachanún	תַּחֲנוּן

Táchles	תַּכְלֵייס
Tafásta merubéh, lo tafásta	תָּפַסְתָּ מְרֻבֶּה לֹא תָּפַסְתָּ
Tahará	טָהֳרָה
Taharát mishpachá	טָהֳרַת מִשְׁפָּחָה
Tallít	טַלִּית
Tallít katán	טַלִּית קָטָן
Talmíd	תַּלְמִיד
Talmíd chachám	תַּלְמִיד חָכָם
Talmúd	תַּלְמוּד
Talmúd Toráh	תַּלְמוּד תּוֹרָה
Tamúz	תַּמּוּז
Tanách	תַּנַייךְ
Taryág mitzvót	תַּרְיַיג מִצְוֺת
Tashlích	תַּשְׁלִיךְ
Techína	טְחִינָה
Techiná	תְּחִנָּה
Techiyát ha-metím	תְּחִיַּת הַמֵּתִים
Tefilá	תְּפִלָּה
Tefilát ha-Dérech	תְּפִלַּת הַדֶּרֶךְ
Tefilín	תְּפִלִּין
Tehilím	תְּהִלִּים
Tekiá	תְּקִיעָה
Tenách	תַּנַייךְ
Tenaím	תְּנָאִים
Teruá	תְּרוּעָה
Teshuvá	תְּשׁוּבָה
Tevét	טֵבֵת
Tikún Leyl Shavuót	תִּקּוּן לֵיל שָׁבוּעוֹת
Tinokót shel bet rabán	תִּינוֹקוֹת שֶׁל בֵּית רַבָּן
Tishá be-Av	תִּשְׁעָה בְּאָב
Tishréy	תִּשְׁרֵי
Tóches	תַּחַת
Tochó ke-varó	תּוֹכוֹ כְּבָרוֹ
Todá (rabá)!	תּוֹדָה רַבָּה
Toráh	תּוֹרָה

Toráh she-be'al peh	תּוֹרָה שֶׁבְּעַל פֶּה
Tovél ve-shérets be-yadó	טוֹבֵל וְשֶׁרֶץ בְּיָדוֹ
Tóyvl	טוֹבֵל
Treyf	טְרֵפָה
Tsáar baaléy chayím	צַעַר בַּעֲלֵי חַיִּים
Tsáar gidúl baním	צַעַר גִּדּוּל בָּנִים
Tsabár	צַבָּר
Tsadéket	צַדִּיק
Tsadík	צַדֶּקֶת
Tsarát rabím chatsí nechamá	צָרַת רַבִּים חֲצִי נֶחָמָה
Tsarot	צָרוֹת
Tsava'á	צַוָּאָה
Tsedá la-dérech	צֵידָה לַדֶּרֶךְ
Tsedaká	צְדָקָה
Tsedaká tatsíl mi-mávet	צְדָקָה תַּצִּיל מִמָּוֶת
Tseniút	צְנִיעוּת
Tsevát bi-tsevát asuyá	צְבָת בִּצְבָת עֲשׂוּיָה
Tsibúr	צִבּוּר
Tsitsít	צִיצִית
Tsom Gedalyá	צוֹם גְּדַלְיָה
Tu bi-Shvat	טְיִּיו הִשְׁבָט
Túches	תַּחַת
Tumá	טוּמְאָה
Ulpán	אֻלְפָּן
Vayikrá	וַיִּקְרָא
Vidúy	וִדּוּי
Yam ha-Mélach	יָם הַמֶּלַח
Yam Kinéret	יָם כִּנֶּרֶת
Yamím Noraím	יָמִים נוֹרָאִים
(The) Yardén	יַרְדֵּן
Yatsá secharó be-hefsedó	יָצָא שְׂכָרוֹ בְּהֶפְסֵדוֹ
Yehudá ve-Shomrón	יְהוּדָה וְשׁוֹמְרוֹן

Yeridá　　　　　　　　　　　　　　　　יְרִידָה

Yeridá le-tsórech aliyáh　　　יְרִידָה לְצֹרֶךְ עֲלִיָה

Yeridát ha-dorót　　　　　　　יְרִידַת הַדּוֹרוֹת

Yerushá　　　　　　　　　　　　　　יְרוּשָׁה

Yerusháláyim　　　　　　　　　　　יְרוּשָׁלַיִם

Yesh me-áyin　　　　　　　　　　יֵשׁ מֵאַיִן

Yeshivá　　　　　　　　　　　　　　יְשִׁיבָה

Yétser ha-rá　　　　　　　　　　　יֵצֶר הָרָע

Yetsiát Mitsráyim　　　　　　　יְצִיאַת מִצְרַיִם

Yichúd　　　　　　　　　　　　　　　יִחוּד

Yichús　　　　　　　　　　　　　　　יִחוּס

Yimách shemó　　　　　　　　　　יִמַח שְׁמוֹ

Yishár kóach!　　　　　　　　　　יִישַׁר כֹּחַ

Yisraél　　　　　　　　　　　　　　יִשְׂרָאֵל

Yisurím　　　　　　　　　　　　　　יִסּוּרִים

Yiyéh tov　　　　　　　　　　　　יִהְיֶה טוֹב

Yizkór　　　　　　　　　　　　　　　יִזְכּוֹר

Yom ha-Atsmaút　　　　　　　יוֹם הָעַצְמָאוּת

Yom Kippúr　　　　　　　　　　　יוֹם כִּפּוּר

Yómtov Shéyni　　　　　　　　יוֹם טוֹב שֵׁנִי

Yom Yerusháláyim　　　　　　יוֹם יְרוּשָׁלַיִם

Yóntef　　　　　　　　　　　　　　יוֹם טוֹב

Yoréd　　　　　　　　　　　　　　　יוֹרֵד

(To be) Yotsé　　　　　　　　　　יוֹצֵא

Zécher la-churbán　　　　　　　זֵכֶר לַחֻרְבָּן

Zécher tsadík livrachá　　　זֵכֶר צַדִּיק לִבְרָכָה

Zechút　　　　　　　　　　　　　　זְכוּת

Zemirót　　　　　　　　　　　　　　זְמִירוֹת

Zenut　　　　　　　　　　　　　　　זְנוּת

Zerizím makdimím le-mitzvót　　זְרִיזִים מַקְדִּימִים לְמִצְווֹת

Zichronó/zichroná livrachá　　זִכְרוֹנוֹ/זִכְרוֹנָה לִבְרָכָה

(The) Zóhar　　　　　　　　　　　זֹהַר

The Hebrew Form of Some Familiar Biblical Names

This is essentially a guide to pronunciation. The Jewish spellings of these names in English have not been standardized.

Note: When used as modern given names, the stress is often put on the syllable before last, even in the Israeli pronunciation. Thus *cháva, yítschak* rather than *chavá, yitschák.*

English form	Sephardi and Israeli pronunciation	Ashkenazi pronunciation
Aaron	Aharón	Áaren
Abigail	Avigáyil	Avigáyel
Abraham	Avrahám	Avróhom
Adam	Adám (ha-Rishón)	Ódom (ho-Ríshen)
Asher	Ashér	Ósher
Bathsheba	Bat-Shéva	Bas-Shéve
Benjamin	Binyamín	Binyómin
Bezalel	Betsalél	Betsálel
Daniel	Daniél	Doníel
David	Davíd	Dóvid
Deborah	Dvorá	Dvóre
Dinah	Diná	Díne
Eliezer	Eliézer	Eliézer
Elijah	Eliyáhu	Eliyóhu
Ephraim	Efráyim	Efráyim
Esther	Estér	Éster
Ethan	Eytán	Éyson
Ezekiel	Yechezkél	Yechézkel
Ezra	Ezrá	Ézre
Eve	Chavá	Cháve
Gabriel	Gavriél	Gavríel
Gideon	Gid'ón	Gídon
Hadasa	Hadasá	Hadáse
Hannah	Chaná	Cháne

291

English form	Sephardi and Israeli pronunciation	Ashkenazi pronunciation
Isaac	Yitschák	Yítschok
Isaiah	Yeshayáhu	Yesháye
Israel	Yisraél	Yisróel
Issachar	Yisachár	Yisócher
Jacob	Ya'akóv	Yáakov
Jair	Yaír	Yóir
Jeremiah	Yirmiyáhu	Yirmiyóhu
Joel	Yoél	Yóel
Jonah	Yoná	Yóhne
Jonathan	Yonatán	Yóhnoson
Joseph	Yoséf	Yóhsef
Joshua	Yehoshúa	Yehoshúe
Judah	Yehudá	Yehúde
Judith	Yehudít	Yehúdis
Leah	Leá	Léye
Levi	Leví	Léyvi
Manasseh	Menashéh	Menáshe
Michael	Michaél	Michóel
Miriam	Miryám	Míryem
Mordechai	Mórdechay	Mórdechay
Moses	Moshé	Móhshe
Nahum	Nachúm	Náchem
Naomi	Nóami	Nóemi
Naphtali	Naftalí	Naftóli
Nathan	Natán	Nósn
Noah	Nóach	Nóach
Pinchas	Pinchás	Pínches
Rachel	Rachél	Róchel
Rebecca	Rivká	Rífke
Reuben	Re'uvén	Rúven
Ruth	Rut	Rus
Samson	Shimshón	Shímshen
Samuel	Shmuél	Shmúel
Sarah	Sará	Sóro
Saul	Shaúl	Shóel
Shlomith	Shlomít	Shlómis
Shulamith	Shulamít	Shulámis
Simon	Shimón	Shímen
Solomon	Shlomó	Shlómoh
Susanna	Shoshaná	Shosháne
Zebulun	Zevulún	Zvúlun
Zipporah	Tsiporá	Tsipóre